RECOLLECTIONS

OF

James Anthony Gardner

COMMANDER R.N.

(1775–1814)

EDITED BY

SIR R. VESEY HAMILTON, G.C.B.

ADMIRAL

AND

JOHN KNOX LAUGHTON, M.A., D.Litt.

HON. FELLOW OF CAIUS COLLEGE, CAMBRIDGE

PROFESSOR OF MODERN HISTORY IN KING'S COLLEGE, LONDON

PRINTED FOR THE NAVY RECORDS SOCIETY

MDCCCCVI

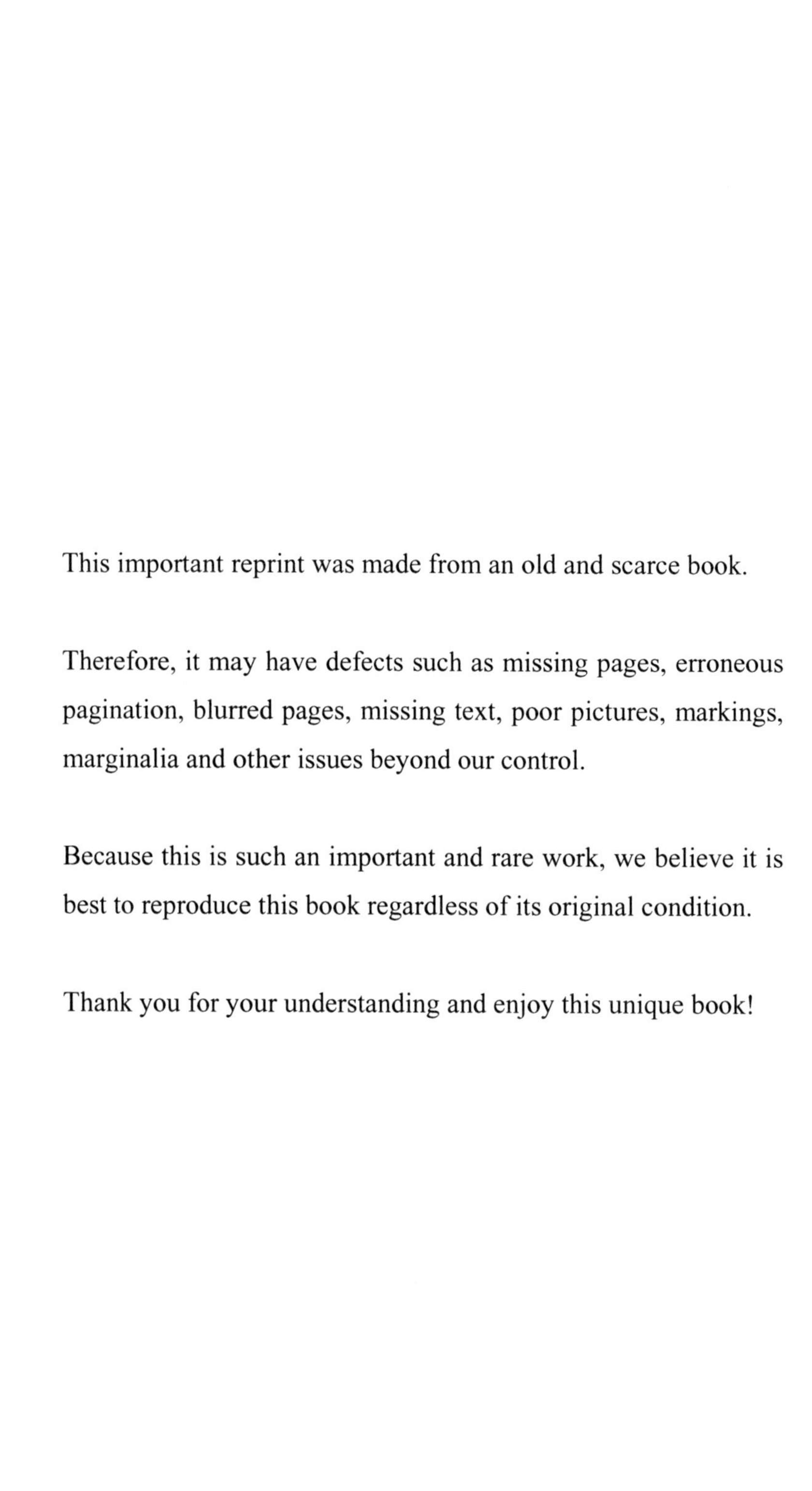

THE COUNCIL

OF THE

NAVY RECORDS SOCIETY

1906–1907

INTRODUCTION

In many respects the present volume differs from the most of those which have been issued by the Society; there is in it very little history, as commonly understood. The author, it is true, lived in a stirring time, and was himself an actor in some of the incidents which have shed a glory on our naval records; but his account of these is meagre and of little importance. The interest which attaches to his 'Recollections' is entirely personal and social; we have in them sketches roughly drawn, crude, inartistic, and perhaps on that account the more valuable, of the life of the time; of the men who were his companions in the berth, or the gun-room or the ward-room; on deck, in sport or in earnest.

In all this, there is perhaps little that we did not know before in an otiose sort of way. We knew that the men of the time were often coarse in speech, rude in action; but it may be that the reality, as portrayed by Commander Gardner, exceeds anything that we had imagined. It seems to carry us back to the days of Roderick Random, and to suggest that there had been but small improvement since Smollett wrote his celebrated description. A closer examination will correct this impression; will convince us that there had, on the contrary, been a good deal of improvement; that the life was less hard, the manners less rude; and if the language does not show very much difference, it has to be considered that Smollett was writing for the public and Gardner was not; that Smollett's dialogues are more or less literary, and Gardner's are, for the most part, in the vernacular.

Occasionally, indeed, the language has been modified, or its undue strength merely indicated by a ——; but where oaths and expletives formed such a large part of the conversational currency between intimates; when 'son of a bitch' was the usual equivalent of the modern 'chappie' or 'Johnnie' or 'rotter'; when 'damned' was everywhere recognised as a most ordinary intensitive, and 'damn your eyes' meant simply 'buck up,' it has been felt that entirely to bowdlerise the narrative would be to present our readers with a very imperfect picture of the life of the day.

Independent of the language, the most striking feature of the portraits is the universal drunkenness. It is mentioned as a thing too common to be considered a fault, though—if carried to excess—an amiable weakness, which no decent commanding officer would take serious notice of. Looking down the lists of old shipmates and messmates, the eye is necessarily caught by the frequency of such entries as 'too fond of grog,' 'did not dislike grog,' 'passionately fond of grog,' 'a drunken Hun,' a term of reprobation as a bully, rather than as a drunkard, 'fond of gin grog,' 'mad from drink,' 'insane from drink,' and so on, *passim.* For the officer of the watch to be drunk scarcely called for comment; it was only when, in addition to being drunk, he turned the captain out at midnight to save the ship, that he narrowly escaped being brought to a court martial; 'but we interceded for him, and the business was looked over' (p. 217).

It is, of course, familiarly known that during the later years of the eighteenth century, such drunkenness was almost more common on shore than afloat; and when more than half the peerage and the most distinguished statesmen were 'habitual drunkards,' there was, from the social point of view, some excuse for the many of Gardner's messmates. For good or ill, the navy has always been very conservative in its customs; and at a much later date, when hard drinking was going out of fashion on shore, except among very young men, it still continued prevalent in the navy. Some of our older officers will remember at least one instance in which a great public scandal was averted only in consideration of the social connections of the principal offender; and courts martial, bringing ruin and disgrace to the individual, long continued to be pain fully frequent. Absolute reform in this direction was slow; but there are few things more remarkable than the change which has come over the service during the last quarter of a century.

But in the eighteenth century this hard drinking brought in its train not only the terribly frequent insanity, such as is recorded in so many of Gardner's pages; not only the gross lapses, some of which Gardner has indicated, but also numerous irregularities, which we may suspect where we do not know, and of which, quarrels and free fights in the ward-room or in the steerage—such, for instance, as brought on the series of Phaëton courts martial (pp. 73-4)—were only one type. Coarse practical joking among men no longer young was another characteristic of the life which seems subversive of true discipline. Here, of course, we are met by the great change which has everywhere taken place; and the horse-play of Billy Culmer and his friends —stupid vulgarity as it now appears—can scarcely be considered more childish than the pranks and hoaxes of Theodore Hook or Grantley Berkeley twenty or thirty years later. But the very serious objection to such practices on board ship was that—as is now common knowledge—the most inveterate practical joker is the most annoyed when the tables are turned and he himself is made the victim of the joke; that quarrels are certain to arise, which, in a small society and among armed men, are both dangerous in themselves and detrimental to the service. It is, too, difficult to draw the line between practical joking, ragging, or 'hazing' and actual bullying. There is no doubt that they merge into each other, and, in the present state of public opinion, could not possibly be tolerated.

Gardner himself, so far as we can judge from his own story, was a good, capable man, who took the life around him as quite a matter of course, without falling into its worst characteristics. He seems, too, to have been a man of singularly equable temper; and it is worthy of special notice that, amid much to annoy and irritate him, he has preferred to say what is good, rather than what is bad, of his messmates and superiors. It used to be so very much the custom to speak evil of dignities, that it is quite refreshing to meet with a young officer to whom his captain did not necessarily seem a bullying, tyrannical blockhead; who could see that the senior might have a proper motive and have formed a correct judgment, even though he did thwart the junior's wishes or act contrary to the junior's opinion. Gardner had, for instance, no particular cause to love Calder, but he could still speak of him as 'a brave and meritorious officer, and of first-rate abilities, a man that had the service at heart' (pp. 101, 107). Leveson Gower he did not like—no subordinate did; but, though he relates several incidents, which of themselves are sufficiently damning, he does not seem to have set down aught in malice, nor has he made any spiteful commentary. His worst remark is 'I have said enough of him' (p. 90).

First lieutenants were, of course, the natural enemies of a youngster; but with few exceptions his comments, even on them, are good-humoured. Of one only does he speak bitterly; it is Edward Hamilton (p. 172), whose celebrated recapture of the Hermione might induce us to suspect that Gardner was merely expressing the spleen roused by the loss of his kit, did we not remember that, at this time, Hamilton was only 23, and that he was but 30 when his active career was brought to a premature end by a court martial dismissing him the service for cruelty and oppression. It is true that he was specially reinstated six months later, but he never afterwards commanded a sea-going ship, nor, as an admiral, did he ever hoist his flag. It is indeed a remarkable fact, and one giving much food for thought, that other young captains, whose brilliant courage before the enemy won for them a reputation little, if at all, inferior to that of Hamilton, were also tried by court martial for tyrannical and excessive punishments. It is difficult to avoid the suspicion that this was in great measure due to utter want of training in the art of command. The way in which the ships' companies were raised, the vicious characters of the men, almost necessarily led to severity which easily might and too often did degenerate into brutality.

On all this, however, Gardner offers no opinion. He took the service as he found it, content to do his duty honestly and faithfully. The story of his career, which is related at length in the following pages, may be summarised from the memoir in

O'Byrne's *Naval Biographical Dictionary*, the first draft of which was almost certainly written from information supplied by himself.

James Anthony Gardner, son of Francis Geary Gardner, a commander in the navy, who died at St. Lucia in September 1780, was born at Waterford in 1770–1. Francis Geary Gardner, captain of marines, was his brother. Sir Francis Geary Gardner Lee, who began life as a midshipman (p. 202) and died a lieutenant-colonel of marines, was a cousin. Two other cousins—Knight and Lee—captains in the 17th regiment, are mentioned (p. 208), and yet another, 'son of the late Alderman Bates of Waterford' (p. 221). His grandfather, James Gardner, who died, a lieutenant in the navy, in 1755, was, in 1747–8, a lieutenant of the Culloden, with Captain, afterwards Admiral Sir Francis, Geary, the godfather of James's son, who, on 2 February, 1768, married Rachel, daughter of Anthony Lee of Waterford, and niece of Admiral William Parry. It will be noticed that the younger Gardner, having been born in Ireland, son of an Irish mother, considered himself Irish, is especially Irish in his sympathies, and that throughout his 'Recollections' the word 'Irish' is very commonly used as denoting 'exceptionally good.'

From 1775, when he was not more than five years old, Gardner was borne, as his father's servant, on the books of the Boreas, the Conqueror, and the Ætna; and he might, according to the custom of the day, have counted these years as part of his time at sea. As, however, when he went up for his examination (p. 174), he had more sea time than enough, he only counted it from his entry on board the Salisbury in December 1783 (p. 41). Really, he first went to sea in May 1782 (p. 19) in the Panther, and in her, under—in succession—Captains Thomas Piercy and Robert Simonton, he saw the loss of the Royal George, and was present at Howe's relief of Gibraltar and in the 'rencounter' with the combined fleets of France and Spain off Cape Spartel on 20 October, 1782 (pp. 24, 27, 30 *seq.*).

During the ensuing peace he served on the Newfoundland and Home stations, as midshipman and master's mate in the Salisbury, 50, flagship of Vice-Admiral John Campbell (pp. 41–55); Orestes, 18, Captain Manley Dixon (pp. 56–63); Edgar, 74, flagship of Rear Admirals the Hon. John Leveson Gower and Joseph Peyton (pp. 64–96); Barfleur, 98, bearing the flags of Admirals Roddam, the Hon. Samuel Barrington, Sir John Jervis, John Elliot and Jonathan Faulknor (pp. 97–120), and Queen, 98, Captain John Hutt (pp. 121–5). After a further service, chiefly in the Mediterranean in the Berwick, 74, Captains Sir John Collins, William Shield, George Campbell and George Henry Towry (pp. 126–154); in the Gorgon, 44, Captain James Wallis, for a passage to England (pp. 155–171); and in the Victory, 110, Captain John Knight, at Portsmouth (pp. 172–7), he was promoted, 12 January 1795, to be lieutenant of the Hind, 28, Captains Richard Lee and John Bazely (the younger), on the North American and Irish stations, and in January 1797 was sent in to Plymouth in charge of a prize, La Favorite privateer, of 8 guns and 60 men (pp. 178, 202).

His next appointments were—8 March 1798, to the Blonde, 32, Captain Daniel Dobree, under whom he assisted in conveying troops to Holland in August 1799 (pp. 203–225); 13 April, 1801, to the Brunswick, 74, Captain George Hopewell Stephens, which, after a year in the West Indies, returned home and was paid off in July 1802 (pp. 226–249). After a short service as agent of transports at Portsmouth (p. 250), he was appointed, in January 1806, in charge of the signal station at Fairlight in Sussex, where he continued till 7 December 1814 (pp. 251–263). From that date he remained on half pay as a lieutenant, till on 26 November 1830, he was placed on the retired list with the rank of commander.

Reading this summary of Gardner's service, in connection with the longer narrative, we are naturally inclined to say: Another instance of a good man choked out of the line of promotion by want of interest; there must have been something radically wrong with the system that permitted want of interest to shelve, at the age of 32, a sober, punctual and capable officer, with a blameless record and distinguished certificates. But would such a presentment of the case be quite correct? Gardner was excellently well connected, and had relations or good friends—including the comptroller himself (p. 97)—in many different departments of the public service. He must have had remarkably good interest; and we are forced to look elsewhere for what can only be called his failure.

The first reason for it—one, too, that has damaged many a young officer's prospects—was his determination to pick and choose his service. This is apparent throughout. He wasted his interest in getting out of what he considered disagreeable employments. He quarrelled with Captain Calder and wearied Sir Henry Martin by his refusal to go to the West Indies, as it 'did not suit my inclination' (p. 97); he scouted McArthur's suggestion to try his fortune on board the Victory (p. 148), and got himself sent to the Gorgon for a passage to

England, only to find that his cleverness cost him five months' time and the whole of his kit (pp. 172–3). The same daintiness is to be observed throughout. But if one thing is more certain than another in calculating the luck of the service, it is that a whole-hearted devotion to it, a readiness to go anywhere and to do anything, pays the best.

Later on, there was another reason for Gardner's want of this readiness. He married early—on 11 December 1798—and his future career does not contravene the frequently expressed opinion of our most distinguished admirals, from Lord St. Vincent downwards, that—as far as the service is concerned—a young lieutenant might as well cut his throat as marry. 'D'ye mind me,' says the old song—

> 'D'ye mind me! a sailor should be, every inch,
> All as one as a piece of the ship;'

and for a young man, with a young wife at home, that is impossible. His allegiance is divided; the wife on shore has the biggest share and continually calls for more, till the husband gets a home appointment—a guardo, a coast-guard, or a signal station—pleasant for the time, but fatal to all chance of promotion. No doubt there have been exceptions. It would not be impossible to cite names of officers who married as lieutenants and rose to high rank; but either under peculiar conditions of service, or because the wife has had sufficient strength of mind to prevent her standing in the way of her husband's profession; possibly even she may have forwarded him in it. *Exceptio probat regulam*; but Gardner was not one. His direct connection with the service ended with the peace in 1814. It does not appear that he either asked for or wished for any further employment; but spent the rest of his life in a peaceful and contented retirement in the bosom of his family, at Peckham, where he died on 24 September 1846, in his 76th year. He was buried in the churchyard of St. Mary's, Newington Butts, where a head-stone once marked the site of the grave. But the churchyard has been turned into a pleasure-ground, and the position of the stone or the grave is now unknown.

The 'Recollections' which by the kindness of the author's grandsons, Francis William and Henry James Gardner, we are now permitted to print, were written in 1836, and corrected, to some small extent, in later years. We have no information of the sources from which he composed them. He must have had his logs; and we may suppose either that these took the form of journals, or that he had also kept a journal with some regularity. Certainly it is not probable that, without some register, he could have given the lists of his shipmates, correct even—in very many cases—to the Christian names. That their characters and the various highly flavoured anecdotes were matters of memory is more easily believed.

What is, in one sense, the most remarkable thing about the work is the strong literary seasoning which it often betrays. The manuscript is a little volume (fcap. 4to) written on both sides of the paper, in a small neat hand. This, of itself, is evidence that Gardner—leaving school, after six or seven broken years, at the age of twelve—did not consider, or rather was not allowed to consider, his education finished in all branches except in the line of his profession. Of the way in which it was continued, we have no knowledge. It is quite possible that Macbride, the drunken and obscene schoolmaster of the Edgar, may, in his sober intervals, have helped to inspire him with some desire of learning. The educational powers of Pye, the schoolmaster of the Salisbury and of the Barfleur, can scarcely have stretched beyond the working of a lunar. In the Berwick he was shipmates with the Rev. Alexander John Scott—in after years chaplain of the Victory and Nelson's foreign secretary—a man of literary aptitudes, who was 'always going on shore to make researches after antiquities' (p. 150), and Gardner may sometimes have been allowed to accompany him in his rambles.

However this may have been, it is very noteworthy that a tincture of polite learning was shared by many of his messmates. To those whose notions of life afloat are gathered from Roderick Random and other descriptions of the seamy side of the service, it will seem incredible that such should have been the case. We are not here concerned to prove it as a general proposition. It is enough to refer to the particular instances before us—that of Gardner and his messmates. He tells us that Macredie, who was with him in the Edgar, and afterwards in the Barfleur, was 'an excellent scholar, well acquainted with Greek and Latin, ancient history and mathematics' (p. 80), which must mean something, even if we allow a good deal for exaggeration. In the Edgar they were with that disreputable but amiable and talented sinner, Macbride; and it was also in the Edgar that the assumption of Homeric characters was a common sport, in which Macredie figured as Ajax Telamon, Culverhouse as Diomede, and Pringle won the name of 'Ponderous and Huge' (pp. 84, 93).

This does not, perhaps, go for very much; but it cannot be lost sight of that, as concerns Gardner, it was accompanied by a readiness to apply quotations from Pope's *Iliad* and from the *Æneïd*, sometimes in Dryden's version, sometimes in the original. He was certainly, also, as familiar with *Hudibras* as ever Alan Quatermain was with *The Ingoldsby Legends*. Shakespeare he does not seem to have studied; and though it is but a small thing in comparison that he should have read *Ossian* and *A Sentimental Journey*, his knowledge of, his familiarity with, Roman history may be allowed as a make-weight, unless indeed—which is quite possible—it was drilled into him by Scott on each separate occasion. Thus, when the Berwick goes to Tunis and Porto Farino, he is reminded of the fate of Regulus (p. 136); he connects Trapani with the destruction of the Roman fleet under Claudius (p. 137), and knows that the concluding battle of the first Punic war—the battle which, as Mahan has shown, decided the result of the second Punic war—was fought off the Egades (p. 138). Incomparably more attention is nowadays paid to the instruction of our youngsters; but we are confident that very few of them could note such things in their journal unless specially coached up in them by a friendly senior.

In this, again, there have been exceptions. Until recently there has probably always been a sprinkling of officers who kept up and increased the knowledge of Latin they brought from Eton or Westminster[1] or other schools of classical learning; and Hannay, the novelist, who had a personal acquaintance with gun-room life of sixty years ago, has represented the midshipmen and mates of his day bandying quotations from Horace or Virgil with

[1] It is not out of place to mention here what we were told many years ago by an officer of the Conway, that the late Professor Montague Burrows, when a lieutenant of the Winchester, was initiated in the mysteries of the Greek Grammar by the late Sir Anthony Hoskins, then a cadet fresh from Westminster. Burrows afterwards took a first class in classics at Oxford

a freedom which many have thought ridiculous, but which, we must admit, might sometimes be met with. We were told by an officer who served in the Hibernia under the flag of Sir William Parker, that it was easy to fit names to all the principal characters in Hannay's novelettes; and it may be assumed that what was true for the captains was equally true for the midshipmen.

Such familiarity with the Latin poets was, of course, very exceptional then; it has now, we fancy, entirely dropped out. The Latin which our present youngsters bring into the service must be extremely little, and they have no opportunity of continuing the study of it; and though English history and naval history form part of the curriculum at Osborne and Dartmouth, there is but little inducement to a young officer to read more when he goes afloat. But there are certainly many of our older officers who would say that a sound and intelligent knowledge of history is more likely to be profitable to the average captain or admiral than the most absolute familiarity with the processes of the differential or integral calculus.

A considerable, and what to many will be a most interesting, part of the volume is occupied by lists of names and thumb-nail sketches of character. No attempt has been made to amplify these beyond filling in dates and Christian names [in square brackets] from *Navy-lists* and *Pay-books*. More would generally have been impracticable, for most of the names are unknown to history; and where otherwise, anything like full notices would have enormously swelled the volume, without any adequate gain. It has seemed better to add a mere reference to some easily accessible memoir, either in the *Dictionary of National Biography* (*D.N.B.*), Charnock's *Biographia Navalis*, Marshall's *Royal*

Naval Biography, or O'Byrne's *Naval Biographical Dictionary*; sometimes also to James's *Naval History*, Schomberg's *Naval Chronology*, or to Beatson's *Naval and Military Memoirs*—all books which are quite common, and are or ought to be in every naval library.

It remains only for the Editors to express their grateful thanks to the Messrs. Gardner, who not only permit them to publish the 'Recollections,' but supplied them with a copy of the MS., typed at their expense; to the Very Rev. the Dean of Waterford, who has most kindly had all the registers at Waterford searched (though vainly) in the endeavour to determine the exact date of Commander Gardner's birth; and to the numerous friends and even strangers who have so kindly helped them in answering the various queries which have presented themselves. These are too many to name; but the Editors must, in a special degree, mention their obligations to Commander C. N. Robinson, R.N., whose very exceptional knowledge of the byways of naval literature has been most generously put at their service. That some of their queries have remained unanswered and that explanatory notes are thus sometimes wanting will serve to emphasise the importance of the assistance referred to. What, for instance, is the meaning of the phrase 'My hat's off' (p. 108)? Apparently 'Not a word!' but why? or again, what are 'ugly podreen faces' (p. 214)? To a mere Englishman the epithet looks as if it might be Irish; but Irish dictionaries and three competent Irish scholars are positive that it is not. Once more, they express their warmest thanks for the help that has been so freely given them.

CONTENTS

NAVAL RECOLLECTIONS
IN SHREDS AND PATCHES
WITH STRANGE REFLECTIONS
ABOVE AND UNDER HATCHES.

I know nothing of grammar;
At school they never could hammer
    Or beat it into my head.
The bare word made me stammer,
    And turn pale as if I were dead.
And here I may as well be telling
I'm often damned out in my spelling.
And this is all the apology
I offer for my chronology,
And biographical sketches
Of mighty men, and lubberly wretches,
From seventeen hundred and seventy-seven—
Their rank, their titles, and their names are given.

14th June 1836.

BOREAS, 28

Ye bloods of the present day!
To you I have nothing to say,
Except ye are able
To splice a chain cable
Or get a sheer hulk under way.
But to my veteran friends,
I submit here my odds and my ends.

I BEGIN at the good old times when luxury was not known in the service, when we were carrying on the war against the Yankees and the French. My father, the late Captain Francis Geary Gardner, was appointed through the interest of Admiral Francis Geary [1] (afterwards Sir Francis), and of my mother's uncle, Admiral William Parry,[2] to be master of the Boreas, a new frigate of 28 guns fitting at Chatham, and commanded by Captain Charles Thompson, with the promise of Lord Sandwich (then first lord of the admiralty) to be promoted when opportunity offered; which promise his lordship performed by appointing him lieutenant of the Conqueror, 74, as will be seen hereafter.

It has pleased God to give me a good memory, and I have perfect recollection of almost every circumstance from very early life. My objection writing my naval recollections is to amuse my family

[1] *D. N. B.*—In 1780, commander-in-chief in the Channel; baronet in 1782. Died in 1796.

[2] Charnock, v. 350. Died in 1779.

when I am moored head and stern; and I shall first state for their information that my naval ancestors held the rank from admiral of the white to that of commander, and in the soldiering line from general to major. Having settled this point I shall now commence by stating that, while the Boreas was fitting, we took lodgings at the house of a cross old maid at Brompton, named Patty Pankhurst, who I have reason to remember; for having unfortunately cut up some carrots she had for dinner, and upsetting her potatoes down an alley, she for this innocent amusement never forgave me. I well recollect a ghostly story the old hussy related about the boatswain of the Bonny Broom who was drowned going off to his ship near Gillingham, and how he used to be seen cruising up and down along the shore and hailing 'Board the Bonny Broom ahoy!' three times, and then go to the churchyard exactly at 1 o'clock and disappear! She would kindly tell me this at night, adding 'Hark, don't you hear him?' and then I would be afraid to go to bed. This had ten times more effect upon my nerves than the little cane she kept for active service,

> With which she laid about more busily
> Than the Amazonian dame Penthesile (*Hudibras*);

and if Patty would only say 'I think I hear the boatswain,' I would be off without further trouble.

My father, mother, and Charley Buchan, the purser, took it into their heads to walk to Cobham on a Sunday in very warm weather. When they got there, it was near church time in the afternoon; they wanted to get dinner, but nothing could be obtained at any of the houses; and when asked if they had anything, the answer was, 'We have ate it all up,' and Buchan would reply, 'The devil choke you with it.' He then set off to forage while we remained at an inn. After waiting some time we heard a shouting, and on going out saw him marching at the head of the people who were going to church, waving a shoulder of mutton and singing a stave from the 41st Psalm:

> Happy the man whose tender care
> Relieves the poor distressed.

On his coming in, the landlord took my father aside and requested to know if the gentleman (meaning Buchan) was right in his intellect. To keep up the joke my father told him he was subject to sudden fits of insanity and would frequently bite people, and always took the piece out. 'God save us!' said the landlord; 'I wish his honour had gone to some other house, for I don't like the look of him.' The mutton, however, was put down to roast, and when about half done was brought in, and the landlord, bending his eye, not on vacancy but on Buchan, said he hoped everything was to his honour's liking, and adding that when the company had dined he would be glad to have the room, as it was engaged for the evening; upon which Buchan got up and, flourishing the carving knife, sang with a voice of thunder, 'Farewell to Lochaber,' which made the landlord back out as if he had been at the levee. We soon after relieved him from his troubles and returned to Brompton.

When the ship was fitted we sailed for Sheerness; and on paying a visit to the Mars, 74, a guardship at Black Stakes (the captain being a relation of my mother) we got swamped alongside, but luckily escaped drowning. While at Sheerness we had an invitation to dine with a merchant whose name was Simmers, and among the number Buchan the purser was invited. At the table sat Mr. Simmers' dog Pompey, with a plate laid for him.

It was laughable to hear Buchan (who was a wag) ask Pompey if he should have the pleasure of drinking wine with him; and on taking leave he gave the dog an invitation to dine on board with him the next day, saying he should be most happy to see him and his father (Mr. Simmers), and to be sure not to come without him. The old man felt the rebuke and gave no more invitations.

After getting our powder we sailed for the Downs, and soon after proceeded to Spithead, where we remained a short time until we received orders to take shipwrights to Halifax from Portsmouth and Plymouth; and when everything was ready, we got under way from St. Helen's in the evening; but in consequence of the man in the chains giving the wrong soundings—the leadline being foul—the ship struck on the Dean, where the old Invincible, 74, was lost, and after considerable damage was got off and returned to Spithead and then to Portsmouth Harbour to refit. My father was tried by a court martial and honourably acquitted. While in the harbour alongside the jetty, a cat flew at the sentry on the gangway and fixed on his shoulder, and it was with great difficulty the animal could be removed; the sentry fell in a fit and dropped his musket overboard and was subject to fits while he remained in the ship. The Boreas when refitted was ordered to the West Indies, and I left the ship for school,[1] and again joined her on her return, and sailed for Plymouth and went into Hamoaze, when Lord Sandwich promoted my father and appointed him fifth Lieutenant of the Conqueror, 74, fitting in the harbour.

[1] It was then, and for many years afterwards, quite usual for a youngster to be at school while his name was on the ship's books When—as in this case—the boy was his father's servant, he might be on board while the ship was in a home port.

We took lodgings at the house of a hop merchant in North Corner Street; he was also carpenter of a line-of-battle ship, and a very eccentric character. His name was John Cowdray, and on his table linen was marked in large letters Sir John Cowdray, Baronet and Knight of the Bath. His wife was also a strange being and was perpetually calling out 'Bet Waters! Bet Waters!' (the name of her servant) from morning until night, with a voice that sounded like a sow-gelder's flageolet. The day before my father left the Boreas, he gave at this house a dinner to the captain and officers; and I remember his saying to Captain Thompson that Sir Francis Drake taught the people of Plymouth to walk upright: before that they went on all fours. He had hardly made the observation when the door opened, and in came one of the servants upon all fours, having fallen and upset a couple of roast fowls with all the contents upon Sir John Cowdray's fine carpet, and bespattered my father's white lappels. 'There,' says Captain Thompson, 'is a specimen of grown people taught to walk upright by Sir Francis Drake.'

While the Boreas lay in Hamoaze, a violent quarrel took place between her crew and that of the Foudroyant, and several hard battles were fought, to the advantage of the former, who always came off conqueror when not overpowered by numbers. We had a fellow by the name of Waddle who was coxswain of the pinnace, and a noted boxer. This man fought and beat three of the best men belonging to the Foudroyant, one after the other, to the great satisfaction of his shipmates, who made a subscription and handsomely rewarded their champion.

During the time this frigate was in the West Indies and also on the home service, she sailed superior to any of the men of war, and was one of the first of the copper-bottomed. The following are the names of the officers that I can recollect :—

CHARLES THOMPSON, Esq., Captain.

Dead [1799]. A baronet and vice-admiral of the red.—[*D.N.B*].

JOHN LAUGHARNE, 1st Lieutenant.

Dead [1819]. A vice-admiral; a most indefatigable first lieutenant, and one of the best seamen in the service.

JOSEPH PEYTON, 2nd Lieutenant.

Dead [1816]. A rear-admiral [superannuated].

CHARLES HOLMES EVERITT, 2nd Lieutenant.

Dead [1807]. An admiral [took the name of Calmady].

[RICHARD] HAWFORD, 2nd Lieutenant.

He commanded the Rover sloop of war when she upet in a white squall on the West India Station and all hands unfortunately perished [on or about 29 October 1781].

FRANCIS GEARY GARDNER, Master.

Dead. A captain in the Royal Navy. He was considerd one of the first seamen in the navy, and also a most skilful pilc for the coast of America.

CHARLES BUCHAN, Purser.

Dead. A most worthy gentleman.

CORREY, Surgeon.

Dead. Remember little of him. I believe he was drowed when the Royal George upset.

[WILLIAM] WILLIAMS, Lieutenant of Marines.

Dead.

J[OHN] MONKTON, Mate.

Dead [1827]. A rear-admiral. He was first lieutenant of te Marlborough, 74, in Lord Howe's action, June 1, 1794, and behaved with great bravery. He was made commander and soon afte got his post rank. He commanded the Mars, 74, the flagship of Admiral Berkeley. When the promotion of flags took place to the astonishment of every person, he was placed on the *retird* list of rear-admirals.—[Marshall, iii. 12.]

LENOX THOMPSON, Mate.

Dead [1835]. A post captain [1802]; a very good officer

GEORGE WANGFORD, Midshipman.

Dead. See Edgar.

[JACOB] SWANSON, Gunner.

Dead. A very good man, but had a very bad wife.[1]

[THOMAS] WILSON, Surgeon's Mate.

Uncertain. He could play a little on the flute, and used to annoy all hands by everlastingly playing the King's Minuet.

The above are all the officers I can recollect that belonged to the Boreas.

[1] The heroine of a low-class chap-book, *The Adventures of Moll Swanson of Portsmouth*, which may still occasionally be met with.

CONQUEROR, 74

My Lord, you give a fight in sham,
A Spithead fight not worth a damn,
And that's your Lordship's epigram.

My father joined the Conqueror in December 1777 as fifth and then fourth lieutenant, the late Admiral Thomas Lord Graves captain, fitting in Hamoaze; and after a cruise or two the ship was ordered to Spithead to join the fleet assembled there for the sham fight, and to be reviewed by his Majesty King George III. Sir Thomas Pye, admiral of the white, was port admiral and senior officer, and Admiral Keppel (blue at the main) had his flag on board the Prince George, 98. When his Majesty went afloat, the flag officers and captains attended in their barges, Sir Thomas Pye leading the van. The royal standard was hoisted on board the Prince George, and a grand salute took place from the whole of the men of war, which was repeated several times during the day. Thousands of boats full of spectators attended at Spithead; several of the nobility were on board the Conqueror. The ladies didn't much like the firing, and one of them had a tooth knocked out by biting the frame of the quarter-gallery window when the after gun on the main deck went off. Soon after the review, a fleet being ordered to sail for America with all possible dispatch, we were sent to Plymouth to join them.

They consisted of the following men of war under the command of the Honourable John Byron, vice-admiral of the blue:—

Princess Royal	98	Flag Ship
Conqueror	74	Commodore Graves Captain H. Harmood
Cornwall	74	
Sultan	74	
Grafton	74	
Fame	74	
Bedford	74	
Albion	74	
Culloden	74	
Russell	74	
Invincible	74	
Royal Oak	74	
Monmouth	64	
Guadeloupe	32	

The fleet sailed from Cawsand Bay in 1778 soon after the review and a short time before Keppel's action, and I left the ship for school. It is in the remembrance of many that this fleet had a dreadful passage and separated. The Princess Royal arrived at her destination alone, and it was a long time before they could be collected. The Conqueror was eleven weeks on her passage, and had three hundred of her crew in the sick list. The Invincible put into St. John's, Newfoundland, in distress, and all the squadron suffered more or less. I hope it will not be presumptuous to state that my father was considered one of the best seamen in the service, and a very able and skilful pilot, particularly for the coast of America; which is well known to some of the oldest officers of the present day. In this gale he exerted himself with such ability that when Admiral Hyde Parker hoisted his flag on board the Conqueror, he told my father that he should remember him when opportunity offered, which promise he performed by removing him to the Princess Royal, his flagship, when he took the command of the fleet on the return of Admirals Byron and Barrington to England. The rear-admiral was a very strict officer, and from his austere disposition got the nickname of Old Vinegar, and it was a very difficult task for an officer to get into his good graces. When he shifted his flag (blue at the mizen) from the Conqueror to the Princess Royal in the West Indies, he also removed Mr. McInerheny, the master of the former (an officer and seaman of first-rate abilities), to the flagship, and, in February 1780, he promoted my father and appointed him Captain of the Etna, wishing him success as a meritorious officer and deserving of promotion, and said he would recommend him to Admiral Rodney as soon as he should take command of the fleet. I shall just mention that Patrick Gibson,[1] who died about four years ago, aged one hundred and eleven, was purser of the Princess Royal and a messmate of my father's. I shall state further particulars of this extraordinary man when I come to the Blonde.

The following are the names of the officers.

THOS. GRAVES, Esq., Captain and then Commodore.

Dead [1802]. An admiral of the white. When made a rear-admiral he had his flag on board the London, 98, at the Chesapeake, but failed in preventing the Count de Grasse getting there with succours for the American Army. Owing to this unfortunate circumstance, Lord Cornwallis was obliged to capitulate with 5,000 men to the Americans. He had his flag on board the Ramillies when that ship foundered in the gale of September 1782, coming home with the West India convoy, of which he had

[1] Born in 1720; died 1830. His portrait, painted shortly before his death, is in the Painted Hall at Greenwich. See *post*, p. 213.

charge, and showed uncommon presence of mind in the dreadful situation that ship was in. The Ramillies was lying to under a main sail[1] (a sail that a ship should never be laid to under) on the larboard tack with her head to the westward, when she was taken aback, and if her mast had not gone she must have foundered. She had six feet of water in the hold, which increased to nine feet, and it was found impossible to keep her free. Fortunately the gale abated for a short time, and the ship's company were removed to a merchantman, the admiral being the last to quit. He did everything that an able seaman could do to save her, in setting a good example and showing undaunted courage in a situation that would have shaken the nerves of the philosophers of Greece and Rome. Admiral Graves was port admiral at Plymouth, and when the war broke out in 1793 he hoisted his flag on board the Royal Sovereign, 110; was in the action of the 1st of June 1794; was wounded and made a peer.—[*D.N.B.*]

HARRY HARMOOD, Esq., Captain
Dead. Commissioner of the Navy.

[CHARLES] OSBORNE, 1st Lieutenant.
Dead.

[ELLIS] TROUGHTON, 2nd Lieutenant.
Dead. A commander.

[THOMAS] FLOYD, 3rd Lieutenant.
Dead. A dandy.

FRANCIS GEARY GARDNER, 4th Lieutenant [5th, 4th, 3rd, 2nd.]
Dead. Captain. [James Gardner, his servant; both D. August 28, 1779, to Princess Royal.]

WILLIAMS, 5th Lieutenant.
Dead. A mad fellow.

N[ICHOLAS] McINERHENY, Master.
Dead. An excellent officer and seaman. [William McInerheny, his servant.]

SIR JOHN DALSTON, Baronet, Captain of Marines.
Dead.

WALTER SMITH, Lieutenant of Marines.
Dead. A colonel.

WILLIAM BARKER, Lieutenant of Marines.
Dead. A captain in the army.

---

[1] This was then usual. Probably the fate of the Ramillies had a good deal to do with putting it out of fashion, as it certainly had with forcing seamen to consider that there was a right and a wrong tack on which to lie to; and may thus be said to have brought about the discovery of the Law of Storms.

[Henry] Hutchins, Purser.
Dead.

[Robert] White, Surgeon.
Dead.

[John Stode] Foote, Chaplain.
Dead.

[Thomas] Mears [or Mayers], Gunner.
Dead.

[Benjamin] Hearle, Carpenter.
Dead.

Richard Nash, Midshipman.
Dead. A lieutenant R.N.; was first of the Impregnable, 98, the flagship in Hamoaze; and while standing on the gangway was killed by a man falling on him from the mainyard.

[John] Nash, Midshipman [Captain's servant].
Dead [1824]. Captain, brother of the above.

[James] Nash, Midshipman [Captain's servant.]
Dead [1827]. Captain, brother of the above.

John Blake, Midshipman [Captain's servant].
Dead. A commander.

Robert Rolles, Midshipman.
A vice-admiral, and a most active and able officer. [Died, 1839 —Marshall, ii. 676.]

NAVAL ACADEMY, GOSPORT

> In Mathematics he was greater
> Than Tycho Brahe, or Erra Pater.
> For he by geometric scale
> Could take the size of pots of ale;
> Resolve by sines and tangents straight,
> If bread or butter wanted weight;
> And wisely tell what hour o' th' day,
> The clock does strike by algebra.—*Hudibras.*

THE name of the master of this school was Orchard, and a very good man he was; but who the devil taught him navigation is more than I can say. He was a great disciplinarian, and used to flourish with direful sway an infernal horsewhip, that I have reason to remember. It was called 'black pudding,' and he was no way stingy in serving it out. I recollect one of the scholars coming very late one morning quite out of breath, and when asked the reason by old Orchard, he replied: 'The man said that the boy said that the woman said that Mr. Browell said if he did not hold his tongue he would knock him down dead.' This set the whole school in a roar of laughter, and I for one got three or four cuts across the shoulder with the before-mentioned black pudding, that I have perfect remembrance of to the present day. While at this school we used to bathe in a lake that runs near the Horse-field on the Stoke Road. On one occasion we drove a cow into the mud so that we could not extricate the animal, and it was fast sinking up to the neck. A militia regiment happened to be encamped near the spot, and it took several of the soldiers a long time to get it out. I never shall forget the terror we were in when the owner swore he would send the whole of us to jail; and Buck Adams, the keeper of the Bridewell, passing near the spot by chance, we thought he was come to seize us, and several of the party set off and ran naked into the town covered with mud. We had to pay near twenty shillings to make the matter up, besides treating the soldiers, who enjoyed the fun. As I'm in a hurry to get to sea again I shall only relate one or two circumstances that happened before I took my departure.

I was standing on Gosport beach when the prisoners were landed from some of the prizes taken by Rear-Admiral Kempenfelt (the ablest tactician in the navy), who with only twelve sail of the line by a masterly manœuvre captured most of the convoy from the French admiral, Count de Guichen, who had nineteen sail of the line, and frustrated the expedition. A party of soldiers assembled on the beach to escort them to Forton prison, a lieutenant of the navy and several midshipmen also attending, when a *posse* of women rushed out of Rime's 'noted alley' and, pointing to the soldiers, sang the following beautiful ditty:

Don't you see the ships a-coming?
    Don't you see them in full sail?
Don't you see the ships a-coming
    With the prizes at their tail?
Oh! my little rolling sailor,
    Oh! my little rolling he;
I do love a jolly sailor,
    Blithe and merry might he be.

Sailors, they get all the money,
    Soldiers they get none but brass;
I do love a jolly sailor,
    Soldiers they may kiss—
Oh! my little rolling sailor,
    Oh! my little rolling he;
I do love a jolly sailor,
    Soldiers may be damned for me.

Then, catching hold of the lieutenant and midshipmen, they began to hug and kiss them, and it was some time before they could get out of their clutches. They then began to pelt the soldiers, who took it very patiently and seemed very glad when the order was given to march with the Frenchmen.

In holiday time we used to set off to a place called Grange, about two miles from Gosport, where the gipsies had a camp, and many a desperate battle we have had with them. I well recollect about fourteen of us going out, and after many manœuvres we succeded in capturing some of their donkeys and rode off in triumph; but the swarthy squad got a reinforcement, with which they attacked us; and with sticks and stones, we maintained a running fight until driven into Stoke, after abandoning our donkeys and giving up the contest. The clergyman at Stoke (Mr. Shield) who had witnessed the engagement, said it was the defeat of the long-eared cavalry by the Egyptian infantry.

The following are the names of the gentlemen at this Academy :—

Orchard, the Master.
Dead. A very worthy and upright character.

Edward Bingham, Midshipman.
Dead. A very worthy young man.

J. Bingham, Midshipman.
Dead. A rear-admiral—proud enough.

Robert Bingham.
Dead. A clergyman, Royal Navy.

John Merrett.
Dead. A surgeon at Portsmouth.

J. A. Gardner, Midshipman.
A commander.

William Vosper, Midshipman.
A lieutenant of the Royal Hospital at Greenwich.

William Kitten.

Uncertain. Like all kittens made too much of.

Richard Nicholson, Midshipman.

Dead. A commander.

W. P. Nicholson, Midshipman.

Dead. Unfortunate.

John Wilkinson.

Dead. A lawyer at Gosport.

W. Coet, Midshipman.

A commander; a very good fellow; we used to cal him Old Owl. Since dead. [Possibly William Coote.—Marshall, x. 364.]

William Bowler.

Dead. A surgeon in the Royal Navy, called Squiney; a very good fellow.

John Barton.

Dead. Sir John Barton, treasurer of the Queen's household.

Skene, Midshipman.

Uncertain. Called Jaw-me-dead.

Sol. Saradine.

Dead. A droll, wicked fellow.

Taylor.

This unfortunate man was surgeon of H.M. ship Jamaica, and by the sentence of a court martial was hanged at the yardarm at Spithead.[1]

Richard Carter.

Dead. A very worthy fellow.

---

[1] There is no reason to doubt the fact; but, in the absence of Christian name and date, the court martial cannot be traced; nor can any man of the name be found, as surgeon, in the pay-books of the Jamaica.

PANTHER, 60

When I remember all
    The friends so link'd together,
I've seen around me fall,
    Like leaves in windy weather;
    I feel like one
    Who treads alone
Some banquet-hall deserted,
    Whose lights are fled,
    Whose garlands dead,
And all but me departed.
Thus in the stilly night,
    Ere slumber's chain has bound me,
Sad memory brings the light
    Of other days around me.—MOORE.

WHEN I was on board the Boreas and Conqueror with my father I had nothing to do with the midshipmen, as I lived in the gunroom of the former and wardroom of the latter. But in this ship I took my degrees (not as a doctor of Oxford, thank God!) but as a midshipman in the cockpit of H.M. ship Panther, with some of the best fellows that ever graced the British navy. I joined her early in 1782 fitting in Portsmouth Harbour, commanded by Captain Thomas Piercy of glorious memory. I had eleven shillings given me by some friends in Gosport, and I thought my fortune was made.

On my introduction to my new shipmates I was shown down to the starboard wing berth. I had not been long seated before a rugged-muzzled midshipman came in, and having eyed me for a short time, he sang out with a voice of thunder: 'Blister my tripes—where the hell did you come from? I suppose you want to stick your grinders (for it was near dinner-time) into some of our a la mode beef;' and without waiting for a reply, he sat down and sang a song that I shall remember as long as I live. The first verse, being the most moral, I shall give:

A Duchess from Germany
  Has lately made her will;
Her body she's left to be buried,
  Her soul to the devil in hell.

This gentleman's name was Watson; and notwithstanding the song and his blunt manner of speaking, he proved to be a very good fellow, and was the life and soul of the mess.

I must now describe our starboard wing berth and compare it with the manners and customs of the present day. In this ship our mess-place had canvas screens scrubbed white, wainscot tables, well polished, Windsor chairs, and a pantry fitted in the wing to stow our crockery and dinner traps with safety. The holystones and hand organs,[1] in requisition twice a week, made our orlop deck as white as the boards of any crack drawing-room, the strictest attention being paid to cleanliness; and everything had the appearance of Spartan simplicity. We used to sit down to a piece of salt beef, with sour krout, and dine gloriously with our pint of black-strap[2] after, ready at all calls, and as fit for battle as for muster. Here mark the difference. The cockpit abandoned, and my lords and gentlemen ushered into the gunroom fitted up in luxurious style, with

[1] Large holystones, fitted with beckets, were drawn about by two men. The smaller ones, used in the hand, were 'hand organs.'

[2] Coarse red wine of any country, but very commonly Spanish or Portuguese.

window curtains, blinds, buffets, wine coolers, silver forks, and many other appendages of that delicate nature, unknown in the good old times; and, if I am correctly informed, a brass knocker[1] fixed at the gunroom door, which ever and anon announces the approach of the mighty members with as much pomp as a Roman consul with his lictors thundering at the door for admittance. But enough of this. When war comes we shall see.

When I joined the Panther, Mr. Price, the purser, who I knew nothing of, furnished me with everything I stood in need of, as the ship was hurried off to join Lord Howe and I had not time to get fitted out. When the ship was paid, he refused to take any remuneration when I called to repay the obligation, but said he would do the same again with pleasure. I stand indebted to his kindness, which I shall remember for ever with heartfelt gratitude and respect for his memory, and grieved I am that the service should have lost so good an officer, lamented by every person who had the pleasure of his acquaintance.

We sailed (I think) in May with the grand fleet under Lord Howe, to cruise in the North Sea after the Dutch. On our arrival in the Downs, Captain Piercy, from ill health, left the ship, to the great regret of every officer and man on board, and was succeeded in the command by Captain Robert Simonton.

> Nor he unworthy to conduct the host,
> Yet still they mourned their ancient leader lost.—*Iliad.*

During our cruise the influenza carried off great numbers in the fleet. Our ship's company (a most excellent one) was turned over to the Raisonnable, 64,

[1] The brass knockers, when met with, were probably trophies of a night's foray. Such things have been known within the memory of not-very-old men.

and that of the Ripon, 60, sent on board of us, and we shortly after left the fleet, and returned to the Downs to relieve the old Dromedary, and hoisted the flag (blue at the fore) of Vice-Admiral Sir Francis William Drake as port admiral, for about a month; when we were relieved by the Ripon, and then proceeded to St. Helen's, where we remained a short time, and sailed with a flying squadron to the westward, consisting of four sail of the line and three frigates, under the command of Captain Reeve[1] as commodore, as follows:

Crown .	. 64	(Captain Reeve, senior officer)
Suffolk .	. 74	[Captain Sir George Home][2]
Vigilant.	. 64	[Captain J. Douglas][2]
Panther.	. 60	[Captain R. Simonton]
Monsieur	. 36	[Captain Hon. Seymour Finch][2]
Recovery	. 32	[Captain Hon. G. C. Berkeley][2]
Cerberus	. 32	

About the middle of July, in the Bay of Biscay we took, after a long chase, three prizes, the Pigmy cutter, Hermione victualler, with ninety bullocks for the combined fleet, and a brig laden with salt. A day or two after, when blowing very hard and under a close-reefed main topsail and foresail, on the starboard tack, a fleet was seen to leeward on the beam and lee bow. The commodore made the private signal which was not answered, and then the signal for an enemy and to wear and make sail on the other tack. Wore accordingly, and set close-reefed topsails, with fore and main tacks on board, which worked the old ship most charmingly. In loosing the mizen topsail, and before letting it fall,

[1] Samuel Reeve died a vice-admiral, in 1802. Cf. *N.R.S.* xx. 111.

[2] The names are filled in from Beatson.

I slipped my foot from the horse[1] and fell off the yard into the top, and saved my life by catching hold of the clewline, having fallen from the bunt of the sail. The captain saw this and gave me a terrible rub down for not taking more care of myself. One of the prizes (the brig with salt) was retaken. The next morning, the weather being moderate, saw the enemy about three leagues to leeward. Sent down one of our frigates, the Monsieur who sailed remarkably well, to reconnoitre; in the evening they were out of sight. Soon after, we fell in with the Sandwich, 90, Vice-Admiral Sir Peter Parker (white at the fore), with the Count de Grasse[2] on board a prisoner, and a large convoy from the West Indies bound to England. Parted company from Sir Peter. Several ships of the line joined our squadron, which proceeded to cruise off the coast of Ireland for a short time, and then returned to Spithead, where we found the grand fleet fitting for the relief of Gibraltar. Caught fire in the marine storeroom near the after magazine, which damaged several knapsacks before it could be got under. We had only one boat alongside, the others being absent getting off the stores from the dockyard. A quartermaster's wife and three others jumped out of one of the lower-deck ports into this boat, and casting off the painter pulled away for the hospital beach as well as any bargemen, leaving their husbands to take care of themselves.

August the 29th, one of our fleet, the Royal George, 100, Rear-Admiral Kempenfelt (blue at the mizen), being on a careen, to the astonishment of every person upset at Spithead, and more than two

[1] *Sc.* the foot-rope.

[2] Commander-in-Chief of the French fleet in the battle of the 12th April.

thirds of her crew drowned, and among the number that brave and meritorious officer Admiral Kempenfelt, a man that has never been surpassed as an able tactician. We saved twenty-seven of her hands. One of them told a curious story. He said he was boat-keeper of the pinnace, whose painter was fast to the stern-ladder; and just as the ship was going over, the hairdresser took a flying leap out of the stern gallery with a powder bag in his hand and had nearly jumped into his boat. He was so much alarmed that he could not cast off the painter, nor could he find his knife to cut it, and was obliged to jump and swim for his life, when our boat picked him up. His own boat went down with the ship. It was a sad sight to see the dead bodies floating about Spithead by scores until we sailed. The poor admiral and several officers were never found. Captain Waghorn (the admiral's captain) was saved and tried by a court martial and acquitted. God knows who the blame ought to light on, for blame there must have been somewhere, for never was a ship lost in such a strange and unaccountable manner. The ship might have been weighed had proper steps been taken. A stupid attempt was made, but failed, as well it might; for neither officers nor men exerted themselves. The Royal William and Diligente were placed one on each side, and would have raised her, but energy was wanting, and there she remains, a disgrace to this day.[1]

[1] The very persistent way in which this story of the loss of the Royal George was spread abroad from the first, the entire suppression of the evidence (on oath) to the contrary, as given at the court martial, and the fact (here and elsewhere so strongly commented on) that care was taken to prevent the success of the proposed attempts to raise her, all point to one conclusion from which it is difficult to escape—the conscious guilt of some high-placed and influential officials of the Navy Board. Cf. *Naval*

Lord Howe having hoisted his flag (blue at the main) on board the Victory, 110, and the fleet being ready, the signal was made on the 11th of September to get under way, and that we were to take charge of the convoy as commodore with a broad blue pennant, and the Buffalo, 60, to bring up the rear. The convoy consisted of fifty sail of victuallers for the relief, with which we went through the Needles and joined the grand fleet at the back of the Isle of Wight, the Bristol, 50, and East India fleet under her charge, in company. In forming the line of battle the Goliath was to lead on the starboard tack and the Vengeance on the larboard. The fleet consisted of thirty-four sail of the line, besides frigates, and their names I shall give when I come to the action with the combined fleets.[1] We had moderate weather down Channel, and the number of convoys collected, and under the protection of the grand fleet to a certain distance, made up several hundred sail, which cut a fine appearance.

But, when the fleet got well into the Bay of Biscay, things began to alter, the wind shifting to the SW, with heavy squalls, which increased from a gale to a furious hurricane. I remember being at dinner in the wardroom when the height of the gale came on, the ship being under a close-reefed main topsail, and a very heavy sea running, which made her labour prodigiously. Our third lieutenant (Montagu) came down and said: 'Gentlemen, prepare for bad weather; the admiral has handed his main topsail and hove to under storm staysails. Our main topsail was not handed ten minutes before she gave a roll that beggared all description; 'chaos seemed to have come again,' and it appeared

Miscellany (*N.R.S.* xx.) p. 216; and *D.N.B.* *s.nn.* Durham, Sir Philip; Kempenfelt, Richard; Waghorn, Martin.

[1] *Sc.* of France and Spain.

doubtful whether she would right. The quarter-deck guns were out of sight from this lee lurch, and the weather roll was equally terrible. The scuttle butts[1] broke adrift and were stove; a lower-deck gun started and with great difficulty was secured; one of our poor fellows was lost overboard, and serious apprehensions were entertained for the safety of the ship, who cut such dreadful capers that we expected she would founder. I must here mention that when the Panther came from abroad, the devil tempted the navy board to order her proper masts to be taken out, and [a] fifty-gun ship's placed in their room, and this occasioned her to roll so dreadfully. It was in this gale that the Ville de Paris, Glorieux, Hector, Centaur, and others were lost on their passage to England from the West Indies. It lasted a considerable time, and it was near the middle of October before the fleet entered the Gut of Gibraltar.[2]

His lordship made the signal to prepare for battle, and while he stood up the Straits with the fleet, we were ordered to lead in the relief. In doing so we had near been relieved for ever, for we were taken in a sudden squall with our lower-deck guns run out, that had nearly swamped the ship before we could get them in and the ports down. Stood in for the Rock, but unfortunately got black-strapped[3]

[1] A 'scuttle' is defined by Falconer as 'a small hatchway cut for some particular purpose through a ship's deck, or through the coverings of the hatchways'; 'scuttling' is 'the act of cutting large holes through the bottom or sides of a ship.' A 'scuttle-butt' was a large cask, whose bung-hole had been cut into a small scuttle, secured on the main-deck in some convenient place, to hold water for present use. It may be well to say that 'scuttles' to light the orlop deck were quite unknown till long after the great war.

[2] October 11th. Cf. *N.R.S.* xx. 217 *seq.*

[3] So in MS.; but the word is 'back-strapped,' carried by the current to the back of Gibraltar. The writing 'black' shows

with part of the convoy, and with difficulty got them safe into Rosia Bay. Had three cheers given us by the garrison. The enemy's fleet, consisting of forty-five sail of the line, at anchor at Algesiras; one of their ships, the St. Michael, 70, a prize to the Rock; she had driven in the late gale under the batteries near the Old Mole and was captured. A constant cannonade kept up between the garrison and the Spanish lines; shot and shells flying in every direction; not a house left standing in the town, and the forts that were abreast the junk ships[1] (sunk before we arrived) beaten down to the water's edge; the inhabitants living in the bomb-proof, the only place of safety; and with the exception of the old Moorish Tower, that bid defiance to shot and shells, everything had the appearance of desolation and ruin.

While we remained in Rosia Bay, one of the enemy's line-of-battle ships (a three-decker) had the temerity to stand in and attack us and the convoy at anchor; but when within gunshot, the batteries opened such a heavy fire that she was obliged to haul off after being severely handled, doing us little damage—we had none killed or wounded. It was laughable to see the convoy blaze away with their pop-guns at this great hulk of a ship.

I have lately seen a volume [i. 106 *seq.*] of Lieutenant Marshall's *Naval Biography*, where he mentions, in the Life of Admiral Holloway, who commanded the Buffalo, 60, several particulars respecting the relief. Anyone not knowing better must suppose from reading his account that Captain Holloway had the sole charge, when, in fact, he only brought up the rear, and was under our orders.

how entirely the meaning of the term had been lost sight of. It is so with very many of the old nautical expressions.

[1] More commonly known as the 'floating batteries.' They were burnt.

No mention is made of the Panther being the commodore, and leading in a great part of the victuallers. Now, without wishing to take from the merits of Captain Holloway (who was a most able officer) I must beg leave to state that Captain Simonton, who was intrusted with the convoy, did his duty full as well as Captain H., although Lieutenant Marshall takes no notice of the Panther or her commander.

The same gentleman quotes an anonymous author[1] who reflects upon Lord Howe, and, among other incorrect statements, says it was injudicious in his lordship to place the Buffalo the rear ship in the action. Now I for one flatly contradict this, and I say that the Vengeance, 74, and not the Buffalo, was the rear ship. Lord Howe was too good an officer to place a ship in a situation where she was likely to be cut off, and his lordship's character is above the animadversions of an author who was afraid to put his name to his work. One of the convoy under charge of the Buffalo was captured, with the baggage and soldiers' wives, the only loss sustained.

The enemy's fleet having got under way on the 17th or 18th October, we also weighed; but were obliged to anchor, the enemy having made demonstrations to attack us. They, however, gave up the point for fear of the batteries; and we soon after left the Bay and joined the fleet preparing to anchor in Tetuan Bay, until his lordship was made acquainted of the combined fleet being at sea and standing up the Straits. The next morning, the 19th of October, the weather 'rather hazy, a kind of a mizzle,' the admiral made the signal to prepare for battle, the wind having shifted to the eastward, and

[1] Neither Marshall nor Gardner seems to have realised the utterly worthless character of the scurrilous book referred to—*The Naval Atalantis*, by 'Nauticus Junior,' said to have been Joseph Harris, sometime secretary to Admiral Milbanke.

the enemy in sight. His lordship soon after made the signal to bear up and sail large through the Gut, it not being his intention to engage until clear of the Straits. The enemy's fleet stood after us with every sail they could pack. It was a very beautiful sight to observe the evolutions of the two fleets and a fair trial of who could sail best. I well remember the Victory, Edgar, Raisonnable, and Royal William, with their topsails on the cap, running ahead of some with topgallant sails set. Our old ship, once called the Flying Panther, would have out-sailed any of them, had her masts not been altered. As we and the old Buffalo were not in the line of battle, because we had charge of the convoy before we saw them safe in, we imagined our station would be with the frigates to look on and see the fun, and we were laughing to think we should have a cool view of a battle, and one of the officers (who had read a little) observed he should be like Scipio the Younger, who, when sent on a mission to Africa, saw from an eminence a battle between that old vagabond Masinissa and the poor Carthaginians that lasted from morning until night. 'But mortal joys, alas! are fleeting;' for behold Lord Howe made our signal to come within hail; and while passing under the stern of the Victory we received directions to take our station in the line of battle between the Ruby and the Foudroyant in the van division. Nothing more about Scipio and Masinissa! The Buffalo was sent to the rear between the Union, 90, and Vengeance, 74. What do you say to that, Lieutenant Marshall, in your *Naval Biography*?

It took the fleet the whole day to clear the Gut. The next morning, off Cape Spartel, the signal was made to form the line of battle on the starboard tack and to prepare for action; the enemy coming down in line of battle abreast, with light winds and every sail set, making numerous signals, which had a very fine effect, as every ship repeated the signal and their fleet had the appearance of being dressed in colours. Our line was drawn up in the finest style, and so close and correct that you could only see the ship ahead and the other astern.

So close their order, so disposed their fight,
As Pallas' self might view with fixed delight ;
Or had the God of war inclined his eyes,
The God of war had owned a just surprise.

Owing to the light winds and the enemy repeatedly hauling up and then bearing away, it was near 6 P.M. before he formed his line. A three-decker (supposed to be the Royal Louis) leading his van began the action by firing into the Goliath, who led ours. The action continued from 6 P.M. until ¾ past 10 ; the van and rear chiefly engaged ; the centre had little to do. The enemy's centre extended to our rear-most ship, so that eleven or twelve of them (the whole of their rear) never fired a shot. We had four killed and sixteen wounded ; among the former Mr. Robert Sturges, midshipman doing duty as mate, a gentleman highly respected and lamented by every officer and man on board. I was placed with another youngster under his care, and he took the greatest pains to teach us our duty. He was as brave a fellow as ever lived, and when his thigh was nearly shot off by the hip, he cheered the men when dying. It was a spent shot that killed him, and weighed 28 pounds ; and what was remarkable, it took off at the same time the leg of a pig in the sty under the forecastle.[1]

I had a very narrow escape while standing on the quarter deck with Captain Forrester of the

[1] The pigsty, with its inmates, 'under the forecastle,' when going into action, seems indeed 'remarkable' on board an English ship, even in 1782.

marines. The first lieutenant (the late Admiral Alexander Fraser) came up to us, and while speaking a shot passed between us and stuck on the larboard side of the quarter deck. We were very close at the time, so that it could only have been a few inches from us. It knocked the speaking-trumpet out of Fraser's hand, and seemed to have electrified Captain Forrester and myself. The shot was cut out and weighed either 12 or 18 pounds—I forget which. Our rigging fore and aft was cut to pieces; the booms and boats also, and every timber-head on the forecastle, with the sheet and spare anchor stocks, were shot away, and the fluke of the latter. Our side, from the foremost gun to the after, was like a riddle, and it was astonishing that we had not more killed and wounded. Several shot-holes were under water, and our worthy old carpenter (Mr. Cock) had very near been killed in the wing, and was knocked down by a splinter, but not materially hurt. The enemy set off in the night and could only be seen from the masthead in the morning. It was supposed they went for Cadiz.

A curious circumstance took place during the action. Two of the boys who had gone down for powder fell out in consequence of one attempting to take the box from the other, when a regular fight took place. It was laughable to see them boxing on the larboard side, and the ship in hot action on the starboard. One of our poor fellows was cut in two by a double-headed shot on the main deck, and the lining of his stomach (about the size of a pancake) stuck on the side of the launch, which was stowed amidships on the main deck with the sheep inside.[1] The butcher who had

[1] Sixteen years later, before the battle of the Nile, the live stock was ruthlessly thrown overboard. Cf. *Log of the Zealous* (*N.R.S.* xviii. 12).

the care of them, observing what was on the side of the boat, began to scrape it off with his nails, saying, 'Who the devil would have thought the fellow's paunch would have stuck so? I'm damned if I don't think it's glued on!'

We had a fellow by the name of Mulligan who ran from his quarters and positively hid in the coppers! and had put on the drummer's jacket. When the firing had ceased he was seen coming out, and was taken for the poor drummer, and ran forward taking off the jacket, which he hid in the round house; but one of the boatswain's mates observed the transaction and Mr. Mulligan got well flogged just as the action was over. The poor drummer had greatly distinguished himself, and had taken off his jacket in the heat of the action, which this fellow stole to hide his rascality.

[Lists of the fleet, killed and wounded, of detachments to the West Indies and the coast of Ireland, follow. They are in close agreement with the lists given by Schomberg (*Naval Chronology*, iv. 390 *seq.*) and were probably copied from them, or the published lists which Schomberg reproduced. In any case, they have no special authority and are therefore omitted.

In November, on the Panther's arriving at Plymouth, where Vice-Admiral Lord Shuldham had his flag in the Dunkirk—]

a court martial was held on board the Dunkirk on one of our midshipmen (Mr. Foularton) on some trifling charge brought against him by Lieutenant Hanwell of the Dublin, on which he was fully acquitted. One of our main-top men (Martin Anguin), in sending down the topgallant mast, fell from the fore part of the main topmast crosstrees and pitched on the collar of the main stay, from which he went down, astern of the barge upon the booms, into the hold, the gratings being off. He was sent to the hospital without a fractured limb, but much bruised about the breast. He recovered and came on board to receive his pay on the day the ship was paid off. Such a fall and to escape with life, I believe is not to be found in the annals of naval history.[1] Hoisted the flag (blue at the fore) of Vice-Admiral Milbanke as port admiral, second in command.

The peace soon after taking place, a mutiny broke out in the men of war, and some of the ships began to unrig without orders, and were in a high state of insubordination, particularly the Blenheim, Crown, Standard, Medway, and Artois. I do not remember that any examples were made, but this I am sure of, that the ringleaders richly deserved hanging. Having received orders we dismantled the ship and struck Admiral Milbanke's flag, and in a few days after the old Panther was paid off to the great regret of every officer on board. It was like the parting of a family who had lived long together in the strictest friendship; and while writing this, it brings to mind many circumstances that make me bitterly lament the inroads death has made among those worthy fellows.

> The stroke of fate the bravest cannot shun;
> The great Alcides, Jove's unequall'd son,
> To Juno's hate at length resigned his breath,
> And sunk the victim of all-conquering death.

Before closing my account of the Panther, I must relate a few anecdotes that happened during the time I belonged to her. I was placed with another youngster, by the name of Owen, under the tuition of the captains of the fore and main top. We were

[1] The statement is curious, for instances of similar escape are by no means rare. In the days of sailing ships there can have been few officers of any seniority who had not known of at least one.

both in the same watch, which we kept first in one top and then in the other, to learn to knot and splice and to reef a sail; and for their attention we remunerated them with our grog. I remember the captain of the fore top (Joe Moulding), a very droll fellow, teaching us what he called a catechism, which we were obliged to repeat to him at two bells in every middle watch. It was as follows:

> 'So fine the Conflustions!! of old Mother Damnable, who jumped off the fore topsail yard and filled the main topgallant sail; run down the lee leach of the mizen and hauled the main tack on board, that all the devils in hell could not raise it; clapped a sheepshank on the main mast, a bowline knot on the foremast, and an overhand knot on the mizen mast; run the keel athwart ships, coiled the cables in the binnacle, tossed the quarter deck overboard, and made a snug ship for that night; when up jumped the little boy Fraser with a handspike stuck in his jaws to fend the seas off, with which he beat them into peas porridge, and happy was the man who had the longest spoon. AMEN!!'[1]

After repeating this rigmarole we were obliged to start up to the mast head, if topgallant yards were across, to blow the dust out of the topgallant clueline blocks. One night, blowing and raining like the devil, I proposed to Owen about five bells in the middle watch to steal down out of the top and take the raisins that were intended for the pudding next day. When we got down to our berth we found the

[1] The obsolete gibberish seems worth preserving, if only as a parallel to the still familiar 'So she went into the garden, &c.,' attributed to Samuel Foote.

raisins were mixed with the flour and we had the devil's own job to pick them out. After filling our pockets, one of the watch came down for grog and found us out. We ran off as fast as we could and got in the weather main rigging, where poor Owen was caught, seized up and made a spread eagle of for the remainder of the watch and part of the next. I made my escape and remained some time on the collar of the main stay, until all was quiet. One of the watch came up, but not finding me in the top gave over chase; but I got cobbed in the morning, and no pudding for dinner.

While in Hamoaze we had a draught of Irish Volunteers, about sixty in number. One of them was seven feet high, and when the hands were turned up to muster on the quarter deck, he stood like Saul the King of Israel, with head and shoulders above the host. This man used to head his countrymen when on shore upon leave, and was the terror of the people about Dock,[1] particularly North Corner Street, flourishing an Irish shillelah of enormous size, [so] that the constables when called out would fly like chaff at the very sight of him. He was, like the rest of his countrymen, honest and brave, and very inoffensive, but woe betide those that insulted him. Being in the dockyard returning stores, some of the shipwrights called him a walking flagstaff; for which compliment he gave two or three of them a terrible beating, and then challenged to fight twelve of the best men among them, taking two a day, but the challenge was not accepted from so queer a customer.

The night before we were paid off our ship's company gave a grand supper and the lower deck was illuminated. Several female visitors were of the party from Castlerag and other fashionable places,[2]

[1] Now Devonport.

[2] *Sc.* in nautical life.

who danced jigs and reels the whole of the night, with plenty of grog and flip; and what was remarkable, not a soul was drunk in the morning.

I must here mention that my shipmates, though brave as lions, were given to superstition, as the following will show. After poor Sturges was killed it was given out that he was often seen in the tier, and sometimes in the cockpit. This had such an effect that not one of the midshipmen would stay below by himself. I remember one of them (Sm Simmonds) falling asleep on the table in the starboard wing berth; and the rest going on deck, he was left alone. When he awoke, he took to his heels and ran up to the gunroom, where he fainted away and remained so a long time. When he came to, he declared that he saw poor Sturges standing in the berth as pale as death and looking steadfastly at him. This story worked so much upon the minds of the others that they took good care to have company at all times when left below. I had the shot that killed my worthy friend, and intended to have brought it home; but by some means it was lost or stolen on the morning of pay day.

While lying in Hamoaze our midshipmen carried on a roaring trade when rowing guard in the middle watch. They would sometimes set off to Catwater to visit a house where a very handsome girl lived, who would get up at any hour to make flip for them and felt highly flattered at their calling her Black-eyed Susan. I have sometimes been of the party and well recollect the many escapes we have had in carrying sail to get back in time, as the passage from Catwater to Hamoaze is rather a rough one in blowing weather, and the boat would frequently be gunwale under, so that I often thought my life was at stake.

I should have mentioned that our ship's company

mutinied as well as the other ships,[1] and some of our midshipmen that were obnoxious went on shore before the ship was paid off. A gentleman whose name I shall not give, and who had joined us in Hamoaze, had unluckily given some umbrage to the men, and was one of those who kept out of the way; but after the ship was paid off some of the fellows met him at the bottom of North Corner Street and took him on board of a collier and gave him a ducking.

After leaving the old Panther several of the officers were put on board the Rose transport for a passage to Portsmouth; but the wind being unfavourable for more than a fortnight, we left the Rose and her mutinous lot of scoundrels, she being ordered somewhere else. We were then transferred to the Hope transport, and after considerable delay we sailed for Portsmouth with a fine breeze from the westward, which soon after changed to the eastward, and blew like the devil. We were nine days turning up Channel[2]; however, we had a glorious set on board, and the master of the vessel (whose name I forget) did everything in the most handsome manner to make us comfortable. On the tenth day we arrived at Spithead, and on my landing at Gosport I found my poor grandmother at the point of death. She wished much to see me before she died. I followed her to the grave where she was interred alongside of my grandfather, Captain James Gardner, Royal Navy.

[1] *Cf.* Barrow, *Life of Earl Howe*, p. 165 *seq.*; Schomberg, *Naval Chronology*, ii. 131.

[2] *Cf. post*, p. 43.

OFFICERS' NAMES

SIR FRANCIS W. DRAKE, Vice-Admiral.[1]
Dead. Admiral.

MARK MILBANKE, Vice-Admiral.
Dead [1805]. Admiral of the white.—[*D.N.B.*]

THOS. PIERCY, Captain.
Dead. An excellent officer; he was taken prisoner[2] with Sir Richard Pearson by Paul Jones.

ROBT. SIMONTON, Captain.
Dead. An excellent officer. After repeated applications for employment which he could not obtain, he was made, on the promotion of flags, a rear-admiral on the retired list. He commanded the Superb, 74, in the East Indies (1779–81), and had seen a great deal of service.

RICHARD DORREL, 1st Lieutenant.
A commander; a good officer.

FRANCIS BROOKS, 2nd Lieutenant.
Dead. A good officer.

MONTAGU, 3rd Lieutenant.
Dead. A good officer.

ALEXANDER FRASER, 1st Lieutenant.
Dead [1829]. A vice-admiral of the red; a very smart officer.—[Marshall, ii. 458.]

[JAMES] MURRAY, 2nd Lieutenant.
Dead. A quiet, good fellow.

TILLMAN, Acting Lieutenant.
Uncertain.

[JOHN] WADE, Master.
Dead. A brave and meritorious officer.

[BEN.] FORRESTER, Captain of Marines.
Dead. As brave and generous a soul as ever lived, but thoughtless, and died unfortunate.

GEO. NOBLE, Lieutenant of Marines.
Dead. A captain in the militia, a brave and generous fellow.

---

[1] Elder brother of Sir Francis Samuel Drake, Bart., but himself neither baronet nor knight; and a vice-admiral at his death in 1788.

[2] When in command of the Countess of Scarborough, hired ship.

[ROBERT] ANDERSON, Surgeon.
Dead Highly respected.

[JAMES] MALCOLM, Surgeon.
Dead. Highly respected. See Edgar.

[JOHN] PRICE, Purser.
Dead. I want words to express my gratitude and respect for his memory.

[JAMES] BRANDER, Boatswain.
Dead. A worthy veteran sailor.

[THOMAS] DAWSON, Boatswain.
Dead. A good seaman, but severe.

[JAMES] FRASER, Gunner.
Dead. Much respected; kept a stationer's shop at Plymouth Dock.

COCK, Carpenter.
Dead. A good man; no dandy.

ROBERT STURGES, Mate.
Killed in battle [20th Oct. 1782]; a most worthy gentleman.

[THOMAS] CONNELL [Quarter gunner; Mid.], Mate and Acting Lieutenant.
Dead. A brave Irishman.

[EDWARD] FORSTER, Midshipman—[aftds. Mr's Mate].
Dead. Herculean Irishman; a terror to the dockyard maties.

[THOMAS] WATSON, Midshipman.
Dead. A glorious noisy fellow.

SAMUEL SIMMONDS, Midshipman.
Dead. Called Yellow Sam.

[JAMES] TAYLOR, Midshipman.
Dead. A smart fellow.

[JAMES] TAYLOR 2nd, Midshipman.
Dead. A pilot at Deal, called South Sands Head.

[LUKE] CAMPBELL, [Clerk, then] Midshipman doing duty as Schoolmaster.
Dead. A very clever, good fellow.

[WILLIAM] NEATE, Midshipman.
Dead. *Neat* in his dress; a fiery, good fellow.

JOHN FOULARTON, Midshipman.
Dead. A very brave fellow, but half mad.

RICHARD DANTON, Midshipman.
Dead. A respectable pilot at Deal.

MARTIN PERT HARTLEY, Midshipman.
Uncertain. A quiet, good fellow.

[ROBERT] SKIRRET, Midshipman.
Uncertain. A good-natured Irishman.

[ALEXANDER] THOMPSON, Surgeon's Assistant.
Uncertain. A gentleman; skilful in his profession.

[RICHARD] PICKERING, Clerk.
Dead. A worthy fellow while on board, but turned out thoughtless and unfortunate.

FLANAGAN, Under Clerk.
A Purser. A gentleman; since dead.

J. A. GARDNER, Midshipman. [Ord., 8th Feb. 1782; A.B., 1 Oct. 1782; Mid., 1 Jan. 1783.]
A commander.

SALISBURY, 50

Stern tyrants whom their cruelties renown.—Addison.

I joined this old devil of a ship, properly called the Hell Afloat, in December 1783 in Portsmouth Harbour. James Bradby, Esq., captain, and in June 1784 hoisted the flag, white and then red, at the fore, of Vice-Admiral John Campbell, F.R.S., as commander-in-chief and Governor of Newfoundland, and sailed soon after. Nothing remarkable happened on the passage to St. John's, where we arrived in July; the following men of war composing the squadron:—

Salisbury	50	Vice-Admiral Campbell. Captain James Bradby.
Santa Leocadia	36	Captain Alexander Edgar.
Proselyte	32	Captain Jonathan Faulknor, jun.
Æolus	32	Captain
Thisbe	28	Captain
Merlin	18	Captain J. Lumsdale
Echo	18	Captain Nichols.
Thorn	18	Captain Lechmere.
Lawrence brig		Lieutenant Carter, acting.

If I remember correctly it was this year that an extraordinary court martial was held on the master of the Proselyte for cutting the lanyards of the weather main shrouds when the people were up reefing topsails. The charge not being proved, he was acquitted. While laying in the harbour, a French frigate with a commodore came in, saluted the admiral, and remained a few days. The 28th October is the time for the men of war to sail for England; but owing to unfavourable winds, we were not able to leave St. John's before November. The admiral having given permission for any person that pleased to take home a dog, 75 were actually embarked. We took our departure with a sloop of war in company. I am not certain whether it was this year or the next, when about 60 leagues to the SW of Scilly we were covered in the night with a flock of crows and caught several. When near the Channel we fell in with a vessel from the coast of Africa in want of provisions, the crew living on parrots and monkeys, and in great distress; supplied them with provisions and parted company, and after a passage of near three weeks arrived at Spithead, and then into harbour, where we remained as a half-and-half guard-ship until May, when the admiral hoisted his flag, and we soon after sailed for our station, in company with a sloop of war.

When on the banks of Newfoundland, in a thick fog at night, going about three knots, a field of ice struck us on the weather bow and carried away the starboard bumpkin and head sails, besides knocking off several sheets of copper. On the banks we picked up a cask of brandy covered with weeds and barnacles, and saw the yards and spars of the line-of-battle ships that were lost on and near the banks in the gale of September 1782 on their passage to England from the West Indies. Fell in with several islands of ice. Arrived at St. John's, and remained there the usual time. We had a brewery on shore which supplied the squadron with spruce beer.[1] I was on shore at this brewery when one of

[1] Esteemed a good antiscorbutic. Our ships continued to brew it, up to 1840.

our men unfortunately fell into the boiling coppers and died the same day in a most deplorable condition. It was said that the beer was sent off (of course by mistake) to the squadron, and I think some little demur was made about drinking it and it was sent back.

On the 29th of October (1785) we left St. John's with a thundering gale right aft. A merchant who had never been out of St. John's harbour took a passage for England. We had a tremendous sea following that almost turned his brain with horror. One sea that measured heights with the mizen peak had a prodigious effect upon him, and with a look I cannot describe, he called out, 'Lord, Lord, Lord, Have mercy on me, and pray do let go the anchor!' His bawling out so horribly, frightened the man at the wheel so that the ship was in danger of broaching to. This gale lashed us on at a devil of a rate, and we had 294 and 296 knots on the log in 24 hours. Our passage was very short as far as the Lizard, when the wind shifted to the eastward, and I think it was nineteen days before we arrived at Spithead, having a dish of turnips [1] all the way up Channel. Went into Portsmouth harbour, where the old Salisbury was paid off the latter end of 1785 or beginning of 1786.

This was the most hateful and disagreeable ship I ever had my foot on board of—so unlike the Panther. Mastheading upon every trifling occasion. The senior midshipmen (with the exception of a few) were tyrants; and petty tyrants are generally the worst. The captain was a very good man at times, but often harsh and severe in his remarks. He once told me (and I have never forgotten it) I

[1] Possibly a pun on '*turn*-ing *up* Channel' (*cf. ante*, p. 37); or a variation on the familiar 'playing hell and turn up Jack'= 'making things lively' (*cf. post*, p. 65).

would never be fit for anything but the boatswain's store-room. This was because I was down with the keys in my turn, a midshipman being always sent to see that lights are not taken into the store-room except in a lantern, which is the custom in every man of war. He had missed me in the watch and thought I was skulking; and though I explained to him how it happened, it was all to no purpose. Great men don't like to be put right. I well remember the cutting taunt; but I thank God his prophecy did not come to pass, as the certificates I am proud to say I produced from some of the first officers in the service will testify; and when I went to pass for lieutenant at Somerset House, the commissioners told me my certificates would get me promoted without interest. Upon this hint I transmitted them to Earl Spencer, the first lord of the admiralty, and by return of post he gave me a commission and appointed me second lieutenant of the Hind, 28. This may be considered as sounding my own trumpet. It may be so; but it is the truth. Enough of this digression, and let me return to the old bundle of boards and relate a few circumstances.

I have positively, after keeping the first watch while in the harbour of St. John's, been turned out with other youngsters, to keep the morning watch and most of the forenoon without being relieved. Had we complained we knew what we had to expect from the overgrown tyrants, some of whom were members of the Hell-fire Club. I remember my old messmate, Ben Morgan (poor fellow! now dead and gone), having the lower part of his ear detached from his head because he kicked a little at the tyranny.

Our admiral was a great astronomer and took delight in lunar observation. One Sunday morning he sent four of us down with Pye the schoolmaster to work a lunar. While we were below, the hands were turned up to muster, and we were going to attend, but Pye said there was no occasion. Presently down came the quartermaster saying Lieutenant Stiles (who had the watch) wanted us. On going up he, in a very knowing way, demanded why we were not up to muster, and on our acquainting him with the reason he said it was all very well, and it would be better if we were to step up to the masthead and look out for squalls, as it was too thick to take a lunar. So two of us (I was one) were sent to the main topmast head and two to the fore, where we remained some hours. This was on the banks; a thick fog having just come on, with drops from the topgallant rigging which wetted us through in a short time; but that was of no consideration. On another trifling occasion, the same worthy was going to trice me up to the mizen peak, but this he thought better of. I could relate many more cases, but let this be sufficient. Lieutenant Stiles lately died a rear-admiral. One of the laws of Solon says, 'Speak not ill of the dead; no, not if their sons offend you.' I shall attend to this and say no more on the subject until I come to the Edgar, and then naught in malice.

When at St. John's, a playhouse was got up by Graham, the admiral's secretary, with considerable ability, and several of the officers used to perform. The scenery was very good and did Mr. Graham a deal of credit. Only the favoured few could get leave to see the performance. The kindhearted first lieutenant would send us that were not descended from the Kings of Cappadocia and Pontus on board at sunset, for fear we should catch cold if we stayed out late. This was making game; and I remember some of us meeting the admiral, who kindly gave us leave to pick fruit in his gardens for two hours, when this same Lieutenant Deacon happened to come up at the time; and when the admiral was gone, he started us on board, when we had not been there a quarter of an hour, saying he was fearful the fruit would gripe us. Kind soul!—the devil thank him. He was a most facetious gentleman, and when a seaman once asked him for slops, he replied, 'Certainly, my man, what slops do you want?' 'A jacket, sir, if you please.' 'And cannot you think of something else?' 'Yes, sir,' says the man, 'I will be glad of a shirt and trowsers.' 'Very well, you shall have them. But do think of something more that you stand in need of.' 'Why, sir,' says the man, 'If you have no objection I should like a pair of shoes and stockings, and a smock frock.'[1] 'Very well, my man, you shall have them all in good time. I expect a vessel in with some blue chalk from the Straits of Baffleman, and then I shall chalk out all your wants; so be off, or I shall get the boatswain's mate to measure you with the end of the fore brace before her arrival, which you may think rather premature.'

When asking him for leave to go on shore he would frequently say, 'As soon as I have time to chalk you out a barge to take you, I shall attend to this most important business.' Once on a rainy day he was making some of those remarks, when his foot slipped and he fell on his bottom on the quarter deck. One of the lieutenants said, 'Had the deck been chalked, sir, it would have saved your fall.' This vexed him greatly, and seeing us laugh he started us up to the masthead for the remainder of the watch, saying, 'Take care! As the rigging is not chalked you may slip and get an ugly fall.'

I have already mentioned our bringing home 75

[1] The list is interesting, as showing that, in 1785, a 'smock frock' was in the slop-list.

dogs. I messed in the main hatchway berth on the lower deck, with four midshipmen and a scribe. We had eight of those dogs billeted on us. One of them had the name of Thunder. At dinner I once gave him a piece of beef with plenty of mustard rolled up in it. The moment he tasted it, he flew at me and I was obliged to run for it. He never forgot it, and whenever I offered him victuals he would snap at me directly. Another of those dogs used to sleep at the foot of Charley Bisset's cot, and when the quartermaster would call the watch this dog would fly at him if he came near Bisset, who would often plead ignorance of being called, and by that means escape going on deck for the first hour of the watch. We had a drunken Irishman, by the name of Collins, who, when sent to the hospital at St. John's, contrived to get liquor in spite of all precaution to prevent it. At last it was found out by the following circumstance. He had one of those dogs that could do anything but speak. He used to sling a bottle round his neck and then put a shilling in his mouth and send him off in the evening. The dog knew well where to go, for he had been often there with Collins. It was to a public-house, between the hospital and St. John's. He'd howl as soon as he got there; the landlord knew well what he wanted, and would fill the bottle with rum. The dog would then drop the shilling, but not before, and scamper off to return to his master; not at the gate of the hospital—he was too cunning for that—but like a Roman conqueror, through a hole in the wall; when one night he was discovered by the watch going their rounds, and by that means the business was brought to light. From the ingenuity of the master and his dog, both escaped punishment.

Our armourer was a man who would drink like a fish, and one morning coming to the brewery complaining of thirst, the cooper, a droll and wicked fellow, gave him some essence of spruce, and the armourer took a good swig before he found out his mistake. The moment he could speak he asked what it was he had taken. The cooper said he was very sorry for what had happened, but he thought it right to acquaint him it was some stuff they had to poison rats. The armourer was struck dumb with terror, but at last, in a paroxysm of rage, swore that the cooper should die first; and drawing out a large knife, gave chase and certainly would have put an end to his joking had he not locked himself up in the brewery in great tribulation, as the armourer was trying all in his power to break open the door. However, the poor fellow was at last made sensible it was a joke, and had some double spruce given him to make amends—which had the desired effect.

Our second assistant surgeon was another wet soul, and coming from the play half drunk went to sleep in an empty cask that was lying on Quigley's Wharf, when a squall of wind rolled the cask overboard and poor old Andrew Reardon would have been drowned, had it not been for the boat-keeper of the cutter. Old Andrew is now dead. He dearly loved grog, and when told that new rum was a bad article he said he didn't care; if it fractured the brain it was all he wanted.

With a few exceptions we had a terrible lot of wild midshipmen. Some of them were members of the Hell-fire Club,[1] and used to dress, when going to that place, in scarlet coats with black velvet collars

[1] This would seem to have been a mere short-lived association, with its head quarters at St. John's, and may, perhaps, be compared—with a difference—to the nearly contemporary 'Order of Marlborough,' described in *N.R.S.* vi. 387. There are obvious geographical reasons why it cannot have been connected with any foul club of the name (there was a long succession of such) in London.

and cuffs, black waistcoat, breeches, and stockings, and hair powdered. Those chaps would play all manner of wicked pranks on board, such as pouring molasses under the heads of those who slept in the tier, and others would have a hook and line with which they'd haul our quilts and blankets off in the night, and then heave water over us, at the same time making a squeaking noise; while others, in the secret, would say it was the gibbering of a ghost, and that the tier was haunted; but that they would ask the parson (a wet soul) to lay the spirit, not in the Red Sea, but in the large pond near St. John's. One poor fellow, a clerk whose name was Newnham, but nicknamed Newcome, they got in the tier one night in the dark, and swore it was the admiral's cow that had got adrift. It was no use for the poor fellow to say he was not that personage; for a selvagee was clapped round him in an instant with a hauling line made fast, with which they roused him up the hatchway in a moment, terrified almost to death.

I must here mention the shifts my old messmate, Ben Morgan, and myself were put to the last year we were at St. John's. Our captain used to pay our mess and washing bills, for which he was repaid on our return to England. It happened one morning when the washing bill was sent in, that he observed our towels were inserted with other articles; upon which he sent for us, and after a severe reprimand upon our extravagance, adding that we ought to have washed the towels ourselves, he dismissed us, saying he should give no more money to be fooled away in that manner, and that we deserved to be well flogged in the bargain. We were glad enough to steer clear of him. In respect of the money he was as good as his word; for devil a farthing more would he let us have, and we were sadly put to it;

for we had only Tom Cod (caught alongside) for breakfast, salt beef or pork for dinner, and Tom Cod for tea in the evening. At last we in some measure got over our difficulties by going to the hills and gathering a weed called maidenhair, a good substitute for tea; and with molasses instead of sugar, poor Ben and myself fared gloriously.

While at St. John's two of our seamen deserted and got into the woods on their way to an out port; and they had nearly been devoured by the wolves who attacked them in a hut, where they remained three days without provisions, and had great difficulty and danger in coming back to the ship, where they were treated with two dozen apiece.

Our captain to keep us in good order placed a Mr. Stack as father of our mess. He was cursed surly and disagreeable, but I believe meant well; only [he had] an ugly way of showing his kindness. When in good temper (which was seldom) he would say 'My son,' when he addressed any of us; but generally, 'I'll split your ear.' This man drew a very long bow and would frequently tell the most unaccountable stories. I have heard him relate that the ghost of Commodore Walsingham[1] (who he had served under, and who was lost in the Thunderer, 74, in the West Indies, in the hurricane of 1780) appeared to him when he was a slave on the coast of Barbary, where he was chained by the leg for upwards of a twelvemonth, and after undergoing innumerable hardships he was released by a Moorish lady who fell in love with him and paid his ransom to a considerable amount. This was too much to swallow from a fellow as ugly as the old Diligente's [figure-] head.

When at Spithead and in the harbour, our ship's company had a violent quarrel with the crew of the

[1] See Charnock, vi. 284.

Grampus 50, commanded by Ned Thompson[1] the poet, who had the Coast of Guinea station, and several battles were fought with various success. The quarrel originated in some of our fellows saying they of the Grampus, when on the coast, lived chiefly on monkey soup, except on Sundays, and then they were regaled on roast parrots. For this they swore to murder every snow-eating son of a bitch belonging to the Salisbury whenever they could catch them. One of the mates of the Grampus had the impudence, while we were in harbour, to drop under our bows with a launch-load of his people who had been for stores to the dockyard, and challenge ours to fight; for which he had very near been brought to a court martial.

Our quarrelsome blades had another row with the riggers; and when the latter would pass the ship in their launches, our fellows would thrust their heads out of the ports and sing out—'I say, Mortimer, drop in the launch, make fast a hawser to the NW buoy, take three round turns and a half hitch, seize the end back and come on board with the launch.' This occasioned many a battle, and the riggers generally got the worst of it; for we had some from that land which produces the finest peasantry in the world on board, and woe betide those who came in contact with them. We had the O'Ryans, the O'Gallaghers, the Macartys, the O'Donovans, the Murphys, the O'Flahertys, the O'Tooles and the O'Flanagans, and great part of the ship's company were Irish and very quiet when not disturbed. One of those fellows—Darby Collins, who had the dog that I have mentioned at the hospital—did positively beat at the back of the Point, Portsmouth, eleven men by cracking their heads at single-stick one after the other. He was

[1] Died, in command of the Grampus, 1786. See *D.N.B.*

a tall, raw-boned Irishman, a Garry-owen boy that stood up manfully for the honour of his country.

The following are the names of the officers belonging to the Salisbury :—

JOHN CAMPBELL, F.R.S., Vice-Admiral.

Dead [1790]. An admiral; a most able officer and great astronomer. He was captain of the fleet on board the Royal George with Admiral Hawke when he defeated the French under Conflans.—[*D.N.B.*]

JAMES BRADBY, Esq., Captain.

Dead. A retired rear-admiral.

HENRY DEACON, 1st Lieutenant.

Dead. He was the senior commander on the list; had the out-pension of Greenwich Hospital. A good seaman, but satirical, and too fond of mastheading.

RICHARD RUDSDALE, 2nd Lieutenant.

Dead. A commander; a fine-looking fellow and the best officer in the ship.

JOSEPH LORING, 3rd Lieutenant.

Dead. A good sailor, very passionate, and swore like the devil.

JOHN STILES, 4th Lieutenant.

Dead. A rear-admiral of the white. Fond of mastheading for little or nothing. More of him when I come to the Edgar.

[GEORGE] TREMLETT, Master.

Dead. A quiet, good man. [William Henry Brown Tremlett (captain, 1802), his servant].

[JAMES] PIERCE, Captain of Marines.

Dead. A strange fish.

[WILLIAM] GOULD, Lieutenant of Marines.

Dead. A good officer.

THE PARSON (I forget his name).

Dead. Had no dislike to grog.

[JAMES] COCKERELL, Purser.

Drowned. Took care of his eights.[1]

---

[1] The purser 'was allowed one-eighth for waste on all provisions embarked.' Provisions were thus issued at the 'purser's pound' of 14 oz.—Smyth. In the mutiny at Spithead in 1797, the seamen demanded and obtained an order that the pound should in future be of 16 oz.

[Edmund] Peterson, Surgeon.

Dead. Crabbed as the devil.

Aaron Graham, Admiral's Secretary.

Dead. A very clever fellow ; was magistrate at Bow Street.

[Charles] Smith, Gunner.

Dead. Fractious from long illness. [D.D. in pay book: no date.]

D—— (I forget his name) [Edward Dowdall], Gunner.

Dead. Lethargic ; always dozing on the forecastle ; a sleepy, good man.

[Simeon] Brown, Carpenter.

Dead. A quiet, good man; clever in his profession.

[James] Hall, Boatswain.

Dead. An infernal tyrant ; a good sailor ; a sycophant, a Hun, a Goth, a Vandal ; a fellow that was made too much of by those who ought to have kept him at proper distance.

[John] McCurdy, 1st Assistant Surgeon.

Dead. A surgeon at St. John's ; a very excellent fellow, and clever in his profession.

Andrew Reardon, 2nd Assistant Surgeon.

Dead. A surgeon, R.N. A very worthy fellow, who loved his glass of grog.

Dodwell Brown, Master's Mate.

Dead. A lieutenant ; a gentleman very much respected.

[Samuel] Scott, Master's Mate.

Uncertain. A tyrant who I well remember, although it is upwards of fifty years since I saw the blustering, swaggering bully.

Robert Laurie, Midshipman.

Vice-admiral of the white ; a baronet and K.C.B. A most excellent officer, seaman, and gentleman. [Admiral, 1846 ; died 1848. —O'Byrne.]

Charles Bisset, Midshipman.

Dead. Wild and thoughtless, but a good-natured, harmless fellow.

[Henry] Potts, Midshipman [afterwards A.B.].

Dead. A tyrannical fellow and member of the Hell-fire Club.

[John] Sandford, Midshipman [afterwards A.B.].

Dead. A member of the Hell-fire Club ; a dandy and droll fellow.

[Richard] Herbert, Midshipman. [A.B.].

Uncertain. A noisy, tyrannical fellow ; member of the Hell-fire Club ; nicknamed Hawbuck.

[Thomas James] Skerret, Midshipman. [A.B.]
Uncertain. This fellow wanted to be a tyrant, but was too great a fool.

[Campbell] Marjoribanks, Midshipman.
East India House.

[Thomas] Merchant, Midshipman.
Uncertain. A good fellow; called Old Siolto.

[John Wentworth] Holland, Midshipman. [A.B.]
A post captain; played the violin well. [Died 1841.]

Robert Manning, Midshipman.
Dead. A commander. Bob was a good fellow.

R. B. Vincent, Midshipman.
Dead [1831]. A post captain; C.B.; fought well; called Don Diego Del Vinsanti Hispaniola Whiskerando. More of him when I come to the Victory.—[*D.N.B.*]

Philip Brock, Midshipman.
Dead. A loss to the service.

Borromy Bradby, Midshipman, son of the captain. [A.B.]
Dead. A commander; a very worthy character. [Two other (presumably) sons of the captain, Matthew Barton and Daniel, were rated captain's servants.]

Charles Garnier, Midshipman.
This gentleman was Captain of the Aurora, 32, and was unfortunately drowned in Yarmouth Roads, Isle of Wight, going off to his ship in the evening [1796].

James Macfarland, Midshipman.
A commander; good-natured and droll. [Captain (retired), 1840; died 1852.—O'Byrne.]

R. B. Littlehales, Midshipman.
A retired rear-admiral. [Vice-admiral, 1840; died 1847.—O'Byrne.]

John Tyrwhitt, Midshipman.
Marshal at Gibraltar.

Benjamin Morgan, Midshipman.
Dead. A lieutenant. Poor Ben! you and I have spent many an hour at the masthead for little or nothing.

Henry Batt, Midshipman.
Dead. A lieutenant. An old schoolfellow of mine. Harry was passionately fond of grog, which made him an ungrateful return by taking him out of this world before it was agreeable. Nicknamed Ram, Cat, Batt, and Rammon the Butcher.

William Garrett, Midshipman.
Dead. A lieutenant. A very good fellow and good sailor, but fond of grog and boasting.

NORBORNE THOMPSON, Midshipman.
A rear-admiral. [Died 1844.—Marshall, iii. 294.]

INCE, Midshipman.
Dead. A worthy fellow; a loss to the service.

RICHARD STILES TREMLETT, Midshipman.
Killed in a duel with Lord Camelford.

GEO. N[EATE] TREMLETT, Midshipman.
A commander. Brother of the above; a very good fellow. [Died 1865.—O'Byrne.]

ANDREW DUFF, Midshipman.
Dead. A drunken Hun.

FRANCIS GIBBON, Midshipman.
Dead. A lieutenant; wonderfully great, in his own opinion.

[WILLIAM] ELLIOT, Midshipman.
Dead. A commander, sickly and proud.

LORD AMELIUS BEAUCLERK, Midshipman.
An admiral, G.C.B. and G.C.H.; chief naval aide-de-camp to the king. [Died 1846.—*D.N.B.*]

SMITH, Midshipman.
Uncertain. Remember little of him, and that no good.

J. A. GARDNER, Midshipman. [Entered Dec. 12, 1783.]
A commander.

WILLIAM PYE, Schoolmaster.
Dead. A purser; Fit Pye, Fit man.

JOHN ALCOT, Captain's Clerk.
A purser and retired storekeeper of Portsmouth yard.

HENRY ROLAND HARLEY, Admiral's Office.
Was a purser in the navy but resigned the situation; a most worthy fellow. We were in four ships together.

[WILLIAM] WILLCOCKS, Admiral's Office. [A.B.]
Uncertain. A very droll and noisy fellow.

[THOMAS] LANDSEER, Admiral's Office. [Admiral's servant.]
Dead. A purser; a very satirical gentleman.

CRISP, Admiral's Office.
Dead. A purser; another noisy, droll fellow.

NEWNHAM, Admiral's Office.
Uncertain. A quiet, easy, poor fellow; made a butt of.

[THOMAS] STACK, used to keep the forecastle watch as Midshipman
Uncertain. Made a gunner; I have mentioned him before with his long bow.

ORESTES, 18.

I JOINED the son of Agamemnon early in 1786, fitting in Portsmouth Harbour for Channel service, to cruise after smugglers from Dunnose to the Start; Manley Dixon, Esq., commander.

This brig was considered the finest in the service. She measured 32 ft. 9 in. on the beam, and drew 17 ft. 4 in. abaft, 13 ft. 4 in. forward, and [was] nearly 450 tons, mounting 18 long nines, and pierced for 26. She and the Pylades (called the Hercules and Mars) were taken from the Dutch by Macbride in the Artois, 44.[1] She sailed remarkably well, but was a wet soul, shipping seas over the bows and washing the men at the wheel. She would never condescend to rise to a sea, but dash right through. After a few cruises, when off the Isle of Purbeck we observed two large Hogboats [2] among the rocks, and several people on horseback upon the cliffs above the spot. Sent our boats to examine, and found them to be smugglers with seven hundred tubs of liquor, which we seized, and landed the smugglers at Swanage. After landing our tubs at the Custom House, Portsmouth, we anchored at Yarmouth, in the Isle of Wight, our place of rendezvous, where we remained a short time, and then resumed our cruising; sometimes in

[1] December 3, 1781.—Beatson, v. 424.

[2] Or 'Heck-boats.' See Smyth, *Sailors' Word Book.*

company with the Hebe, 36, on the same station; and then put into Guernsey, where we stayed but a short time and ran out in a gale of wind. Caught fire in the master's cabin over the magazine, by the candles rolling against his curtains. It created great alarm, but was soon got under. During the time, it occasioned the utmost terrors among the ship's company. Several of them got into the forechains, the head, and on the bowsprit, ready to jump overboard. However, they seemed to have as much dread of water as they had of the fire and remained stationary. It was ludicrous to see the captain with a speaking trumpet, exerting himself to keep order, and the carpenter's wife catching him round the legs, and while he was calling for Water, she was screaming out Fire.

When our cruise was over we returned to Yarmouth, where our surgeon turned mad and cut some unaccountable capers. One morning early, he came upon deck and gave some orders to the officers of the watch, who paid no attention to them. Upon this he got hold of a crow[1] that was in the becket over one of the guns, and began to run a muck,[2] and cleared the deck in a moment. Sentries and all took to their heels, and it was some time before an opportunity offered to get him below. At last he was got to his cabin in the gunroom, with four marines and a midshipman to guard him; but he soon made a start from his den and made no more of the marines than if they were sparrows. He first caught hold of two and knocked their heads together, and then punished the others, who from fear, made little resistance. He next attacked Patterson, the master, and swore he should stand auctioneer as it was his intention to sell his effects.

[1] *Sc.* crow-bar. *Cf.* Smyth, *Sailors' Word-Book.*
[2] More correctly, *a-mok*—a Malay term.

I never saw a more ludicrous scene when the master, to humour him, began to put his things up to auction and we, outside (for we were afraid to go in) the gunroom, bidding for them. After the sale was over, he made Patterson put on two of his coats—one of them the Windsor uniform [1]—and then upset him and rolled him about the gunroom, swearing he was a beer cask. Then rushing out, he belaboured all that he met with, and went upon deck and remained cock of the walk until he came down of his own accord, and went to bed, saying, 'You shall hear from me presently.' However, good care was taken to secure him, and he was soon after sent to sick quarters, being a dangerous subject, and glad enough we were to get rid of him.

There was at Yarmouth a truly hospitable gentleman, a Captain Urry [2] of the Royal Navy, well known to officers in the service, who kept open house and gave large parties. He was the life and soul of Yarmouth, which place has never been worth going to since his death. On one of these parties, our barge (for we had a barge) was ordered to attend and tow a sloop full of company (it being calm) from Yarmouth to Lymington, and I was the midshipman sent, and had directions to land them, and to take orders from a captain in the navy, who was one of the party. This being done, a half-guinea was given to the men to drink, and I was desired to let them go on shore for that purpose. After they had their grog I missed the strokesman of the barge, a tall Irishman named McCarthy, who was nowhere to be found; in fact he had deserted. On my return I reported this to Lieutenant Jeynes who abused me and said he would write against me to the captain (who lived on shore) for suffering this

[1] The full-dress is perhaps meant.

[2] John Urry, a captain of 1768; died 1800.

tall Paddy to run away. The next morning he was as good as his word, and sent me with the letter. The captain, on reading it, gave me a severe reprimand, and sent me on board in a hurry, saying I should hear more of it very shortly. In a day or two after he came on board and we left Yarmouth for Spithead. I was in hourly expectation of some terrible explosion, as my friend the lieutenant was constantly reminding me of the subject. After the ship was moored the captain went on shore, and Jeynes soon followed. The master being commanding officer, I asked him permission to go and see my friends, which he granted, and I never joined the Orestes after.

I was but a youngster then. Had I known as much as I did soon after, I would have demanded a court martial on myself, and would have brought Lieutenant Jeynes to another for tyranny and oppression, which he was guilty of in many instances and had laid himself open to anyone who might think proper to bring the charges forward. He was obliged to leave the Orestes soon after. He had formerly (as I have understood) been a purser, and was broken by court martial; but having served his time as midshipman, got to be made a lieutenant, and died a retired commander.

Whenever the Orestes came in I used to keep out of the way. I lived at Gosport and was always on the watch, and when she came into Spithead I had timely notice and would set off for the country. After returning from one of those excursions, I was hiding behind a screen in our parlour; on the other side sitting by the fire was an old schoolfellow of mine and a young lady in earnest conversation about me. The former among other remarks said he believed I had made away with myself. This observation I could not brook, and catching hold of a large family Bible that was on a table near me (and which I have at this moment) I hove it over the screen and hit my friend on the jaw and knocked him down as flat as a flounder. I set off as fast as I could, leaving them in the utmost consternation; and he told me a long time after that he thought it was the devil that had felled him, until he saw the Bible. Captain Dixon, I believe, was aware that Lieutenant Jeynes had blamed me wrongfully, as he sent me my prize money and gave me a good certificate, and offered to take me again, for which he has my most grateful thanks, and I hope to live to see him admiral of the fleet.[1]

He was a very smart officer, and did everything in his power to teach the midshipmen their duty. We used to take helm and lead, and reef the main topsail; also pull in the boats upon particular occasions, such as going along shore in the night after smugglers, &c. When we were at Guernsey, the captain in the kindest manner allowed the petty officers a moderate quantity of liquor in each of their messes; but the sergeant of marines, not content with this indulgence, smuggled twenty kegs into the ship. When this was told the captain, he ordered all the kegs to be brought on deck and stove. The sergeant stood, like Niobe, in tears for his loss. It was a most laughable sight, as the liquor was running out mixed with salt water (for the ship rolled a great deal), to see the fellows laying down like beasts on the deck and licking up, while the boatswain's mates were thrashing them to no purpose. The sergeant, I believe, was reduced to the ranks.

I shall mention a few strange fellows we had on board, and first Mr. Quinton the mate. This gentleman was a good sailor, and was very fond of

[1] He died, admiral of the red, in 1837.

gin grog, and used to say it agreed with him so well and made his flesh so firm. It was determined one day to count how many glasses he drank from morning until evening; and, if I remember correctly, twenty-six tumblers of good Hollands and water made the number; for in the good old times we never sported Cockney gin. I must in justice declare that Mr. Quinton was no drunkard; I never saw him disguised with liquor the whole time I belonged to the ship. The next was Mr. Stevens, who went by the nickname of Tommy Bowline, a rough knot; full of wise saws and strange dry sayings, but rather slack in his movements, and was what we call a hard officer and droll middy. When belonging to a guard-ship commanded by Sir Roger Curtis, while lying at Spithead the mizen topsail was ordered to be loosed, to swing the ship the right way. Tommy Bowline was the first to go aloft and was highly complimented by Sir Roger for his activity, saying 'You are a fine fellow, Mr. Stevens; a most active officer, Mr. Stevens; you are a wonder, Mr. Stevens.' Now it unfortunately happened that Tommy was left behind by the other midshipmen and was last on the yard. Sir Roger observing this called out 'I recall all my compliments, Mr. Stevens; you are a damned lubber, Mr. Stevens; a blockhead, Mr. Stevens; come down, Mr. Stevens.' This poor Tommy never heard the last of.

Our gunner (McKinnon) was another strange hand. He was troubled with sore eyes and would sit in his cabin damning them from morning till night. Two of our men having deserted while in Yarmouth Roads, our boat, manned by midshipmen with Lieutenant Jeynes, left the ship in the evening and pulled for Cowes, where we arrived about eleven at night. Mr. Jeynes having received some information respecting the deserters, set off in the boat for Ryde, leaving me at Cowes with two marines to go round by land and meet him there. I had no money to get any refreshment, and never shall I forget the fatigue I went through that night. After pulling in the boat thirteen miles, I had to walk seven miles on a wild goose chase, for we never heard anything more of the runaways; and the wind shifting, we had to pull all the way back to Yarmouth. Before I close my account of the Orestes, I must say a word or two respecting Lieutenant Jeynes (letting the law of Solon sleep for a day). He was without exception the most cold-blooded and bad fellow I ever met with. I have seen him thrash the men with the end of a rope in the most unfeeling manner, until he was tired, making use of the most abusive language; and for his tyranny was obliged to quit the ship; but, to give the devil his due, [he] was what we call a bit of a sailor, and if he pleased (which was seldom) could make himself agreeable. In the year 1793, the Orestes was lost in the Indian Seas and every soul perished.

NAMES OF OFFICERS

MANLEY DIXON, Esq., Captain.

An admiral and K.C.B. He commanded the Lion, 64, when the William Tell, 84, was taken. The Foudroyant, 80, and Penelope, 36, in company. He was also port admiral at Plymouth. Since dead.—[Marshall, i. 375.]

THOS. JEYNES, Lieutenant.

Dead. I have said enough of him. A commander on the retired list.

[GEORGE] PATTERSON, Master.

Uncertain. Was master attendant abroad.

DUSAUTOY, Lieutenant of Marines.

A barrack-master.

[JAMES] STREET, Purser.

Took care of his eights.

WALLIS, Surgeon.
Uncertain. Mad from drink.

[ALEXANDER] PROCTOR, Surgeon's Assistant.
A surgeon. Proud as the devil.

[HUGH] LAND, Clerk.
Uncertain. A clever little pedant.

[JOHN] HILL, Boatswain.
Uncertain. A good sailor.

[TIMOTHY] SCRIVEN, Carpenter.
Uncertain. A good man, and good bread-and-cheese carpenter.

[PETER] MCKINNON, Gunner.
Uncertain. A good sailor, but used to damn his poor eyes so.

[JOHN] QUINTON, Mate.
Dead. A good sailor; fond of gin grog.

D. HAMLIN, } Brothers, Midshipmen.
HAMLIN, }
Dead. Good young men.

[CHRISTOPHER] GULLET, Midshipman.
Dead. A lieutenant. See Queen.

STEVENS, Midshipman.
Tommy Bowline. Was made a gunner.

WM. MOUNSEY, Midshipman.
Dead [1830]. A captain, C.B.; a very good fellow.—[Marshall, vi. 20.]

ALEX. GILMOUR, Midshipman.
A commander; a good old sailor.—[Died 1853.—O'Byrne].

NICHOLA, Midshipman.
Dead from insanity.

MAUNDRELL, Midshipman.
Dead. A lieutenant. Was broke for tyranny, which he richly deserved. Afterwards restored to his rank. Nicknamed Mantrap, from taking up deserters.

J. A. GARDNER, Midshipman.
A commander.

EDGAR, 74

Early in 1787 I joined the Edgar, a guard-ship in Portsmouth Harbour—Charles Thompson, Esq., captain, formerly of the Boreas; and soon after went to Spithead and hoisted the broad pennant of the Honorable John Leveson Gower as commodore of the squadron of observation; but the Dutch armament taking place prevented their sailing. Several ships of the line assembled at Spithead, and others fitting in the harbour; but to no purpose, as the business was soon settled, and the ships returned to their stations, and those fitting were paid off. Next spring we were again ordered to Spithead, and a promotion of flags having taken place, we hoisted the flag (blue at the mizen) of Rear-Admiral the Hon. John Leveson Gower, as commander-in-chief of the fleet of observation, consisting of the following men of war:

Edgar, 74	Rear-Admiral Honorable John Leveson Gower.[1] Captain Charles Thompson.[1]
Colossus, 74 . . .	Captain Hugh Cloberry Christian.[1]
Magnificent, 74 .	Captain Hon. Geo. C. Berkeley.[1]
Culloden, 74 . . .	Captain Sir Thomas Rich, [Bart.][2]
Crown, 74	Captain Charles Morice Pole.[1]

[1] *D.N.B.*

[2] Rear-admiral, 1794: died 1804.

Scipio, 64 . . . Captain Skeffington Lutwidge.[1]
Hebe, 36 . . . Captain Edward Thornbrough.[2]
Andromeda, 32 . Captain H.R.H. Prince William Henry.[2]
Trimmer, 18 . . Captain Charles Tyler.[2]

Sailed with the squadron to the westward of Scilly, and off the Irish coast for nearly two months, putting in occasionally to Cawsand Bay and Torbay, and then returned to our station as guard-ship on Portsmouth Harbour. We were very glad to get rid of our admiral. He was what we call a tight hand of the watch; one that would make a fellow jump where there was no stile. He used to play hell and turn up Jack, and would spare nobody. He had an ugly trick of getting up as early as three and sometimes before it in the morning, and would walk the quarter-deck in a flannel jacket, and most of the time without a hat, until breakfast was ready; a happy dog of a midshipman walking between two of the quarter-deck guns with a signal book, which ever and anon he would call for in the voice of Stentor—

> Stentor the strong, endued with brazen lungs,
> Whose throat surpassed the force of fifty tongues.

Coming out of his cabin early one morning in a great hurry, he fell over a signal lantern, and was going to play hell with the lieutenant of the watch for having lanterns upon deck at that time of day—about half-past two in the morning. The Crown being out of her station, he was going to make the signal for an officer from that ship, and going to the office to write the order he could not get in, the clerk having the key; which put him into such

[1] Rear-admiral, 1794; died, admiral of the red, 1814.
[2] *D.N.B.*

a rage that he swore he would flog the clerk and those that wrote under him. However, his rage abated and he did not make the signal, it blowing very hard; but he would not suffer the clerk or his under-scribes to show themselves in the office while his flag was flying.

Culverhouse was at this time signal lieutenant and was not so quick in getting up this unlucky morning as the admiral, although a very active and able officer. The admiral, not seeing him, roared out to me (which made me jump a foot off the deck) 'Where's that little son of a bitch? Go down for him directly.' Down I went to the gunroom where Culverhouse slept, and told him the news. In great tribulation he instantly got up and came upon deck, and kept some time behind the admiral thinking to weather the storm; but the moment he got sight of him he sang out like a lion, 'Go on the poop and be damned to you. Why were you not out of your nest before?' I must here state that, notwithstanding this, the admiral was a great friend to Lieutenant Culverhouse, and I have been told first took notice of him from the following circumstance. When on board the Victory, he was on the gangway with his glass, sitting on the weather clue of the mainsail, when the main tack suddenly gave way and threw him into the lee clue of the sail unhurt. He was an excellent signal officer, a good sailor, an agreeable messmate, and in every respect a very clever fellow. He was made a post captain, but was unfortunately drowned at the Cape of Good Hope.[1] The admiral was like Sylla the Dictator;

[1] John Culverhouse, 1st lieutenant of the Minerve, was made commander for the capture of the Spanish frigate Sabina, on the special recommendation of Nelson. Captain, 1802. Drowned when agent for transports at the Cape of Good Hope in 1809.—Nicolas, *Nelson Despatches* (Index).

that is, he would go any length to serve his friends, but was the reverse to those he had a dislike to. He appeared to be well acquainted with the character of most of the officers in the service; his memory in that respect was astonishing. He was an able tactician, and in every respect a great officer, with a look 'that withered all the host.'

He was a mortal foe to puppyism, and one of our midshipmen going aloft with gloves on, attracted his eye; for which he got such a rub down that I am certain he remembers to the present day, although he is a post captain, and as proud as the devil, without any reason. Another of his freaks was threatening to have a bowl put upon our heads and our hair cut round in the newest fashion by that measure. He told one of our midshipmen (Pringle) who was a very stout man and who happened to be in his way when looking at the compass, 'That he was too big for a midshipman but would do very well as a scuttle butt,' and, Pringle having his hands in his pockets, he was going to send for the tailor to sew them up. When he first came on board to muster, a little before we sailed, everyone was dressed in full uniform to receive him. He took notice of this, and with a smile (a lurking devil in it), complimented us on our good looks, at the same time observing, 'You knew who was coming; but notwithstanding your looking so well, I think I can see a little rust on you yet which I shall endeavour to rub off.'[1]

Our captain was as gruff as the devil, and had a voice like a mastiff whose growling would be heard superior to the storm. He was very particular respecting dress as the following order will shew:—

[1] Byam Martin's recollection of Leveson Gower was even more unfavourable than Gardner's. *Cf. N.R.S.* xix. 292.

Memo. :—

If any officer shall so far forget himself as to appear when on shore without his uniform, I shall regard it as a mark of his being ashamed of his profession and discharge him from the ship accordingly.

(Signed) Charles Thompson,
Captain.

He had very near caught some of us in Middle Street, Gosport, but fortunately an alley was at no great distance through which we made a hasty but safe retreat, and by that means prevented a few vacancies for midshipmen taking place in the Edgar.

And now according to promise let me speak a few words about my old mast-heading friend, Lieutenant John Stiles. When the guard-ships went out for a cruise to blow the dust off the harbour duty men, their complement was made up of men and officers from those ships that remained in port. It happened that my aforesaid friend was sent on board of us. Now it so turned out that he had not so much to say on board the old Edgar as he had when on board the Salisbury (of cruel memory). In the latter ship he had lambs to look after; in the Edgar he had devils to look after him. In working ship this gentleman was stationed on the forecastle, and got the nickname from the admiral of 'Knight of the Belfry,'[1] because he always planted himself there when the hands were turned up; and from being in such a conspicuous situation, when things went slack—which was sometimes the case—

[1] The 'Belfry'—which has long been obsolete—is defined by Smyth as 'an ornamental frame or shelter, under which the ship's bell is suspended.' It would seem to have been commonly fixed on the break of the forecastle, and is so shown in the models in the Museum of the Royal United Service Institution.

the admiral, who had an eye like a hawk, would damn him up in heaps, and the captain, as an able assistant, would run forward like a bull-dog, and roar out the second part of the same tune. I was also stationed on the forecastle, and when those freaks were going on, I used to look at my old mastheading friend and grin, and he knew damned well what I was grinning at, as the good old times could not be forgotten. And now, John, I am done with you.

I subscribed to a concert in Gosport and one evening I went with a messmate (the late Captain Philpot) and some girls who I gave tickets to; we did not break up until 12 o'clock and then went on board. It happened unfortunately to be our middle watch, and the rest of the watch being on shore we relieved the deck; but, being tired and sleepy, we thought it no harm to go to our hammocks instead of keeping a vile watch; so, singing the old song:

> I hate this damned watching and trudging the deck;
> The most we can get, boys, at best is a check;
> Sit still then, and let the lieutenants all rail,
> We'll ride out the breeze—says Commodore Gale—

we thought ourselves perfectly secure; and so we should have been, had not a quarrel taken place between two of the quartermasters' wives, for which one of them was turned out of the ship; but in revenge she accused the other of smuggling four tubs of liquor into the ship, stating the time to the first lieutenant. Now as ill luck would have it, it proved to be on the concert night, or rather the morning, when the transaction took place. He then made his report to the captain, who sent for us and with a ferocious aspect demanded the reason of our leaving the deck. We could give none, only Philpot said, 'The concert, sir.' 'The concert, sir?' retorted the captain; 'What had the concert to do with liquor getting into the ship, and officers sleeping in their watch? I have a great mind to try you both by a court martial;' and turning to the first lieutenant he said, 'Mr. Yetts, let them be prisoners for three months'—or, in other words, not to be suffered to leave the ship, even upon duty, during that time.

Our first lieutenant (Yetts) was a very droll and strange personage, in dress as well as in manners. When he commissioned the Edgar he had on a uniform coat made in days of yore, with sleeves that reached to his hips, a very low collar, huge white lappels and cuffs, the buttons behind at a good fighting distance, and the skirts and pockets of enormous size. A red waistcoat, nankin breeches, and black worsted stockings, with great yellow buckles on round-toed shoes, a hat that had been cocked, but cut round, with a very low crown, so that he was obliged to keep his hand to his head to prevent its blowing off in the lightest breeze. When he came on board in this costume, the warrant officers thought he had made his escape from a madhouse; and Grey, the gunner, swore he was an understrapper from Bedlam that was come to take Johnny Bone the boatswain (at that time half mad from drunkenness) to the lunatic hospital. When this was told Johnny it brought him to his reason, and in great tribulation he locked himself up in his storeroom and remained there the most of the day, to the great amusement of everyone on board.

This Johnny Bone was a devil of a fellow at Cap-a-bar,[1] and would stick at nothing. It is

[1] Misappropriation of government stores (Smyth, *Sailors' Word-Book*). *Cf.* *N.R.S.* xxviii. 48. A writer in *Notes and Queries* (X. ii. 397) refers the term to the Dutch 'te kaap varen' = to go a-privateering (*N.E.D.*, *s.v.* Cape); a not improbable derivation.

related that the late Lord Duncan, when he commanded the Edgar, once said to him, 'Whatever you do, Mr. Bone, I hope and trust you will not take the anchors from the bows.'

But to return to Lieutenant Yetts; he was a very active old man; extremely passionate, and swore as well as his brother officers of the present day; an excellent sailor, and though violent at times, would hurt no one. He was also well read in ancient and modern history. In asking him leave to go on shore, his answer was (if out of temper), 'No; damn my brains if you shall go.' It happened one night when he went on shore that Jack Kiel (one of the midshipmen) and myself took the opportunity and set off on a cruise in the long boat's punt (small boat), and landed on Gosport beach; and having secured the boat, we took a stroll up Middle Street, when who should pop upon us but old Yetts, who, we thought, had gone to Portsmouth. We took to our heels and he called after us, but was not certain (so it appeared) to our persons. We, without loss of time, got on board and went to our hammocks. The moment he returned, down came the quartermaster to acquaint us that Mr. Yetts wished to see us. When we came upon deck he addressed us with '——, Mr. Kiel and Mr. Gardner, who gave you leave to go on shore? and why did you not come when I called you?' We brazened it out that we had not been on shore and had gone to our hammocks a considerable time, and that he must have mistaken somebody else for us. This seemed to stagger him, but he swore, 'damn his brains, but it must be us.' He then made inquiry of the midshipmen of the watch, but we had taken devilish good care not to come up the side but crept in through the gunroom port, so that they could give him no information. By these means we weathered him; but for more than a week after, whenever he saw us on deck, he greeted us with, 'Damn my brains, but it was you.'

There was a song at this time by Storace[1]—it began as follows:

I left the country and my friends
 To play on my little guitar;
It goes tang-tang-tang,
It goes tang-tang-tang,
It goes tang-tang-tang,
It goes ta— etc.

One of our midshipmen (Vosper) altered this, and used to sing with a thundering voice the following burlesque to the same tune.

The other day I asked old Yetts
 For leave to go on shore;
He said no, no, you shall not go,
He said no, no, no, he said no,
He said no no, you shall not go,
By Christ, you shall not go, etc.

I had nearly got into a second scrape about the confounded middle watch. My friend Jack Kiel and myself relieved the deck at 12. The rest of the watch were absent as before. The night was as dark as pitch, and blowing and raining most furiously, when about five bells we got rather hungry and went to our berth in the cockpit to stew beef steaks. This was done by lighting several pieces of candle in the bottom of a lantern, and sticking forks (not silver ones) in the table round it with a plate resting on them over the candles (the head of the lantern being off), which stewed the steaks remarkably well. We had scarcely finished when old Davy Jacks, the quartermaster, came hobbling down the cockpit ladder to inform us that the Endymion was going

[1] Musical composer, died 1796. *Cf. D.N.B.*

out of harbour, and had made the signal for assistance (we had then the command). 'Why, Davy,' says Kiel, 'you must be mad to think of such a thing. Is that all the news you have?' 'Nothing more, sir,' says Davy; 'only Mr. Yetts wants you.' This was the unkindest cut of all. Away we flew upon deck, saw how things were, and went into the wardroom to answer the bell for the officer of the watch, and found the old man nearly dressed. 'J—— ——,' say he, 'What's the matter? and why did you not come when I rung before?' I told him we were looking out on the Endymion, who had broke from her moorings and had made the signal, and that I was just coming to acquaint him of the circumstance. This satisfied him, and we took good care never to be off deck again.

The Phaeton, 38, having arrived from the Mediterranean and a court martial ordered on her captain (Geo. Dawson), and also on Messrs. Wall and Lucas, the first and second lieutenants, and likewise on a man by the name of Wilkie, her master—Rear-Admiral J. Peyton hoisted his flag (white at the mizen) on board of us as president of the court. The lieutenants were tried the first, and sentenced to be dismissed from their ship; and then the above-named Wilkie, as prosecutor, exhibited fifteen charges against Captain Dawson. The trial lasted several days, when twelve of the charges and part of another were brought in Scandalous, Malicious, Ill-founded, and Derogatory to the discipline of his Majesty's Service; but two of the charges and part of another being proved, he was dismissed from his Majesty's Service.

Captain Dawson then tried Wilkie on four charges; part of which being proved, he was sentenced to be dismissed from his ship—a sad punishment, she being paid off the next day. The surgeon

(Wardrope) had been tried before the ship arrived and was a long time under sentence of death.[1]

Captain Dawson was an officer who had greatly distinguished himself in the American War when he commanded the Hope [schooner]. He was captain of the Renown, 50, when she engaged and would have taken a French 84,[2] one of the Count D'Estaing's fleet, had she not been rescued by some of the enemy's ships coming to her assistance. This trial occasioned a great party spirit among the midshipmen, some siding with Wilkie the prosecutor, and others with Captain Dawson. I was for the latter, because I thought there was malice prepense in the prosecution. I hated the basilisk look of Wilkie, and wished him at the devil. A violent altercation taking place upon this subject, my old messmate Philpot, a strong adherent to the house of Wilkie, in the moment of irritation threw a black jack full of beer in my face; for which compliment I instantly knocked him down, and after a hard battle in which he got two black eyes, I came off conqueror. Things were going to be carried farther, but a stop was put to it and we made it up.

Like all ships we had some droll hands, and with the exception of about half a dozen, all good and worthy fellows. One or two of the half dozen I shall mention, and begin with Geo. Wangford,

[1] See in the Record Office (*Admiralty, Sec. In Letters*, 5326), the minutes of these curious and remarkable courts martial—on David Wardrope, the surgeon, for drunkenness, quarrelling and beating the lieutenants: death; on William Wall and John Lucas, lieutenants, for permitting themselves to be beaten: dismissed the ship; on George Dawson, captain, for tyranny, oppression, malversation, suttling and such like: dismissed the service; and on John Wilkie, the master, for neglect of duty, disobedience, disrespect and drunkenness: dismissed the ship.

[2] Le Languedoc, 80, D'Estaing's flagship. She had been previously dismasted in a gale. *Cf.* Beatson, iv. 348; Chevalier, i. 117.

who had been in the Boreas, and was a follower of the captain. He was an immoderate drinker, and from his fiery countenance had the nickname of Bardolph. While in the Edgar his mother died and left him one thousand pounds. He lived about six months after receiving the money in one scene of debauchery; and with the assistance of a noted prostitute, named Poll Palmer, in that short time made away with nearly five hundred pounds. I remember his being taken ill after a hard drinking match, and then he got religious and requested one of the midshipmen (Patrick Flood), another strange fish, to read the Bible to him. This Patrick readily agreed to; but before he got through a chapter pretended to have a violent pain in his stomach, upon which Wangford requested him to take capillaire[1] and brandy, and that he would join him, and desired that, in mixing, two thirds should be brandy. Flood was immediately cured, and began to read a chapter in Job; and when he came to that part, 'Then Job answered and said,' Wangford started up and roared out—'that I am going to hell before the wind.' I lay close by them and heard every word. He soon after turned to upon Hollands, his favourite beverage, and thought no more of Job or the Bible. Soon after he was sent to the hospital, where he remained some time and died mad. A little before his death Pringle (one of the midshipmen) went to see him, and while sitting on the foot of his bed he started up and seized hold of Pringle by the hair singing out, '—— —— ——, catch that bird'; the other calling out for the nurse to assist him, which was of little use for he nearly broke her arm before others came up to secure him. Several of us attended his funeral.

Our time passed cheerfully in the harbour;

[1] Syrup of maiden-hair, flavoured with orange-flower.

plenty of fun and going on shore. One night several of us supped in the main hatchway berth on the orlop deck, when old Andrew Macbride, the schoolmaster (a man of splendid abilities but unfortunately given to drinking, though the goodness of his heart made him much respected and did away in a great measure with that infirmity) on this occasion got so drunk that Ned Moore (my worthy messmate) handed him a couple of tumblers of the juice of red pickled cabbage and told him it was brandy and water, which he drank without taking the least notice. I believe it did him good as an aperient, for he was cruising about all night and next day, and could not imagine what it was that affected him so.

One of our midshipmen (Millar), as worthy a fellow as ever lived, told me the following anecdote of himself and Macbride. On his joining the Hector, 74, a guard-ship in Portsmouth Harbour, Morgan, the first lieutenant, came up to him and said, 'Millar, my boy, how glad I am to see you. You must dine with me to-day.' Millar, who had never seen him before, thought it rather queer that he should be so friendly at first sight; however, he accepted the invitation. When dinner was over, Morgan declared that he was under a great obligation to him and that he should at all times be happy to acknowledge it. Poor Millar said he was really at a loss to understand him. 'Well then,' says Morgan, 'I'll tell you. It is this. I was considered the ugliest son of a bitch in the fleet before you came on board, but you beat me dead hollow, and surely you cannot wonder at my being sensible of the obligation.' Millar laughed heartily, and they were ever after on the best terms. It happened in about three months after this, Macbride also joined the Hector. The moment he came on board, down came the quartermaster to Millar saying that Lieutenant Morgan wanted to see him immediately. As soon as Millar came on the quarter-deck, Morgan went up to him and wished him joy; and pointing to Macbride observed, 'You, Millar, are a happy dog for being relieved so soon. I was considered the ugliest son of a bitch in the fleet for more than a year; you then came on board and outdid me; but there stands one that beggars all description, and if they were to rake hell they could not find his fellow.' Then going and shaking Macbride by the hand, asked him and Millar to dine with him that day to celebrate the happy relief.

Poor Andrew once made a vow that he would not get drunk, and said that not only the taste but the smell of the liquor was so disagreeable that he could not bear to stay where it was. He also gave Watson, the boatswain, leave to thrash him with his cane if ever he found him drunk. Poor fellow, he kept his promise for about three months, and then turned to as bad as ever, and Watson did not forget to give him a lacing with his cane, which occasioned the following song written by John Macredie:—

Of all the delights that a mortal can taste,
A bottle of liquor is surely the best;
Possessed of that treasure my hours sweetly glide,
Oh! there's nothing like grog, says sweet Andrew Macbride.

When I sit in my school I think my time lost
Where with dry sines and tangents my temper is crossed;
But how sweetly I smile with the glass by my side:
Grog helps mathematics, says Andrew Macbride.

The boatswain, God damn him, would fain me control
With a promise when sober I made like a fool;
With his cursed rattan he so curried my hide,
That I'll drink his damnation, says Andrew Macbride.

When the sweet powers of grog have my reason betrayed,
And free from sad care on the deck I am laid,
Then the boys black my face, and my actions deride;
The whelps may be damned, says Andrew Macbride.

[illegible] the raptures of grog shall a sage be controlled,
[illegible] like myself submit to be schooled?
[illegible] drink, the lieutenant and captain may chide:
[illegible] drink till I die, says sweet Andrew Macbride.

[illegible] said the smell hurt me, the fools did believe:
[illegible] my dear friends, I did you deceive:
[illegible] the taste or smell hurts me, may hell open wide.
[illegible] damned there with water to drink, says Macbride.

Nothing disrespectful was intended by this song. Every officer in the ship was a friend to poor Andrew, and Macredie would have been one of the the first to resent an insult offered to him. It is a strange coincidence that on the day we were paid off, I saw Macbride sitting on the taffrail reading Ossian's poems, and looking at a fine engraving of the Spirit of Crugal.[1] Twelve years after in Port Royal Harbour, Jamaica, I went to answer the signal for lieutenant on board the Leviathan, 74 (I then belonged to the Brunswick), and going on the poop to write the order, I saw a figure sitting on the taffrail, who I thought I knew, in deep meditation. On going up to him I recognised my old messmate Macbride, with the identical book and the engraving of the Spirit of Crugal in his hand. The poor fellow was most happy to see me, but how altered! He went back with me to dinner, and I gave him some classical books that pleased him greatly. His bones are lying at the Palisades. He was one of the first mathematicians in Europe; an excellent

[1] There are not so many readers of Ossian now as there were a hundred years ago, and the description given of this Spirit may be novel. 'Connal lay by the sound of the mountain stream, beneath the aged tree. . . . At distance from the heroes he lay; the son of the sword feared no foe. The hero beheld, in his rest, a dark red stream of fire rushing down from the hill. Crugal sat upon the beam, a chief who fell in fight. . . . His face is like the beam of the setting moon. His robes are of the clouds of the hill. His eyes are two decaying flames. Dark is the wound of his breast. . . .' *Fingal*, ii.

writer in prose and verse, an able disputant, and possessed a mind remarkable for the strictest integrity. 'Tread lightly on his ashes, ye men of genius, for he was your kinsman.' [1]

I must here say a word about poor unfortunate Patrick Flood. When first I knew him in the American War, he was a fine officer-like looking fellow; but when he joined the Edgar he was sadly reduced from long illness in the West Indies; and from domestic troubles, and disappointment at not getting promotion, grew regardless of himself and reckless of his character. Cynical to a degree and used to caricature us upon every occasion, I remember his making a very ludicrous drawing of Macbride, representing him sitting on the deck with the boys blacking his face and a bottle and a glass alongside of him; and [underneath it, some scurril-

[1] Without quite being 'one of the first mathematicians in Europe,' it is probable enough that Macbride was really an able man. The old schoolmasters were of two sorts: either they were respectable, half-educated men, who were rising in life and sometimes became pursers, occasionally even lieutenants; or, and more commonly, they were clever, highly educated men, ruined by drink, and on the down grade. We may believe that Macbride was a man of this stamp. *Cf.* also Byam Martin's experience on board the Pegasus (*N.R.S.* xxiv. 57). Some of our most distinguished captains and admirals endeavoured, at their own expense, to remedy this utterly disgraceful state of things:—*e.g.* Pellew in the Caledonia, Sir Samuel Hood in the Centaur; but it was not till 1836 that the Admiralty tried to make an entirely new departure by the institution of naval instructors. Complete success, however, came very gradually. Some of the earlier officers so appointed were not uncommonly put to bed by a *posse* of their pupils; and even less than fifty years ago, one of them—a capable instructor and a clever writer—went on four days' leave to his cabin, in company with half a dozen of brandy. All might have gone well—from his point of view—had not the supply run short after two days, and the wretched man, in his night-shirt and a state bordering on *delirium tremens*, appeared in the ward room clamouring for drink.

ous verses, which Macbride answered with others still more indecent].

When the Edgar was paid off, Captain A. J. P. Molloy[1] was appointed to the command of her, and Flood was continued as one of the midshipmen. Having obtained leave to go to London to try and raise friends to get his promotion, he succeeded in getting the promise from Lord Chatham; but unfortunately having staid a short time above his leave, Captain Molloy, in answer to Lord Chatham's letter respecting him, cruelly said he considered Mr. Flood in no other light than that of a deserter. This was the ruin of poor Flood, who died in penury, but lived long enough to witness the downfall of his enemy. And now let me mention my worthy messmate John Macredie, a gentleman that did honour to society and one that was highly respected by a numerous acquaintance. He had seen a great deal of service and was on board the Hercules, 74, in Rodney's action on the 12th of April 1782. He was also on board the Princess Royal, 98, and Pégase, 74, and then joined the Edgar, and was a messmate of mine for three years, and again in the Barfleur for upwards of a twelvemonth. He was an excellent scholar, being well acquainted with the Greek and Latin, and was deeply read in ancient history and nearly equal to Macbride in mathematics. The author of many plays that were never printed, as he would not allow them to be sent to the press, although strongly urged by those who were competent judges of their merit. He was also a good poet and possessed undaunted courage, and was as

[1] Tyrannical and oppressive as a captain, but reputed a brave officer previous to 1st June 1794. His conduct on that day led to his being tried by court martial, and dismissed his ship—whether for cowardice, or for Howe's inability to make himself understood, may be doubted.

generous as he was brave. At the same time he was one of the most absent [minded] men that can be imagined. I have known him when going to answer a signal come on deck with one boot and one shoe on; and when sent below in consequence, come up again with his black stock with the inside turned out. One morning when alongside of the flagship, on stepping from the boat to the accommodation ladder he dropped the order book overboard, and in trying to get hold of it he let go his sword, which sunk in a moment. I have also known him walk nearly two miles out of Gosport before he recollected that he had only to go to his tailor's, who lived near the beach.

I must not forget another worthy fellow and messmate of mine, the late Lieutenant Edward Moore, at this time one of the mates. Ned was as brave and generous a soul as ever lived; a determined enemy to tyranny, as the following circumstance will shew. When the present Retired Rear-Admiral Shield[1] was first lieutenant of the Saturn, 74, at Spithead in the year 1791 or 1792, one evening in the first watch he ordered one of the midshipmen (Mr. Leonard) on some trifling occasion to the masthead for punishment. Mr. L. said he would go there with pleasure if it was on duty, but not for punishment; upon which Mr. Shield had him made fast to a girtline and triced up to the main topmasthead without a guy to keep him clear of the top etc. This made a great stir both on board and on shore, and Mr. Leonard was advised to commence proceedings by entering an action against Shield; and a subscription was set on foot to defray the expenses attending it. My friend Ned at this time belonged to the London, 98, lying at Spithead; and he wrote letters to the midshipmen of the other men

[1] Marshall, iii. 89.

of war to subscribe also. This coming to the knowledge of Lord Hood, he considered it as a conspiracy injurious to the discipline of the navy, and Moore was put under an arrest. A court of inquiry was held, and then a court martial, where Sir Hyde Parker stood as prosecutor; and after a long examination of witnesses, Moore was found guilty of contempt of court and sentenced to be confined in the Marshalsea for one month, a fortnight of which he remained on board the guard-ship. The other charge was not proved. The late Admiral Macbride, who commanded the Cumberland, 74, at that time, was a member of the court, and was a friend to Moore ever after, and made him lieutenant.

One of our midshipmen, who lately died a post captain, was an infernal tyrant. While in the Edgar, this chap one evening began his tricks by thrashing one of the youngsters, a messmate of Ned's, and for so doing Ned gave him, to the great joy of all, the most severe drubbing I ever witnessed. Ned had been a shipmate of this person's before in the Queen, 98, when a guard-ship, and had seen some of his pranks there and now paid him on the old score.

While lying at the Hardway moorings, about three o'clock one morning we heard a voice halloing out 'Come here, you sleepy-headed hounds, and take me out of a hole that I have got into.' It being low water, the voice appeared to come from the mud. Two or three of us got into the cutter (for we always kept a boat out)[1] and went in the direction of the voice, where we found Moore up to his middle, and being a stout fellow it was no easy matter to extricate him. Had we not gone when we did he

[1] It will, of course, be remembered that all boats were then hoisted in; boat-davits were unknown.

would have been suffocated as the tide was flowing. He had been keeping it up and missed his way to the Hard. He was one that would part with his last shilling to serve a friend or assist those in distress. I recollect while lying in Torbay with the grand fleet (we belonged to the Barfleur, 98, then), that I had not a sixpence and no opportunity of sending home; and I wanted to go on shore, and how to raise the wind I did not know; which coming to the ears of Ned, says he, 'Tony, I have got a guinea and I am determined that you shall have half of it'—which he made me take. Would to God that he was alive and that I could shake hands with him now, and the rest of the brave fellows that are no more. *Sit tibi terra levis!*

We had a custom when the officers were at dinner in the wardroom, of dividing into parties; one division was to storm the other on the poop. In one of those attacks I succeeded in getting on the poop, when Kiel (who I have mentioned before) attacked me with a fixed bayonet and marked me in the thigh (all in good part). I then got hold of a musket, put in a small quantity of powder, and as he advanced, I fired. To my horror and amazement he fell flat on the deck, and when picked up his face was as black as a tinker's, with the blood running down occasioned by some of the grains of powder sticking in. I shall never forget the terror I was in, but thank God he soon got well; only a few blue spots remained in his phiz, which never left him. This was the only time I ever fired a musket and probably will be the last. They used to say in the cockpit that he was troubled with St. Anthony's fire (alluding to my name).

Another time when attacking the poop, I was standing on one of the quarter-deck guns, when I received a violent blow on the face from a broomstick, which made my nose bleed off and on for several days. It was thrown at me by J. S. Carden (now Captain Carden [1]) and a hand swab was thrown at him, which falling short, entered one of the office windows, which put an end to the attack. It was laughable to see John Macredie take the part of Ajax Telamon, with a half-port for a shield and a boarding-pike for a lance. Culverhouse used to take the part of Diomede, but instead of a lance would use the single-stick, with which he was superior to anyone in the fleet. He was a very clever fellow, full of fun and drollery, and sung humorous songs in the most comic style. I remember a verse or two of one:

> When first they impressed me and sent me to sea,
> 'Twas in the winter time in the making of hay,
> They sent me on board of a ship called Torbay,
> Oh! her white muzzle guns they did sore frighten me,
> Musha tudey, etc.
>
> Says the boatswain to Paddy, And what brought you here?
> For the making of hay 'tis the wrong time of year.
> By Jasus, says Paddy, I wish I was gone,
> For your small wooden kingdom I don't understand.
> Musha tudey, etc.
>
> Oh! the first thing they gave me it was a long sack,[2]
> Which they tould me to get in and lay on my back;
> I lay on my back till the clock struck one bell,
> And the man overhead he sung out, All is well.
> Musha tudey, etc.

We had a very droll midshipman who lately died an old post captain, and was one of the best officers in the service. This gentleman was a kind of ventriloquist, and when we sat in the officers' seat in Gosport chapel, and opposite to old Paul the

[1] Marshall, iv. 1007.

[2] 'What! put a physician in a bread bag!' is quoted as the remark of a newly caught surgeon's mate, on being shown his bed.

clerk, of beer-drinking memory, whenever this man would begin to sing, the other would go Quack, Quack, Quack; sometimes high and sometimes low, according as the clerk would sing the psalm. I have seen the old fellow look round with amazement, the people whispering to one another, while others could not keep their countenance but would hold their heads down and laugh. I remember him coming on board late one night in a wherry from Gosport, and it being calm we could hear him quacking a long way off. We then lay at the Hardway moorings. When the wherry got alongside the waterman swore he would be damned sooner than have that chap in his boat again. Had he known as much, he would not have taken him off for any money; he certainly was the devil or his near relation, for some hell-hound or other had been following him on the water all the way from Burrow Castle (near the Magazine and reported to be haunted) until he got alongside. He said he knew that Burrow Castle was haunted and he'd take good care to return on the other side of the harbour, and blast him if he'd ever come that way at night. I had the watch upon deck at the time and remember every word, and I thought I should have died a-laughing.

Our first lieutenant had an inveterate hatred to the Barfleur (the flagship) for the following reason. The signal was made for all midshipmen, and I had just returned in the long boat from Spithead, where we had been fishing, and was then going to relieve the deck, it being my watch, when Lieutenant Yetts ordered me to answer the signal. On my asking him leave to go below and get ready, as I was certain they would turn me back if I went in the dress I had on, 'Mr. Gardner, will you dictate to me?' was his reply; 'Go as you are, sir.' When

I got on board the Barfleur, Lieutenant Ross (who I knew very well) was commanding officer. The moment he saw me he came up, and with eyes of a dog fish, asked who I was and where I came from. I could hardly help laughing at the question. However, I explained to him the reason, but all to no purpose, as he sent me into my boat saying, 'Tell your officer that I made the signal for a midshipman, and not for a fisherman, and he ought to have known better from the length of time he had been in the service.'

On my delivering this insolent message to Lieutenant Yetts, it put him in a great rage and he swore, damn his brains, but he'd remember Master Ross for his kindness, the first opportunity. This Ross was a satirist, or would be thought so, because he wrote some poem in doggerel rhymes of scurrilous merit, abusing some of the officers of the guard-ships and many of the respectable people of Gosport. He also wrote a play which was damned and hissed off the stage, and some other pieces of the same description. Soon after this it came to our turn to have the guard, and late in the first watch, Lieutenant Yetts sent for me and gave orders that I should go in the cutter and row guard, and if possible get alongside the Barfleur. Away I went round the guard-ships, and left the Barfleur for the last. On rowing ahead I let the boat drop down with the tide and actually got alongside her accommodation ladder without being hailed. It is the duty of a lieutenant to row guard, so I did not think myself justified in boarding her, which I could have done; but remained some time alongside. At last one of the midshipmen (Mr. Holmes) hailed from the gangway, 'What boat is that?' upon which I called out as loud as I could hollo, 'Guard boat!' and that I had been alongside a considerable time without being hailed—to his great astonishment, as he informed me afterwards. On my telling this to Mr. Yetts, he rubbed his hands and swore that everyone should know how the damned brutes were caught napping.

In the absence of the admiral we, as senior captain, would have the command; and when exercising sails or getting down top gallant yards etc, if the Barfleur only showed a man's head above deck, up would go her signal to call her men down out of the tops and rigging, and old Yetts would exclaim, 'Damn my brains, no starting before us; we are masters now.' Mr. Nowell, our second lieutenant, was a very powerful and active man; and though gloomy and fiery at times, was much the gentleman. He was famous at fencing and jumping, and could, as I have been told, jump across the gateway of Gosport works—about twenty feet. On one occasion he sprained his ankle, when Frost (one of our midshipmen) said in his hearing and mocking the Welsh (Nowell being a Welshman) 'My vather a tevil of a good shumper, shumped twenty veet, came right down, proke his ankle, could no more shumpy.' For this the other gave him a look that spoke volumes.

This Frost was a complete Commodore Gale and went by the nickname of Hard Frost. It is related that when his wife died he gave a dinner on the day of her funeral. When the company arrived, Frost was dead drunk; upon which some of the party laid him out, with a leg of mutton under his head for a pillow, and a bunch of turnips under his feet. In the early time of the guard-ships there was a board held by the midshipmen of the Queen, 98, the flagship, where the midshipmen of the other ships used to go to pass their examination for a blackguard. Frost, who belonged to the

Pégase, 74, went to pass, and on the occasion showed such transcendent abilities, that the board considered him a wonder, and requested he would take his seat as a member. I could relate many of his sayings, but they had better sink into oblivion.

Our first lieutenant was a devil for scrubbing decks, and in the dead of winter we frequently had to shovel the snow from the quarter-deck, and take a spell, about half-past four in the morning, with the holystone and hand organs, while the water would freeze as soon as it was thrown on the deck. The general order, made into rhyme by Flood [was] as follows :

> The decks, as usual, to be washed and scrubbed ;
> And with the holystone severely rubbed.

To show the superstition of sailors I must mention the following anecdote. Not a hundred miles from Portsmouth lived a great nabob, who formerly possessed a large fortune, but from gambling and other bad management had greatly fallen off, and the neighbours used to say he had dealings with the devil, and at night would converse with him in his cellar. We had a raven on board that came from this neighbourhood; and from the number of strange pranks it was in the habit of playing, was supposed by the ship's company not to have been one of this world; and what strengthened this opinion was Macredie giving it out that he had heard the raven speak, and say that he had been the nabob's coachman, and should resume his office as soon as the ship was paid off, and he had got some recruits for his master. This made him be looked at with an evil eye by the ship's company; and one evening when the provisions were serving out and several of the people were in the cockpit about the steward's room, the raven caught hold of the gunner's mate by the trowsers, croaking and snapping at his legs. He then flew on the shoulder of the corporal of marines, took off his hat and hid it in the tier. 'I'm damned,' says old Phillips, the quartermaster, 'if he has not marked you for his master.' He had hardly said this when the raven came hopping back and seized upon the cheese belonging to the quartermaster, and walked off with a large piece of it, the other being afraid to follow.

Another of his tricks I was an eye-witness to. Our sergeant of marines had leave to go on shore, and was on the poop showing a half-guinea to the corporal, saying 'With this bit of gold I shall take a cruise, it will last as long as I like to stay.' He was holding the half-guinea between his finger and thumb, and asked the raven, who was on the poop, if he would take a trip with him. Ralph, ever on the watch, in an instant snapped the half-guinea out of his hand, and flew up to the main topmast head and remained more than an hour aloft, the sergeant all the time in the greatest anxiety, and some of the fellows saying to him, 'Now, don't you believe he's the devil?' At last the raven flew down upon the booms and went into the stern sheets of the barge lying there and hid the half-guinea, which the sergeant found, but swore it was not the same that was taken from him, while several called out 'Sold! Sold!'[1]

I shall now conclude the Edgar after saying a word for Davy Reed, the master. He was what we call a hard officer, as well as a very strange sort of fish, and had the misfortune, like many others, to lose his teeth. I was at dinner in the wardroom

[1] This superstitious dread of the raven was as common on shore as afloat (see *post*, p. 258), and is by no means extinct even now.

when a small parcel was handed in directed for Mr. Reed. 'What the hell can this be?' says Davy (who did not like to have sixpence to pay the waterman), 'and who gave it to you?' continued he. 'Sir,' says the waterman, 'it was a young lady who sent it off from Common Hard.' As several tricks had been played with Davy before, he was afraid to open the parcel, and begged of one of the officers at the table to do so for him, but when opened, what was his amazement to find a set of sheep's teeth for David Reed, Esq., with directions for fixing, and a box of tooth powder that, by the smell, appeared to be a mixture of everything abominable. Poor Davy was in a dreadful rage, and never heard the last of it. The Edgar was paid off in January 1790, and we had a parting dinner at the India Arms, Gosport, and kept it up until twelve that night. With the exception of the half dozen, they were some of the best fellows I ever met with. The Edgar was commissioned immediately after by Captain Anthony James Pye Molloy, and some of the midshipmen rejoined her.

OFFICERS' NAMES

Hon. JOHN LEVESON GOWER, Commodore and then rear-admiral.
Dead [1792]. I have said enough of him.—[*D.N.B.*]

JOSEPH PEYTON, Esq., Rear-admiral.
Dead [1804]. An admiral; a tight hand.

CHAS. THOMPSON, Esq., Captain.
Dead. See Boreas.

JOHN YETTS, 1st Lieutenant.
Dead. Out-pension. A good sailor of the old school, in many respects better than the new.

WILLIAM NOWELL, 2nd Lieutenant.
Dead [1827]. A vice-admiral; gloomy and fiery; but a good officer and gentleman.—[Marshall, ii. 598.]

RICHARD WELLAND, 3rd Lieutenant.

Dead. Had the out-pension, and thirteen children; proud, but a good officer.

JOHN IRWIN,[1] 4th Lieutenant.

Dead [1812]. A post captain [1796]. A very good fellow; always smiling.

WILLIAM BEDFORD, 5th Lieutenant.

Dead [1826]. A vice-admiral; fidgety; he once turned me out of the gunroom because I said Andrew Macbride, our schoolmaster, was formerly Dionysius the tyrant, and kept a school at Corinth, according to the opinion of Pythagoras respecting the transmigration of souls.—[Marshall, ii. 574.]

JOHN CULVERHOUSE, Mate and then flag lieutenant.

Dead. A clever fellow and good officer; a post captain; drowned at the Cape.

JOHN STILES, Lieutenant, lent for the cruise.

Dead. See Salisbury.

HARRY DAWE, Lieutenant, lent.

Dead. A commander [1818]; so-so. [Did not die till 1841.]

DAVID REED, Master.

Dead. An odd fish.

[JOHN] ROSKRUGE, Master.

Dead. A very good man, and one that was better acquainted with rope-yarns and bilge-water than with Homer or Virgil. He said a man's ideas should go no further than the jibboom end.

[JAMES] MALCOLM, Surgeon.

Dead. See Panther.

[THOMAS] TROTTER, Surgeon.

Uncertain. Formerly physician of the fleet; a most excellent fellow with first-rate abilities, an able writer and poet. [Died 1832—*D.N.B.*]

THOMAS KEIN, Surgeon; did duty as first assistant.

A very worthy fellow. Dead since writing this.

TITUS LEVY, Purser and then admiral's secretary.

Dead. Insane before he died.

CHARLES BUCHAN, Purser.

Dead. See Boreas.

JOHN STEVENS, Mate.

Dead. A commander.

---

[1] Captain of the Prince George in the battle of Cape St. Vincent. Grand-uncle of the late Sir George Willes.

[JOHN] WATSON, Mate.

Dead. A lieutenant; sickly and as crabbed as the devil. Cato the Censor never ended a speech without saying 'Delenda est Carthago,' and this man never ended his without saying 'Damn your whistle.'

GEO. WANGFORD, Mate.

Dead. See Boreas; drank himself to death.

FRANCIS SARGENT, Mate.

Dead. Drank hard; a lieutenant.

EDWARD MOORE, Mate.

Dead. A lieutenant; well known in the navy, and highly respected by a numerous acquaintance.

GEO. RULE BLUET, Midshipman, and then mate of the hold.

Dead. A lieutenant; a good-natured fellow with good abilities, but drank hard. I recollect being of a party at Gosport when Bluet wanted to make love to a young lady, but did not know how to begin. At last he took out of his pocket a plan of the Edgar's hold which he begged her to accept, and hoped she would keep it for his sake!

PATRICK FLOOD, Midshipman.

Dead. Good abilities, but thoughtless, and regardless of his character.

CHAS. INGLIS, Midshipman.

Dead [1833]. A post captain; a most able officer.—[Marshall, iv. 699.]

MAURICE BROWN, Midshipman.

Uncertain. A dashing fellow.

TOM EDMONDS, Midshipman.

Dead. A lieutenant; a good fellow, and played the flute delightfully.

FRANK FEARY, Midshipman.

Dead. A lieutenant; a very quiet fellow, who had taken plenty of calomel in his time.

ANDREW JAMES THOMPSON, Midshipman.

Dead. A lieutenant; a mad fellow.

ROBERT PHILPOT, Midshipman.

Dead [1826]. A post captain [1800]; obstinate and stiff in opinion, but quite the gentleman. Called 'Toby Philpot.'—[Marshall, iii. 289.]

GEO. JONES, Midshipman.

Dead [1834]. A commander [1798]; a fiery Welshman; called 'Dog-head.' He used to visit at Fareham, and Billy Lamb drew a midshipman in uniform with a dog's head, which bore a strong resemblance of Jones, and a directing post near him with —'To Fareham,' written on it.—[Marshall, x. 269.]

WILLIAM LAMB, Midshipman and mate.

Dead. A commander; my old and worthy messmate in two ships; a most able officer and seaman.

SOLOMON KING, Midshipman.

Dead. A lieutenant; a very worthy fellow.

WILLIAM KING, his brother, Midshipman.

Dead. A commander; a very worthy fellow.

WILLIAM BROWN, Midshipman, and then mate.

A superannuated master attendant; a good sailor; called 'Billy Beljer,' and 'Hell Sweat Us.'

ROBERT ELLIOT, Midshipman.

A post captain. [Rear-admiral, 1846; died, a vice-admiral, 1854. —O'Byrne.]

JAMES SLADE, Midshipman.

A post captain; wonderfully grand. [Died 1846—O'Byrne.]

WILLIAM WILKINSON, Midshipman.

Dead [1816]. A post captain [1810]; proud without reason.

JAMES SANDERS, Midshipman.

Dead [1834]. A post captain and C.B. Black Sambo, you and I never could agree; we hated one another most cordially: as a midshipman you were tyrannical; as a captain, I know nothing of you.—[Marshall, iv. 635.]

JOHN KIEL, Midshipman.

Dead. A lieutenant. Poor Jack went mad and died.

WILLIAM PRINGLE, first a scribe, and then a midshipman.

Dead. A lieutenant out-pension; nick-named 'Bull Rothery' and 'Ponderous and Huge.' He got the name of 'Ponderous and Huge' from the following circumstance. When we were storming the poop (as I have mentioned before), I was looking at John Macredie who had a boarding-pike for a spear, and repeating the following lines from the Iliad:

> And now he shakes his great paternal spear,
> Ponderous and huge, which not a Greek could rear—

when Pringle, who was standing by, asked me who Ponderous and Huge were, and whether they were Greeks or Trojans.[1]

TITUS ALLARDICE, Midshipman.

Dead [1832]. A commander [1831]; died insane at Haslar.

DAVIS, Mate.

Dead. A lieutenant. Poor fellow, was broke by court martial.

---

[1] As the admiral compared Mr. Pringle to a scuttle-butt (*ante*, p. 67), there would seem to be another meaning in the name.

JOHN BULL CONOLLY, Midshipman.

A lieutenant, out-pension; a very good fellow.

ROBERT YETTS, son of the first lieutenant, midshipman.

Dead. A lieutenant; broke by court martial. Poor Bob with all his faults was a worthy, generous fellow.

HENRY FOULARTON, Midshipman.

Dead. Very religious, and remarkably neat in his dress; but at last drank very hard, and died regretting that a keg of gin (along side of him) should see him out, which was really the case.

HENRY ALLEN, Midshipman.

This unfortunate man was captain of the Rattler sloop-of-war in the West Indies and was hanged at the yardarm by the sentence of a court martial [April 22, 1797, under the 29th Article of War].

GREGORY GRANT, Midshipman.

A commander [1810]; a very worthy fellow. Died 1839.—[Marshall, x. 403.]

WILLIAM VOSPER, Midshipman.

A lieutenant, Royal Asylum, Greenwich Hospital. A very good fellow and seaman; we were at three schools together, and also in the Edgar and Berwick.

RICHARD HEYCOCK, Midshipman.

Dead. A lieutenant. Old Dick was a good sailor, but unfortunately, as deaf as a doornail.

FRAS. ROSKRUGE, Midshipman.

Lieutenant [of Britannia], killed [at Trafalgar] in battle. A very worthy fellow; son of the master.

FROST, Midshipman.

Dead. A master; 'Hard Frost,' I have mentioned you before.

MILLAR, Midshipman.

Dead. A gunner; as worthy a fellow as ever lived; called 'Tom Pepper.'[1]

RICHARD COLE, Midshipman.

Dead. Dicky was an easy, simple fellow.

EMANUEL SILVA, Midshipman.

A magistrate for the county of Surrey; a gentleman; very much respected.

WM. GRANGER, Midshipman.

A vice-admiral of the blue. [Died 1848.—O'Byrne.]

---

[1] The traditional meaning of the name is a curious comment on 'the worthy fellow.'

HUGH DOWNMAN, Midshipman.

A vice-admiral; a very good officer. [Died, admiral, 1858.—O'Byrne.]

[JOHN] HOLLINGSWORTH, Midshipman.

Killed in battle[1]; a lieutenant.

JOHN TWISDEN, Midshipman.

A commander; a droll old guardo! [Died 1853.—O'Byrne.]

JOHN MACREDIE, Midshipman.

Dead [1833]. A commander [1827]; a most worthy fellow whom I have mentioned before.

HUGH COOK, Midshipman.

Dead [1834]. A post captain [1806]; called 'Pot luck and what not.' Billy Lamb gave him this name, because one evening on shore, when half seas over, he was asking every one in the room to come and see him and take 'pot luck and what not.'—[Marshall, v. 160.]

WM. HUGH DOBBIE, Midshipman.

Dead [1830]. A post captain; an excellent character.—[Marshall, v. 136.]

JOHN TRESAHAR, Midshipman.

A commander; my worthy messmate. [Died 1844.—O'Byrne.]

J. S. CARDEN, Midshipman.

A post captain. He commanded the Macedonian when she was captured by an American frigate of superior force. [Died, a retired rear-admiral, 1858.—O'Byrne.]

EDWARD BRACE, Midshipman.

A rear-admiral and K.C.B. [Died, a vice-admiral, in 1843.—Marshall, iii. 253.]

J. A. GARDNER, Midshipman.

A commander.

DAVID SPENCE 1st, Midshipman, lent.

Dead. A lieutenant; worthy fellow.

DAVID SPENCE 2nd, Midshipman, lent.

Dead. A master; worthy fellow.

ROBERT CROSBIE, Midshipman, lent.

Dead from drink; a lieutenant not worth his salt.

JAMES IRWIN, Midshipman, lent.

Dead. A commander; much respected.

---

[1] Whilst in command of the Growler brig, captured by French privateers, 21st Dec 1797.

ANDREW MACBRIDE, Schoolmaster.
Dead. Splendid abilities.

CROMBEY, Assistant Surgeon.
Dead. A surgeon; a man of prodigious strength.

JOHN LIGGATT, Assistant Surgeon.
Dead. A surgeon. Poor Jack lost his leg in action.

GEO. GORDON, Assistant Surgeon.
Dead. George was not very orthodox.

DUNCAN CAMPBELL, Assistant Surgeon.
Uncertain. Much the gentleman.

MARSH, Assistant Surgeon.
Uncertain. Drank like a fish.

LAUCHLIN MACLEAN, Clerk.
Dead. A paymaster at Greenwich Hospital.

JOHN SCOTT, Clerk.
Killed in battle [at Trafalgar]. Lord Nelson's secretary.

GARDNER, wrote in the office.
Dead. A very good little fellow; no relation of mine.

GEO. GRAY, Gunner.
Dead. Much respected.

JOHNNY BONE, Boatswain.
Dead, from drink; Cap-a-bar.

WATSON, Boatswain.
Uncertain. Broke by court martial. Said to have been boatswain with the notorious John Paul Jones when he took Sir Richard Pearson and my old captain (Piercy) in the American War.

DOUGLAS, Carpenter.
Dead. Builder at Antigua; much respected.

BARFLEUR, 98

When the Edgar was paid off, Commissioner Martin[1] of the dockyard at Portsmouth, recommended me to the Barfleur, Vice-Admiral Roddam (red at the fore) port admiral, and Robert Calder, Esq., captain. I had not been long on board when Captain Calder took it into his head to recommend several of us to the Solebay, 32, fitting at Spithead for the West Indies, and I was one of the number. This did not suit my inclination, and I requested my mother to make the circumstance known to the commissioner, who promised her that I should not be sent out against my will. I waited with great anxiety the result, and never shall I forget the manner Captain Calder addressed me the moment he came on board. 'Your mother is a fool, sir; you shall not stay in my ship; take your hat off, sir' (for we were always obliged to stand with our hats off while speaking to him and I was rather slack in doffing mine); 'I will give you one month to provide yourself with another ship, you are disgraced here;' and then turning on his heel went into his cabin. With rage and indignation at such an unwarrantable attack, I sent in to say I would be glad to speak to him if he was at leisure. This he immediately granted, and I was told after by Jefferys, the

[1] Afterwards Sir Henry Martin, Bart., Comptroller of the Navy; died 1794. See *N.R.S.*, vol. xxiv. p. viii.

clerk, who was in the cabin, that he thought I had made up my mind to go, but he was mistaken. I told him I came to return him thanks for his kindness in allowing me to remain in his ship for a month until I could provide myself with another, but if he pleased I would rather have my discharge immediately. He looked at me for some time before he made an answer; at last he roared out in fury, 'You shall not go at all, sir; and mind what you are about.' I answered that I always did mind what I was about. This increased his rage, and turning to the first lieutenant (Dolling), who had just come into the cabin, 'That's a troublesome chap, sir, take care of him.' Now it happened that I had leave to go on shore before Captain C. came on board and only waited till I saw him, and was going into the boat, when Lieutenant Dolling came waddling up to me with the intelligence that I was under arrest, and to consider myself a prisoner at large; and so I was for upwards of ten weeks, and the devil thank Bobby Calder for his kindness.

The Spanish armament taking place, we were ordered to Spithead, and hoisted the flag (blue at the main) of the Honourable Samuel Barrington, Sir John Jervis (rear-admiral of the blue) captain of the fleet, and Captain Calder in command of the ship. Sailed for Torbay, and took command of the fleet assembled there, until the arrival of Lord Howe, which took place soon after, as admiral of the fleet, the union jack being hoisted on board the Queen Charlotte, 110.[1] His Royal Highness the Duke of Cumberland, admiral of the white, attended by Prince William Henry, who commanded the Valiant, 74, came on board to visit

[1] Howe was ordered to hoist the union jack, and considered himself as 'brevet' admiral of the fleet.

Admiral Barrington, who had formerly sailed with the duke. Admiral Barrington having shifted his flag to the Royal George, 110, we hoisted that of Rear-Admiral Sir John Jervis, K.B., and sailed to the westward with the grand fleet, and found the old Barfleur an excellent sea boat. After cruising several weeks the fleet returned, and when off Plymouth we struck the flag of Sir John Jervis, and proceeded to the Downs and hoisted the flag (blue at the fore) of Vice-Admiral Elliot, and sailed with thirteen sail of the line for Spithead, where we found Lord Howe with the remainder of the fleet, Captain Calder having been appointed to the Stately, 64. Captain Robert Carthew Reynolds took command of the Barfleur as flag captain. The chief part of the midshipmen being removed to the Stately, Captain Calder sent for me and introduced me to Captain Reynolds, and spoke to him in the highest terms of my conduct, and among other things said I was particularly active in going aloft, and if I wished to leave the Barfleur he would keep a vacancy open on his books; but that the Barfleur being a flagship and my pay better, he thought it the most eligible of the two to remain. This was a civil way of parting to outward appearance friends.

The Spanish business being settled we remained at Spithead but struck our flag. Soon after a mutiny broke out in the ship, which was soon put a stop to, and the crews of the ships at Spithead (as many as liked) paid off. The Russian armament commencing, Lord Hood hoisted his flag on board the Victory, 100, and took command of the fleet, consisting of thirty-six sail of the line moored in two lines abreast, the frigates between, which had a most beautiful appearance, and thousands from all parts of the country came to gaze, and went back as wise as ever. Rear-Admiral Jonathan Faulknor[1] (red at the mizen) having hoisted his flag on board of us, that excellent officer Captain Reynolds left the ship and was succeeded by Captain John Bourmaster, one of the best men that ever lived. We remained a considerable time at Spithead until the business was settled, and then went into harbour to be paid off.

I shall now relate as well as I remember a few circumstances that took place in the Barfleur during the time I belonged to her. When we had the command in Torbay, before the arrival of Lord Howe, we exercised great guns and small arms every day, with loosing and furling sails, and it was remarked by the fleet that they never looked at the Barfleur without seeing the men crawling up the rigging ready for some manœuvre and keeping them constantly on the alert. I have absolutely been midshipman in the foretop when the sail has been loosed and furled nineteen times; and long Lloyd (one of our lieutenants) calling out from the gratings on the bowsprit, 'Mr. Gardner, will you have your hammock sent up to you?'—a common expression in the navy. I could not help answering, 'I'll thank you, sir, for I'm damnation tired.' He was a good fellow and only laughed.

Our ship's company were never surpassed. We had the pickings of the East India men, and our waisters could take helm and lead, and certainly we could have beaten with ease any two ships of a foreign power of our rate, and a braver officer never stepped between stem and stern than Bobby Calder. I had great reason to dislike him, but I will do him

[1] Son of Samuel Faulknor, captain of the Victory when she was lost on the Casquets in 1744; uncle of Captain Robert Faulknor, the 'Undaunted'; flag-captain with Keppel in 1778. Died, admiral of the blue, 1795.

justice as well as my humble abilities will allow. An error in judgment is what every man is liable to. Even Napoleon, the greatest man the world ever produced, was guilty of three great errors: the first in not entirely crushing the Russian army when he had it in his power after defeating the Emperor Alexander at Austerlitz; the second in not reinstating the Poles; and the third in not marrying a Frenchwoman after his divorce from Josephine. Another great general also made a few blunders; and his retreat from a certain citadel was, I have been told, anything but superior to that of the ten thousand under Xenophon.[1] But to return. Sir Robert Calder was found guilty of an error in judgment by the sentence of a court martial; but no man can deny that he was a brave and meritorious officer, possessing the first-rate[2] abilities of a British admiral.

> To some the pow'rs of bloody war belong,
> To some, sweet music and the charm of song;
> To few, and wondrous few, has Jove assigned
> A wise, extensive, all considering mind.

The newspapers at the time were teeming with abuse; but the braying of those asses soon sunk, and had no other effect than to shew the malignity of their leading articles. One of the blackguard papers was particularly vindictive. It was edited

> by wicked Daniel,
> Who snaps like a cur, and fawns like a spaniel.

From the number of flag officers and captains that were in the Barfleur, we had so many of their followers of every description that it is difficult to remember the whole, and we had six or seven

[1] The reference is possibly to the retreat from Burgos in November 1812.

[2] Many did deny this, while admitting that he was 'a brave and meritorious officer.'

different first lieutenants. However, I shall give as correct a list as possible, but not exactly in rotation. But first I must relate a few anecdotes; and with heart-felt respect for your memory, come forward my old friend Billy Culmer. This gentleman was one of the mates and is or was so well known in the navy that it would be superfluous to say anything respecting him, but for a few anecdotes not generally known which may be interesting.[1]

Billy in person was about five feet eight or nine, and stooped; hard features marked with the smallpox; blind in an eye, and a wen nearly the size of an egg under his cheek bone. His dress on a Sunday was a mate's uniform coat, with brown velvet waistcoat and breeches; boots with black tops; a gold-laced hat, and a large hanger by his side like the sword of John-a-Gaunt. He was proud of being the oldest midshipman in the navy (for he had been in that capacity with Lord Hood since 1757 [2]), and looked upon young captains and lieutenants with contempt. Being on shore at Gosport on a Sunday in the above costume, he tried to get into a tavern when the people were at church, and was thundering at the door to no purpose, when the late Captain N. H. Eastwood of the Royal Navy happened to be passing at the time in plain clothes, made some observations on his conduct, and said, 'Mr. Culmer, you are a disgrace

[1] Billy Culmer is a familiar character in the gossiping memoirs of the old war, *e.g. Greenwich Hospital*, by the Old Sailor (M. H. Barker). From Gardner's account of him, we may fairly believe that Barker's anecdotes are also genuine. It is noted in the Barfleur's pay-book, that he was born in Bridgwater, and was 35 in 1790. Of course, this is by no means conclusive evidence of the fact.

[2] If we are to accept the statement that he was 35 in 1790, he was two years old in 1757. He may have been with Hood in the Romney in 1767–76.

to the service.' Billy at this jumped off the steps, and with his usual oath 'Damn my two eyes,'—though he had but one—'but I'll slit your gullet, you wa wa——,' and with two or three desperate efforts to draw his sword, he at last succeeded, like Hudibras, in getting it out, and then gave chase to Eastwood, whose lean figure, moving like a ghost, had got the start and was fortunate enough to get into his own house just as Billy came up puffing and blowing and bellowing out, 'Stop that lanky son of a —— till I make a razee of him.'

In the American War Billy belonged to the Buffalo, 60. I am not certain that he was on board at the time the Dogger Bank action was fought; however, he used to celebrate the praises of his old ship, which bore a distinguished part in that well-fought battle. The Dutch fleet commanded by Admiral Zoutman had a convoy under charge, when our fleet under Vice-Admiral Hyde Parker fell in with them on the Dogger Bank and bore down immediately to give battle. The Dutch admiral formed his line to windward of his convoy, and waited for our fleet, and to his honour be it said that he never fired a gun until our admiral had formed his line within pistol shot, when up went the colours of both nations and then the action began. After several hours' desperate fighting the Dutch bore away with their convoy for the Texel, and we were so crippled that it was impossible to follow them.

Billy would upon all occasions when sea fights were spoken of sing the following song in honour of his old ship. It was made by a seaman of the Princess Amelia.

'Twas on the fifth of August by dawning of the day,
We spied some lofty sail, my boys, who to leeward of us lay;
They proved to be Dutchmen, with eight sail neat and fine,
We soon bore down upon them, and then we formed the line.

Bold Admiral Hyde Parker commanded us that day,
Who in the noble Fortitude to the windward of us lay;
To engage the Dutchmen closely the signal then he made,
And at his fore topgallant mast the bloody flag displayed.

And when our ships they did engage with seven sail neat and fine,
The Buffalo being one of them, her valour it did shine;
For she engaged six glasses, her shot did on them play,
Though she had three upon her she made them bear away.

There were the noble Berwick, Preston and Dolphin too,
Likewise the Bienfaisant, my boys, who made the Dutch to rue;
The old Princess Amelia was not backward on that day,
She lost her valiant captain all in the bloody fray.

Then our ship being so disabled and our rigging shot away,
And twenty of our brave fellows killed in the bloody fray;
And sixty-four were wounded, a dreadful sight to see,
But yet the rest were willing to engage the enemy, &c.

Billy was once singing the above ditty with a voice as melodious as that of the raven, when old Bob Perkins (a droll old guardo midshipman) began another that annoyed him sadly; but taking great care to be in a place where Billy could not easily get at him, says he, 'Mr. Culmer, you never were a midshipman before you joined the Barfleur, and it's well authenticated that you were cook of the celebrated Huffey so well known in days of yore.' He then began singing the following sonnet:—

Billy the cook got drunk,
Fell down the fore ladder,
And broke his gin bladder,
Then lived upon swipes and salt junk.

Billy the cook got drunk,
Fell into a sty,
And knocked out his eye,
Then into the sick bay he slunk.

As [Billy] had the meanest opinion of any one that would lay by for sickness, the last line of the above threw him into such a rage that Perkins, not finding his situation tenable, was obliged to make a hasty retreat; but not before

> he got a switch
> As quick as lightning on the breech,

which hastened his way down the cockpit ladder. [Billy] was once sitting in the gunroom cleaning a pair of huge yellow buckles, when the same Perkins chalked on a board in large letters, 'To be seen alive—The old blind sea monster, cleaning buckles as large as the main hatchway.' The moment he got sight of the inscription, [Billy] caught hold of a cutlass from the stand and cleared the gunroom in an instant, and had very near given it to Perkins, whom he suspected. He had a custom, when half seas over, of sounding a horn like a huntsman and calling the hounds, and used to swear he would be in at the death.

When he went to pass for lieutenant, one of the midshipmen and Marr the boatswain went up to London with him. They found it no easy matter to keep him in order, and he once swore to have them taken up as runaway soldiers. When he went to the navy board to undergo his examination he asked the commissioners the meaning of the word 'azimuth' and told them he could never find any wa wa that knew a word about it. Some of the board had been shipmates with him and were well acquainted with his ways; and when putting him right when answering a question, he would say, 'Go on, go on, my boy, that's the way; you are very right,' as if he was passing them; and when they told him they had no more questions to ask, he said he was glad of it and would go back to his ship like a lark.

One night soon after his return, when he had the first watch, some of the midshipmen reefed his blankets—this is done by making the ends fast and forming by numerous turns the blanket into the shape of a ring very difficult to undo. As soon as he was relieved he went to his hammock and groping about (for he never would take a light into the tier), he was heard to mutter, 'What the hell have they done with the ends?' and at last roared out, 'A horse's collar, by God.' After several fruitless attempts to shake the reef out, he went upon deck and brought down the ship's corporal and quartermaster with a light, and ordered them to clear his blankets; but they were as unable as himself, while the midshipmen in the tier were convulsed with laughter, and Billy, foaming with rage, drove away the corporal and quartermaster, calling them lubberly wa wa ——s. At this time a cry was heard from a remote part of the tier, 'Lay out, you lubberly rascal, and shake the reef out.' At this Billy lost all patience, and after damning his two eyes he unshipped the orlop gratings and got some billets of wood out of the hold, and in less than a minute the tier was cleared. Soon after some of the watch came down and put his bedding to rights and all was quiet. The same compliment that Cicero paid to Cæsar may also be paid to Billy, "that he remembered everything but an injury." The next morning he thought nothing of the matter.

Speaking about the Roman history respecting the battle of Actium between Augustus and Antony, he said he was in the battle and remembered all about it. The fact was he mistook the name and thought it was some place where he had been in the American war. He never heard the last of this, and when speaking of any battle where he had been present, was always asked if it took place thirty years before Christ. Captain Calder once sent for him to go in the launch for beer to Weevil.[1] 'Go back,' says he to the quartermaster, 'and tell Captain C. that Mr. Wood' (meaning Lord Hood, who he never called by his right name) 'never sent me away at seven bells and I shan't go now without my dinner. As soon as I have got that I will go like a lark—damn my two eyes.' Of course this was not told the captain.

While we had Admiral Roddam's flag in the harbour, a Dutch ship of the line anchored at Spithead and used to fire the morning and evening gun, without our taking notice of the circumstance. However, Bobby Calder soon found it out and came on board in a terrible rage, and gave the commanding officer (Prowse) a severe lecture, and told us all to prepare for a court martial for neglect in not reporting the transaction; at the same time sending a message to the Dutchman that if he persisted in such conduct a ship of the line would be sent alongside of him. This the Dutchman did not relish and took himself off as quick as possible.

Captain Calder was a man that had the service at heart and was a very strict disciplinarian. We dared not appear on deck without our full uniform, and a round hat was never allowed; our side arms always on the quarter deck ready for duty, and when exercising sails the midshipmen in the tops were to be in full dress. I remember when the signal was made for all lieutenants while lying in Torbay, that several came on board not exactly in uniform. He, without hearing a word they had to say, turned them out of the ship with a severe reprimand—old Lieutenant Noah Webb (with his cross-jack brace[2] eye), who commanded a cutter at the head

[1] The victualling yard, whose name was not inaptly transferred to the biscuit-grub.

[2] *Sc.* squinting.

of them; and when the late Sir Joseph Yorke (then a lieutenant) came on board at Spithead with strings in his shoes, Captain Calder came running out of his cabin and desired him to quit the ship immediately; and though Sir Joseph told him he was not on duty, it was all to no purpose; he kept following him to the gangway saying, 'My hat's off, sir; you must go out of the ship,' which the other was obliged to do in high dudgeon.

In working the ship no one was allowed to speak but himself, and I have seen the Barfleur brought to an anchor and the sails furled like magic, without a voice being heard except his own.[1]

> Sedate and silent move the numerous bands;
> No sound, no whisper but their chief's commands;
> These only heard, with awe the rest obey,
> As if some god had snatched their voice away.—*Iliad.*

No ship in the navy was in such high order. The midshipmen's berths were fitted up in great style (the beginning of luxury which the war soon after put a stop to), with rules and regulations. If a candle was taken off the table a fine of sixpence must be paid; and a shilling, if a hat was hung up in the berth or left on the chairs. This was all very well for the dandy aristocracy, but did not suit some of us that formerly belonged to the old Edgar; and Dick Heycock was the first to kick, and refused to abide by the regulations laid down by a proud and usurping few; and we carried our point, and things went on much better when the petty tyranny was abolished. Captain Calder would always bring the nobility that visited the ship to see the midshipmen's berths, and used to say: 'This is the place where all the admirals and captains in the service are tried

[1] Such silence was then very exceptional, and continued so till seventy years later (1861–2), when Sir William Martin, commander-in-chief in the Mediterranean, insisted on it.

every day, and where no one escapes being hauled over the coals.'

No man could be more attentive at his table, and he would particularly address himself to the midshipmen, and even ask their opinion upon different subjects, to give them confidence. Mrs. Calder was very fond of boat sailing, and we had a large double banked cutter in which she would go to Spithead when blowing very fresh, and carrying sail as if in chase until the boat's gunwale was under, so that everyone thought she was mad; and very few liked the trip except in fine weather, as she would always feel offended if any attempt was made to take in sail.

Among the many first lieutenants, we had one that was very pedantic. I shall not mention his name, but his nickname was Soap-Suds. The signal being made for all midshipmen, the order[1] was that a preparative flag would be hoisted before any manœuvre began, but when hauled down it was immediately to take place. Now not content with what was written in the order book, he addressed the midshipmen as follows: 'The idea strikes me thus, that when the preparative is hauled down, the evo-lu-ti-on will most certainly commence, and this pennant is your signal.'

We had another strange first lieutenant—this was Billy Chantrell, well known in the service. In giving his orders at night he used to say, 'Call me at six, and don't come bothering me about blowing and raining and all that damned nonsense.' I was with him in three ships and never met with so droll and strange a fellow. In passing Fairlight, near Hastings, on our way from the Downs to Spithead, Chantrell, pointing out to me the cliff near the church on Fairlight Down, said, 'Jemmy, how

[1] The order which the midshipman brought from the flagship.

would you like to be perched up there in the winter?' Little did he imagine that in some years after, when the war broke out and signal stations were erected along the coast, he should be the first officer appointed to this very spot, and I, the last; which was the fact.

We led a very lazy life at Spithead for several months, and it was expected we should strike upon our beef bones, as we never shifted our berth. We had nothing to do but row guard and go for fresh beef. Captain Bourmaster lived at Tichfield, and if anything particular happened a boat was sent with a midshipman to Hellhead or near it with the orders. On one occasion Mr. S——s, a midshipman, was dispatched in the cutter and took some of the boat's crew with him to Tichfield. On their return, passing by a farmyard, a flock of ducks and geese began to quack and hiss at them. The midshipman considered this as a declaration of war, and ordered his party to prepare for battle and to engage close, which was instantly obeyed, and after a short contest the enemy took to flight and several of the ducks were captured. Now the midshipman had read a little of British history, and particularly remembered that part where Richard the First in Palestine, and Henry the Fifth at Agincourt, put their prisoners to death. He immediately followed their example, and ordered the ducks to be slaughtered. Now the difference between those great men was this, that Richard and Henry buried their prisoners or got somebody else to do it, but the midshipman carried his off; and seeing in an orchard near the farmyard a number of fruit trees heavily laden, he thought it just that those who began the war should pay the expenses, which was no new thing in modern warfare, and gave orders to his party to fill their jackets with pears and apples, observing that it would ease the trees of their burthen and the boughs would be in less danger of breaking down. Now all this was very fair; and peace being restored, the midshipman addressed the farmer (who had come up with the reserve, but too late to assist the main body after their defeat): 'I say, old Hodge, I wish you joy to see your nose and chin come together after being separated for so many years. But harkee, old chap, if I should come this way again, and your feather-bed sons of —— begin their capers, I'm damned if I don't stop the grog of every mother's son belonging to you.' So saying, he returned with his dead prisoners, and the war was considered at an end. But the farmer, being bloody-minded, was of a different opinion, and breathing revenge, went and made his report to Captain Bourmaster. The captain, after coolly and deliberately weighing and investigating the transaction, came to the following conclusion: That Mr. S——s and his party, instead of going direct to their boat, did go this way and that way, and every way but the right way; and on a certain day, and in a certain lane, did kill, or did slay, or did murder or put to death several ducks, and did keep, and did hold, and did maintain the same, without any right law or title; and for such conduct Mr. S——s was sentenced to be dismissed from the Barfleur, and his party to have slops served out to them at the gangway.[1] The midshipman thought this extremely hard, and on leaving observed that had the case been tried before a jury he was sure they would have brought in a verdict of justifiable duckicide.

A curious bet took place between our chaplain and one of the officers. The wager was that the latter would bring a man who would eat eight

[1] A periphrastic euphemism for to be flogged.

penny rolls and drink a gallon of beer before the parson could walk a mile. Now the reverend gentleman was a great pedestrian, and could walk a mile in less than a quarter of an hour. The ground being chosen, one began to eat and the other to walk at the same moment, a gentleman being placed at each end with watches that corresponded to a second, when the parson to his utter amazement, after he had walked three-quarters of his mile, met the other, who had with ease finished his rolls and beer, and was unwilling that his reverence should have the trouble of walking the whole mile and therefore came to meet him. The reverend gentleman, like most clergymen, played well at whist, and once sitting at his favourite game, our signal was made, and the order was for the chaplain to attend a man that was to be hanged next morning. This broke up the game, when one of the officers observed: 'Doctor, you have lost the odd trick; but never mind, the fellow you are going to attend has got nothing by honours.'

OFFICERS' NAMES

[Robert] Roddam, Vice-Admiral, Port Admiral.

Dead [1808]. An admiral. Had his flag on board the old Conquistador, 60, in the American war, as port admiral at the Nore, at the time Mr. Fegan [*post*, p. 214] was sent on board.—[*D.N.B.*]

Hon. Samuel Barrington, Admiral of the blue.

Dead [1800]. A great officer. See his masterly manœuvre in the West Indies.—[*D.N.B.*]

[John] Elliot, Vice-Admiral.

Dead [1808]. This first-rate officer captured after a severe action the French squadron off the Irish coast commanded by Thurot, who fell in the contest. He also commanded the Edgar, 74, in the action when Don Langara was defeated and taken by Admiral Rodney. He commanded at Newfoundland as Governor of that island; a great astronomer and an able sailor.—[*D.N.B.*]

Sir John Jervis, K.B., Rear-Admiral.

Dead [1823]. Earl St. Vincent, admiral of the fleet; needs no comment here.—[*D.N.B.*]

JONATHAN FAULKNOR, Senr., Rear-Admiral.

Dead [1795]. A most able officer who had seen a great deal of service, and no man understood it better.

ROBERT CALDER, Esq., Captain.

Dead [1818]. An admiral, a baronet, and K.C.B. I have already spoken of him.—[*D.N.B.*]

ROBERT CARTHEW REYNOLDS, Captain.

Dead [1811]. A rear-admiral; unfortunately lost on the coast of Denmark, in the St. George, 98; a brave and meritorious officer. —[*D.N.B.*]

JOHN BOURMASTER, Esq., Captain.

Dead [1807]. A vice-admiral; one of the best men that ever did honour to the British navy. [Admiral.]

JOHN DOLLING [*or* DOLING], 1st Lieutenant.

Dead [1795]. A post captain with Admiral Rainier in the East Indies.

PADDY LEE, 2nd and then 1st Lieutenant.

Dead. A commander; a strange, droll hand.

[JOHN] MATHEWS, 3rd Lieutenant.

Dead [1798]. A post captain [1793]; a first-rate seaman.

BENJAMIN HALLOWELL [afterwards CAREW], 4th Lieutenant.

Dead [1834]. An admiral and G.C.B.; a brave and skilful officer. —[*D.N.B.*]

ROBERT SAVAGE DANIEL, 5th Lieutenant.

Killed on board the Bellerophon, 74, at the battle of the Nile; a loss to the service.

WM. PROWSE, 2nd and then 1st Lieutenant.

Dead [1826]. A rear-admiral [1821], C.B.; a worthy man.

Ross, Lieutenant; I forget how he stood.

Dead. A satirical gentleman and would be thought a poet because he wrote a play that was damned, and some poems in doggerel rhymes of scurrilous merit.

JAMES NICHOLL MORRIS, 1st Lieutenant.

Dead [1830]. A vice-admiral, K.C.B.; a very brave and meritorious officer. He commanded the Colossus, 74, at Trafalgar. —[*D.N.B.*]

GEO. GREY, 2nd Lieutenant.

Dead [1828]. Hon. Sir Geo. Grey, Bart. [1814], K.C.B.; late commissioner at Portsmouth yard.

WM. CHANTRELL, 2nd, 3rd, and 1st Lieutenant.

Dead. A very droll and strange fellow.

[ROBERT] LLOYD, Lieutenant.
I believe a vice-admiral of the blue [1837. Died, vice-admiral of the white, 1846.—O'Byrne].

RICHARD SIMMONDS, Lieutenant.
Dead. Was an agent of transports and lieutenant at Haslar Hospital. Nicknamed Gentleman Jack, because he came to see us in our berth in the cockpit, and said he was the gentleman below, but the officer on deck.

JAMES CARPENTER, Lieutenant.
Vice-admiral of the red; since promoted to be admiral of the blue [Jan. 10, 1837. Died, admiral of the white, 1845.—O'Byrne.]

DANIEL DOBREE, Lieutenant.
Dead. A post captain [1802]. See Blonde.

[THOMAS] BOWEN, Lieutenant.
Uncertain. I believe a post captain [1798]; fiery Welshman. [Griffith Bowen, his servant. Died 1809.]

ANDREW BRACEY TAYLOR, Lieutenant.
Dead. A good officer.

[WILLIAM] ELLIOT, 1st Lieutenant.
Dead. A commander. See Salisbury.

PHILIP CHARLES DURHAM, 2nd Lieutenant.
Admiral of the white, G.C.B.; port admiral at Portsmouth. [Died 1845.—*D.N.B.*]

NICHOLAS KEMP, Lieutenant.
Dead. A commander [1797]; a most worthy fellow.

JACKSON DOWSING, Lieutenant.
Dead. All jaw and singing from morn till night.

[EDWARD] MARSH, Lieutenant.
Dead [1813]. A post captain [1797]; steady and quiet.

IRWIN, Lieutenant.
Dead. A very funny officer.

NATHANIEL PORTLOCK, Lieutenant.
Dead [1817]. A post captain; went a voyage round the world; an able navigator.—[*D.N.B.*]

MACKEY, Lieutenant.
Dead. A commander; went a voyage round the world; came safe home; drunk grog and died.

CHARLES MAURICE STOCKER, 1st Lieutenant.
Killed by the wind of a shot on board the Sans Pareil, 84, in Lord Bridport's action.

JOHN RICHARDS, Lieutenant.

Dead [1830, aged 70]. A post captain [1809]. This man belonged to the Boreas at the time my father was on board; he was then before the mast. When Captain Thompson was appointed to the Alcide, 74, he took Richards with him in a low capacity, and afterwards put him on the quarter deck; when his time was served he got made a lieutenant. He was a good sailor, but proud, insolent, and vulgar in his language; full of strange sayings and low wit, and overbearing to those of inferior rank. Lieutenant Daniels once told him to go aboard the Alcide again to his former station. He felt the rebuke severely.—[Marshall, vi. 9.]

[THOMAS] IRELAND, 2nd Lieutenant.

Killed in battle on June 1, 1794.

SAMUEL MOTTLEY, Lieutenant.

A post captain [1802]. I never agreed with him. Since made a retired rear-admiral. [Died, 1841.—Marshall, iv. 684.]

NORBORNE THOMPSON, Lieutenant.

A rear-admiral. See Salisbury.

CHARLES CARTER, Lieutenant.

A post captain; since promoted to be a retired rear-admiral. [Died, a vice-admiral, 1848.—O'Byrne.]

BALDWIN, Captain of Marines.

Dead. Insane from grog.

NINIAN JEFFREYS, Master.

A quiet, good man.

[WILLIAM] MORGAN, Chaplain.

Uncertain. A very worthy gentleman.

[JAMES] KIRK, Surgeon.

Dead. Quiet and inoffensive.

[GEORGE] PURVIS, Admiral's Secretary.

Dead.

[JOHN] DELAFONS, Purser.

Dead.

ROBERT BUSTARD, Mate.

Dead. A lieutenant; a most excellent fellow.

BILLY CULMER, Mate.

Dead. A lieutenant; everyone has heard of Billy.

JAMES ROGERS, Midshipman and mate.

A commander [1806]; since a retired captain.

JOHN TALBOT, Signal midshipman.

Hon. Sir John Talbot, K.C.B.; a vice-admiral of the red. [Died, admiral and G.C.B., 1851.—O'Byrne.]

[Richard Turner] Hancock, Signal midshipman.
A post captain. [Died, a rear admiral, 1846.—O'Byrne.]

[Richard] Bowen, Signal midshipman.
A brave and able officer; he was captain of the Terpsichore, and was killed at the attack at Teneriffe when Nelson lost his arm.

Lord Amelius Beauclerk, Midshipman.
Admiral of the white, G.C.B., G.C.H.; chief naval aide-de-camp to the king. See Salisbury.

Roddam, Midshipman.
Uncertain. A Hun; a Goth; and a Vandal.

Galton, Midshipman.
Dead. A lieutenant; a good sailor.

Robert Perkins, Midshipman.
Dead. A lieutenant; a droll old guardo midshipman.

[Stephen] Skinner, Midshipman.
Dead. A lieutenant; a smart officer.

Tatham, Midshipman.
Uncertain. A lieutenant, but unfortunately broke by court martial; a droll, good fellow.

Henry Richardson, Midshipman.
Dead. A lieutenant; a crabbed old fellow called Long-Belly.

Pitt Burnaby Greene, Midshipman.
A post captain; a very good officer. Since dead [1837.—Marshall, vi. 335].

Charles Otter, Midshipman.
Dead [1831]. A post captain. He commanded the Proserpine, 32, when she was captured by some French frigates in the Mediterranean.—[Marshall, iv. 553.]

Jonathan Christian, Midshipman.
Dead. A commander. One of the few in the service that I disagreed with. I found him waspish, snappish, and disagreeable.—[Marshall, xi. 12.]

Daniel Kirk, Son of the surgeon; midshipman.
Dead. Unfortunate from being a dupe to women of the town. [Borne as his father's servant, then as A.B., then as midshipman.]

John Hinton, Midshipman.
Dead. A lieutenant; crabbed as the devil.

[Thomas] Goddard, Midshipman.
Dead. I believe was a lieutenant and severely wounded at the evacuation of Toulon.—[James, i. 87.]

FRANCIS JOHN NOTT, Midshipman.

A post captain; out-pension, Greenwich Hospital. Dead [1840. —Marshall, vi. 236].

THOMAS H. TIDY, Midshipman.

Dead. A commander. Poor Tom.

Hon. DUNBAR DOUGLAS, Midshipman.

Dead. A commander; a glorious fellow. A follower of Earl St. Vincent. When a midshipman with him in the Foudroyant, 84, he was stationed in the fore-top, and having hold of the main-top bowline by accident when the ship was going about, he was hauled out of the top and pitched into the main rigging without receiving the smallest injury, having the presence of mind to hold fast by the slack of the bowline, and by that means saved his life. This I heard related at Lord St. Vincent's table. Her mainsail was not set at the time.

[JOHN] W. T. DIXON, Midshipman.

Dead. He commanded the Apollo, 36, when that ship was unfortunately lost on the coast of Portugal with several of her convoy, and was drowned. He was brother to Admiral Sir Manley Dixon.

THOS. BYAM MARTIN, Midshipman.

Admiral of the white, G.C.B. [Admiral of the fleet; died 1854. *N.R.S.*, vols. xxiv., xii., xix.]

JOHN HARVEY, Midshipman.

Admiral of the blue, K.C.B.; since dead [1837.—*D.N.B.*].

JACK EATON, Mate.

Dead. My worthy and lamented old messmate; a first-rate seaman. He commanded the Marlborough, 74, in 1797, and in a fit of insanity killed himself at the admiralty.

FRANCIS TEMPLE, Midshipman.

A post captain; since made a retired rear-admiral [1837 Died] admiral, 1863.—O'Byrne].

AUGUSTUS BRINE, Midshipman.

A post captain; since made a retired rear-admiral. [Died 1840.]

P. BROWNE, Midshipman.

A post captain. [Died 1842.—Marshall, vi. 95.]

WM. BUSH, Midshipman.

A commander.

RICHARD SIMMONDS, Midshipman.

Dead. He was made a commander, but broke by court martial, and some years after pût on the list as lieutenant. He fought well, and that was all.

JOHN BRUCE, Midshipman

Dead A commander

JAMES ROSS, Midshipman with one arm.
Dead [1810]. A post captain; son of Admiral Sir John Lockhart Ross.

[JOHN] BULLER, Midshipman.
Uncertain.

JOHN KEY, Midshipman.
Dead. A lieutenant. See Brunswick.

CHAS. INGLIS
JAS. SANDERS
JOHN BELL CONOLLY
SOL. KING
EDWARD MOORE
WM. LAMB
JOHN MACREDIE
RICHARD HEYCOCK
GEO. JONES
EMANUEL SILVA
J. A. GARDNER
} Old Edgars. See Edgar.

JEMMY JOHNSTONE, Midshipman.
Dead [1823]. A post captain [1806]; a rigid disciplinarian, who drank like the devil.

CHAS. GRANT, Midshipman.
Dead [1825]. Commodore at the Cape of Good Hope; C.B.; an excellent officer.—[Marshall, iii. 300.]

WILLIAM DURBAN, Midshipman.
A post captain, LL.D.; a distinguished officer with first-rate abilities; since promoted to be rear-admiral of the blue. Dead [1837.—Marshall, iv. 845].

JAS. DALGLEISH, Mate.
A commander; a good old sailor. [Died, 1846.—Marshall, xi. 135.]

JACKSON, Midshipman.
Uncertain. A good-natured old squinting fellow

MORTON.
Dead. A lieutenant, called 'Red Muzzle'; said to have killed himself.

GEO. CLARK, Midshipman.
Dead. A lieutenant. When we had pudding for dinner, if and was left and put by for next day, he used to call us up in the night

to have a blow out with the remainder. This was called 'puddening[1] the flats.'

[William] Launder, Midshipman.

A most worthy fellow; a lieutenant, killed on board the Bellerophon at the battle of the Nile.

Chas. Came, Midshipman.

Dead. A commander.

Laurie, Midshipman.

A lieutenant; murdered at St. John's, Newfoundland.

[Robert] Spicer, Midshipman.

Dead. A lieutenant.

Chatterton, Midshipman.

Uncertain. All jaw and drink.

John Delafons, Midshipman; son of the purser.

First lieutenant of Bellona at Copenhagen [1801. Died, commander, 1805].

[Thomas] Delafons, Midshipman; son of the purser.

Commander. [Died 1848. Borne as purser's servant, afterwards A.B.—Marshall, xi. 153.]

Wm. Archbold, Midshipman.

A commander. Crab-apple.

Philip Anstruther, Midshipman.

Dead. A commander.

Chas. Anstruther, Midshipman.

Dead. A lieutenant.

Richard Curry, Midshipman.

The senior post captain on the list; since promoted to be rear-admiral of the red [1837]. C.B. [1831. Died, admiral of the blue, 1856.—O'Byrne.]

[George] Johnstone, Midshipman.

A lieutenant, murdered in Five Bell Lane, near Deptford.

[John] O'Connor, Midshipman.

Uncertain. I hated him.

John McDonald, Mate.

A commander; a very smart officer. [Died 1845.—O'Byrne.]

Chas. Bennet, Midshipman.

A commander; since a retired captain. [Died 1843.—Marshall, x. 411.]

---

[1] A puddening is defined as 'a thick wreath of cordage, tapering from the middle towards the ends' (Falconer). The joke, such as it is, seems to refer to the thickening in the middle.

JOHN CHEST, Midshipman.

Uncertain. When he joined the ship he had a very large chest, and had not been on board above an hour when some fellow painted on the lid in large white letters, 'JOHN CHEST HIS BOX.'

HOWELL POWELL, 1st Assistant Surgeon.

Poor Powell was surgeon of the Babet [1801], when that ship foundered with all hands. He was one of the best fellows I ever met with.

JACKY MARR, Boatswain.

Dead. Jacky was as good a seaman as any in the navy, but too severe. He was made boatswain of the sheer hulk and then promoted to the dockyard.

JEFFRIES, Boatswain.

Dead. A good sailor, and a very worthy character.

[WILLIAM] RIVERS, Gunner.

Dead. Very much respected.

STRONG, Carpenter.

One of the oldest warrant officers living ; highly respected ; has been in almost every general action since that of Keppel [1778]. Since dead.

WILLIAM PYE, Schoolmaster.

Dead. A purser. See Salisbury.

[BEN.] JEFFERYS, Clerk.

Dead. A purser ; a very worthy fellow.

QUEEN, 98

Like leaves on trees the race of man is found,
Now green in youth, now with'ring on the ground;
Another race the following spring supplies,
They fall successive, and successive rise;
So generations in their course decay,
So flourish these when those are passed away.—*Iliad.*

In this ship I found a new race of men, all strangers to me with the exception of five. I was recommended to Captain Hutt, commanding the Queen, 98, fitting in Portsmouth Harbour, by my late friend Admiral Bourmaster, and joined her early in 1793. I had not been long on board when I was ordered with a party of seamen to fit out the Conflagration fireship, Lieutenant Laurie (now Sir Robert) superintending. Having received orders to fit for foreign service, we proceeded to Spithead and hoisted the flag (blue at the mizen) of Rear-Admiral Gardner, and having rigged the Conflagration returned to our ship. The Queen being ordered to the West Indies, I made (like a fool) application to Captain Bourmaster to get me removed to the Berwick, 74, commanded by Sir John Collins, Knight, fitting for the Mediterranean, to which place I wished much to go. After long consideration he agreed to my request; at the same time observing that I stood in my own light and that I would lose promotion by taking such a step. This I well knew; but the hatred I had for the West Indies made me blind to my own interest. When

I saw Captain Hutt I found it no easy matter to bring him to my way of thinking, and it was a long time before he would give his consent. I remember when he sent for me in his cabin, I fell over a small case that happened to be in the way and broke my shins, for which he called me a damned clumsy fellow and said I deserved what I got for wishing to leave the ship, and that I would bitterly repent it when I found others promoted and myself left out. However, he gave me my discharge and a very good certificate, shook hands with me and wished me success. He was one of the strictest officers in the navy, an excellent sailor, and woe betide those that were slack in carrying on the duty. He had a stern look, with a penetrating eye that would pierce through those who he questioned, and in him the service lost an officer not easily replaced.

Our first lieutenant, old Constable, was a devil of a tyrant. When first I asked him leave to go on shore for a few hours, he said he would see me in hell first; and on my thanking him for his kindness, he swore if I did so again he would try me by a court martial for my politeness. I was once starting[1] the jolly-boat boys for being slack in getting into the boat, when old Constable being present and observing what I was about, 'Damn my eyes, sir,' says he, 'that's not the way; you should take a handspike and knock their brains out.' He was a good sailor and an indefatigable first lieutenant, but fractious and disagreeable; yet on shore quite the reverse. Our second lieutenant, Billy Bedford, was very particular and fidgety, and would nig-nag all day long about trifles. We had a very droll midshipman (George Milner) who would take him off in the most laughable manner by jumping round a cask, grinning most horribly and singing Nig-nig-nag and Fidgety-

[1] *Sc.* with a rope's end or a cane.

fidgety-fum, until the tears would start from his eyes. This was for getting a rub down from Bedford, who he swore was only fit to be a cooper, and to jump round a cask.

We had many droll and good fellows among our midshipmen. I shall mention a few; and first, Flinders (one of the mates) who I messed with in the main hatchway berth on the lower deck. He was well acquainted with ancient history and wrote notes on what he read with sound observations. He was very fond of a drop, and would expatiate on the character of Alexander the Great, and said had he been present at the drinking party, Promachus would not have won the talent so easy, and he would have pledged Alexander himself with a bowl they had in his family against that of Hercules.

Jack Barrett (who commanded the Minotaur, 74, when she was lost) was another droll hand, the life and soul of the ship. He was a most worthy fellow and departed this life with the character of a brave and meritorious officer, lamented by a numerous acquaintance. James McPherson Rice, my worthy messmate, thou art also gone. A most excellent fellow, a great mathematician, well read, and respected by everyone that knew him. Out of the whole mess I am the only one left—Flinders, Meager, Milner, etc., etc., etc., all gone; and of the forty-eight that were on board, thirty-six have departed for that bourne from whence no traveller returns, as the following list will show:—

OFFICERS' NAMES

ALAN GARDNER, Rear-admiral.

Dead [1809]. Admiral Lord Gardner. He commanded the Duke, 98, in Rodney's action at the taking of the Count de Grasse, April 12, 1782, where he greatly distinguished himself. He had his flag on board the Queen in Lord Howe's action, June 1, 1794. —[*D.N.B.*]

JOHN HUTT, Esq., Captain.

Killed in the action of June, 1, 1794; one of the ablest officers in the navy.—[*D.N.B.*]

LOVE CONSTABLE, 1st Lieutenant.

Dead. A commander; an excellent sailor and an indefatigable first lieutenant. The devil on board, but an angel on shore.

WILLIAM BEDFORD, 2nd Lieutenant.

Dead [1827]. A vice-admiral; a fidgety, good fellow. See Edgar.

JOHN MILLER, 3rd Lieutenant.

Dead [1843]. A retired post captain [1797]; an excellent officer. [Marshall, iii. 114.]

[RICHARD] DAWES, 4th Lieutenant.

Killed on June 1, 1794. [According to James, i. 185, 200, wounded; but his name no longer appeared in the *Navy List*.]

ROBERT LAURIE, 5th Lieutenant.

Vice-admiral Sir Robert Laurie, Bart., K.C.B.; was wounded on June 1, 1794. See Salisbury.

[ROBERT] HOPE, Surgeon.

Dead. Physician at Haslar Hospital.

[GEORGE] GRANT, Secretary and Purser.

Dead.

JAMES KELLOCH, Boatswain.

Dead. A sailor.

WILLIAM IRELAND, Gunner.

Dead. Much respected.

[FRANCIS] ADAMS, Carpenter.

Dead. Builder at Gibraltar.

THOMAS OLIVER, Mate.

A commander; 'Jawing Tom.' [Died 1842.—Marshall, x. 384.]

WILLIAM PADDY RUSSELL, Midshipman.

A commander; a very good fellow. [Died 1828.—Marshall, x. 369.]

CHAS. TINLING, Midshipman.

A retired rear-admiral [1830. Died 1840.—Marshall, iii. 362].

[SAMUEL] BUTCHER, Midshipman.

A post captain; since a retired rear-admiral [1840; died, a vice-admiral, 1849.—O'Byrne].

WM. WOOLDRIDGE, Midshipman.

Dead [1820]. A post captain [1807]; a rough sailor.

[MOSES] CANNADEY, Midshipman.

Dead. A lieutenant.

Noel Swiney, Midshipman.
Uncertain. Was a lieutenant, but broke by court martial and rendered incapable of serving.

John Barrett, Midshipman.
Drowned [1810] in the Minotaur, 74, of which ship he was captain. Brave fellow.—[*D.N.B.*]

James McPherson Rice, Midshipman.
Dead. A lieutenant ; a worthy fellow.

William Dickinson, Midshipman.
Dead. A quiet, good fellow. [D.D. in Queen's pay-book ; no date.]

Francis Dickinson, Midshipman.
Dead. A commander ; satirical.

H. G. Morris, Midshipman.
A post captain. [Died, a retired rear-admiral, 1851.—O'Byrne.]

Geo. Milner, Midshipman.
Dead. No man's enemy but his own.

Robert Jenner Neve, Midshipman.
Dead [1815]. A post captain [1806] ; amazingly grand, and foolishly proud.

[John] Batt, Midshipman.
Dead. A lieutenant.

[Nicholas] Meager, Midshipman.
Dead. A lieutenant ; called 'Mileager.'

[John A.] Hodgskin, Midshipman.
Dead. A lieutenant ; a very worthy fellow ; called 'Pig Hog' and 'Hog's flesh.'

Edmund Rayner, Midshipman.
A commander [1831, on retired list] ; as worthy a fellow as ever lived. [Died 1846.]

[John M.] Seppings, Midshipman.
Dead. A lieutenant ; had a pension from the Custom House.

Peter Hunt, Midshipman.
Dead [1824]. A post captain [1803] ; a very droll fellow.

J. A. Gardner, Midshipman.
A commander.

[John] Davis [Quartermaster, afterwards Midshipman, aged 38].
Dead.

[William] Renwick, Midshipman, lent.
Lieutenant of Greenwich Hospital. [Died 1839.]

[William] Thompson, Clerk.
Dead. A purser.

BERWICK, 74

JOINED the Berwick in April 1793, Sir John Collins, Knight, captain, fitting in Portsmouth Harbour for the Mediterranean, and in May sailed with a division of the fleet under the Vice-Admiral Lord Hood, who had his flag on board the Victory, 100. On the passage the squadron captured a corvette. We arrived at Gibraltar, Vice-Admiral Hotham's Division in company, and having taken in our water sailed for Toulon. When off Minorca we fell in with the Spanish fleet under Don Langara on a cruise. To the best of my recollection our fleet consisted of twenty sail of the line besides frigates, but several men of war joined after.

[The list of the fleet which follows has no authority, and has been frequently printed.]

When near Toulon Lord Hood made the signal to prepare for battle, and also the signal for a general chase which ended in the capture of the corvette L'Éclair. Saw the enemy's fleet at anchor in the inner and outer roads. When sent in to reconnoitre, they would allow us to come as near as we liked; but the moment the ship was put about their forts would blaze away with red-hot shot; and we in the Berwick had nearly got into an awkward situation, which I shall speak of hereafter. In July while cruizing off Toulon the fleet encountered a tremendous gale, and the old Berwick, who always bore the name of a bad sea boat, proved it on this occasion with a vengeance. First the bowsprit went, about two feet before the outer gammoning; bore up, and got the runners and tackles forward to secure the foremast. At daylight made the signal of distress, and parted company from the fleet. The rigging being new, it became so slack that we were obliged to set it up, with a very heavy sea running, which was done in a seaman-like manner; but mark what follows. After the lower rigging was set up, and while before the wind, the main sail, of all sails in the world, was set, and the ship hove to slap at once, by which she was nearly thrown on her beams ends. The main yard went in the slings, the main topmast and half the main top carried away, the fore mast sprung in two places, and the mizen mast in three; of the main-top men of one watch, seventeen in number, one was killed, another drowned, and several of the others severely hurt, but by falling on the splinter netting were fortunately saved. The wreck of the main yard had nearly knocked two ports into one on the main deck, while that of the main topmast got under the counter, damaged the copper, and had almost unshipped the rudder before it could be cleared, which was done with great difficulty. It is a fact that the ship rolled sixteen or eighteen feet of her fore yard in the water,[1] and laboured so dreadfully that on our arrival in port the oakum was found to have worked so much out of the seams, particularly under the counter, that it was astonishing we succeeded in reaching Gibraltar. I must also mention that the force of the wind was so great that it burst the lashings[2] of the jolly boat lying on the booms, and

[1] It is, perhaps, more probable that, at the extreme end of the roll, the sea came up to the yard.

[2] More likely they were carried away by the rolling. The wind might then blow the boat away.

blew the boat away like a feather. So much for the Gulf of Lyons. I do not mean to throw blame on any one, but I cannot help thinking that the ship was somehow or other badly handled, to say nothing of her being a bad sea boat; and if she had not been as strong as wood and iron could make her, must certainly have paid a visit to Davy Jones' locker.

We remained at Gibraltar several weeks in the New Mole, and enjoyed ourselves by going up to the old Porter house on Scud Hill[1] of an evening, and sometimes to the Junk Ships and the Swan; and then cruise about the town, which is not deficient in places of amusement. It was here I first observed the march of intellect; a fellow, whose name was Anthony Strico and kept a wine house, had over his door in large letters,

Tono Strico
Wino Houso.[2]

After the ship was refitted we proceeded to join the fleet at Toulon which had surrendered to Lord Hood during our absence. While off Minorca we were taken in a thundering squall that had almost done for the old Berwick a second time. Next day, fell in with a Spanish frigate dismasted; gave her some assistance which she seemed to want, as they appeared to be deficient in nautical knowledge, or, in other words, the vilest set of lubbers that ever were seen. They positively did not know how to get a jury mast up. On our arrival at Toulon we found Lord Hood with the British fleet and Don Langara with the Spanish; also some Neapolitan men of war. Landed our soldiers, which were part of the 69th regiment of foot doing duty as marines.

[1] See a picture of this by Cruikshank in the Old Sailor's *Greenwich Hospital*.

[2] Looks like an early form of Esperanto.

Plenty of fighting going on in every direction, the Princess Royal and some other ships keeping up a constant fire against the enemy's lines to prevent them throwing up batteries. We had some pleasant trips in our launch in carrying a load of eighteen and thirty-two pound shot to supply the Princess Royal while she was engaging, the shot from the enemy flying more than half a mile beyond us. Fortunately we escaped without injury. One of the lower-deck guns on board the Princess Royal or St. George—I forget which—burst and killed nine men and wounded twenty seven.[1] We remained but a short time at Toulon, and then sailed to join Commodore Linzee at Tunis.

We had a delightful passage running along the Italian shore with a fine view of Elba, Gorgona, Pianoza, Monte Christo, Capraja, etc.

> For here the muse so oft her harp has strung,
> That not a mountain rears its head unsung.—*Addison.*

Stood over for Sardinia and put into Cagliari, the capital, where we found Commodore Linzee and squadron.

October 22, 1793.—Went on shore and dined in company with the Sardinian admiral and several great men of the island, who were very intelligent and gave us an account of the attack made by the French squadron, who were beaten off with loss (according to their account) of 5,000 men.[2] Visited the city, which has a university, and went to some of the convents to purchase articles from the nuns. Found the friars a set of jolly fellows who behaved to us with great civility, not only in this place but

[1] *Cf.* James, i. 78.

[2] The story of this attack and its repulse is given by Chevalier, *Hist. de la Marine Française sous la Première République*, pp. 41 *seq.*

in every other port in the Mediterranean that we put into.

October 25.—Sailed from Cagliari in quest of some French frigates, but had not the good fortune to fall in with them. During the cruise before we put into Cagliari and joined the commodore, we fell in with six sail of the line who, not answering the private signal, were taken for a French squadron. It being late in the evening we made all sail and stood from them; they gave chase the whole of the night, but only two could come up with us, and they took good care not to come alongside, and well for them they did not; all our guns were loaded with round and double-headed shot, and our 68-pounders on the forecastle were crammed with grape and canister, and our fellows (two-thirds of them Irish) were determined to give them a lesson that would never be forgotten. This they seemed to anticipate, as they kept hankering on the quarter until morning, when they hoisted Spanish colours; one of them sent a boat on board of us.

The officer seemed astonished when he saw our men at quarters, their black silk handkerchiefs [1] tied round their heads, their shirt-sleeves tucked up, the crows and handspikes in their hands, and the boarders all ready with their cutlasses and tomahawks, that he told Sir John Collins they put him in mind of so many devils.

After the cruise we put into Tunis, and found lying there the Duquesne, French 74; and higher up in the bay, near the Goletta, her convoy, consisting of fifty sail of merchantmen with valuable cargoes; also the Spanish squadron mentioned

[1] It has, of late years, been so persistently stated that black silk handkerchiefs were introduced into the navy as a mark of mourning for Nelson, that it is most refreshing to meet with this very positive contradiction of the story.

above. Commodore Linzee with the following men of war anchored close to the Frenchman, and the Agamemnon near their convoy :—

Alcide .	. 74	Commodore Linzee; Captain Woodley
Berwick .	. 74	Captain Sir John Collins
Illustrious	. 74	Captain T. L. Frederick
Agamemnon	. 64	Captain Horatio Nelson
Lowestoft	. 32	Captain Cunningham [1]
Nemesis	. 28	Captain Lord Amelius Beauclerk

I must here mention that the Yankee-doodle [2] James in his *Naval History* takes no notice of this expedition, which is to be wondered at as the 'Sea Serpent' was never backward in finding fault, and here he missed a good opportunity. The Agamemnon and Lowestoft were sent, as I have stated, to watch the convoy, and the three seventy-fours anchored one abreast, another on the bow, and one on the quarter of the Duquesne, ready to bring her to action, and six sail of the line (Spanish) to assist in this great undertaking; but all this mighty preparation came to nothing. The cargoes were safely landed from the convoy; and the Duquesne, after laughing at us for several weeks and singing the Marseilles hymn morning and evening, with the English jack spread over her round house, got

[1] Charles Cunningham, at this time commander of the Speedy brig, was not a captain till some months later, and was then posted to the Unité. The captain of the Lowestoft was William Wolseley—*Cf. D.N.B.*

[2] This is an allusion to the absurd story—which Gardner seems to have believed—that James was American by birth. See *D.N.B.* In consequence of his very free comments on the conduct of naval officers, James was far from being a favourite in the service; and it must have been still fresh in Gardner's memory that he had been severely caned by Sir John Phillimore.

under way, and arrived safe at Toulon, which had been evacuated by the fleet and army; and all this because Tunis was a neutral port. Now everybody knew that before the squadron sailed, and also that Tunis was nothing less than a nest of thieves; besides, we were out of gun-shot of their forts and might have taken the whole with the greatest ease imaginable.

We had a rugged-headed, squint-eyed boatswain's mate, who early one morning passed the word for all those who were quartered on the main deck to come below and fight the lower-deck guns. He was instantly obeyed, and the people of their own accord were absolutely going to bring the French 74 to action, and the above boatswain's mate as the head of the party was in the act of setting the example, when the second lieutenant snatched the match out of his hand just as he was going to fire. Lord Nelson, who commanded the Agamemnon, happened to come on board soon after, and when this was told him he seemed quite pleased: 'For then,' says he, 'we must have taken them.' If he had commanded, we certainly should have taken them,[1] and not have stayed wasting our time for months in the bay doing nothing.

Our squadron used to water near the Goletta, a small channel leading to the ancient harbour of Carthage, fortified on each side and a chain across. On the left of this channel they have a gun with marble shot of immense size; the diameter of the bore twenty two inches and a half. On the other side are a few wells dug in the sand, from which the squadron got their water. On one occasion I went

[1] Nelson wrote to his uncle, William Suckling, that, in his opinion, we ought to have taken them—men of war and convoy; and if 'we had given the Bey 50,000*l.* he would have been glad to have put up with the insult offered to his dignity.'

in the launch to fill our casks, a messmate of mine (the present Captain Valobra) taking a trip with me; having given directions about filling, I proposed to cross the Goletta (which has a drawbridge over it) and take a look at the large fort they have close by. On getting into the interior, which is a square, we saw a door open and went into what appeared a guard room, from the number of arms tastefully arranged about the walls, and several Turks rolled up in blankets lying on the floor. Having examined the place we were going away, when one of the Turks, as I approached the door, caught hold of me by the collar and pushed me back. I did not relish this and tried to make the blackguard understand, but all to no purpose. However, I again made a movement to get out, when a young Turk, with a short stick that had something round like a ball fixed to the end of it, made a blow at my head which would certainly have done for me had I not stepped back in time. We had left our side arms in the launch and had nothing to defend ourselves against this ruffian. One of the Turks we heard say 'Spagniolle!' upon which Valobra called out 'Angleise!' Whether this had the effect to liberate us I know not; but an old withered Turk came up, and after a deal of altercation with the fellow who struck at me, he pointed to the door and showed us the way out, and glad enough we were of it. Having filled our casks we returned on board (the rascally Turks pelting us with stones as long as we were in reach), and made a complaint to Sir John Collins, who went on shore the next day to represent the business to the commandant of the fort, and this vagabond had the impudence to say we might think ourselves well off that we were not sent up the country and made slaves. Went with Lieutenant Shirley to see the ruins of Carthage. . . . Saw several remains of antiquity, broken columns, underground passages, pieces of frieze, and the remarkable arches supposed to be the stables of the elephants. I went into a room like a cellar and got a piece of the flooring, of beautiful green and white marble, which I brought home; but some thief in England stole it from me—the devil do him good with it. The ground about the ruins was covered with reptiles of almost every description, which made it dangerous to explore. I carried a piece of frieze several miles intending to bring it home also, but was obliged to leave it from fatigue. As Lieutenant Shirley, who was very tired, sat on a broken column, I observed it might have been the same that Caius Marius rested on when in exile and from which he made this memorable reply (to show the instability of human greatness) to him that was sent by the governor to warn him off: 'Go,' says he, 'and say that thou hast seen Caius Marius sitting on the ruins of Carthage.'

A short time before we left Tunis the bey sent a present to the squadron, of bullocks, butter, poultry, scented candles and some otto of roses. We in the cockpit had some butter, poultry, and a scented candle or two; as for the otto of roses we could smell it near the wardroom, but not a drop could we see in the cockpit. However, we were more regaled with the scent of a seapie, made in a pitch kettle that contained, besides other delicacies, upwards of thirty fowls. We sat round the cauldron in the cockpit, like the witches in 'Macbeth,' and would not have exchanged this glorious mess for all the otto of roses belonging to the bey or his ministers. At the same time, the devil thank some people for their kindness in not paying the compliment; they might have sent us one small bottle to counteract the bilge water; but never mind; they, poor souls, are all dead; and most of us are alive notwithstanding. As for the butter, it was only fit to grease the topmasts, and for that purpose we resigned it. We had a few of the candles, made of beeswax and scented.

The bullocks were very small, and here I must relate a droll circumstance. Our purser's steward was one that dearly loved grog, and it so happened that on the day the bullocks were slaughtered, he got beastly drunk. Some of the midshipmen seeing him in that situation in the first watch, lying near the steward room, agreed to sew him up in one of the bullocks' hides, which was accordingly done. The horns being on, were fixed to a nicety on his head and fastened under the chin, firm as a rock. A little before twelve he came to himself and got up (for his legs and arms were free) and tried to get into the steward room, but the key was secured. He then began to bellow, just as the quartermaster came down to call the watch, and was knocking his horns against the bulk head, his tail near the cockpit ladder. The quartermaster, holding up his lantern, looked at him for some time in amazement; at last, letting it fall, he took to his heels, swearing that the devil was in the cockpit; while those who slept abaft on the lower deck jumped out of their hammocks and followed his example. 'Twas a most laughable sight; particularly so when the officer of the watch came down to see what was the matter and, evidently under the influence of fear, did not venture down the cockpit ladder until one of the midshipmen came up and said it was Colquhoun, the steward, transformed into a bullock. It had a good effect on the steward, as he was afraid ever after to bouse his jib up; and whenever he put his head up the cockpit ladder, those on the lower deck would sing out, 'What's become of your horns?'

Left Tunis for Porto Farino to get a supply of water for the fleet. The plague had made great ravages before our arrival, but had in some measure abated. This place is a Turkish arsenal, and several of their men of war were fitting out. A number of Neapolitan slaves were at work in the different storehouses; some of them could speak English, and gave us an interesting account of the conduct of their masters. I saw an old Turk, upwards of seventy, with a long stick in his hand thrashing several of the poor wretches. I could not refrain from telling him he was a damned old scoundrel; whether he understood or not, I cannot say, but he called out repeatedly, 'Esau, Esau'; and Lieutenant Shirley bawling in his ear, 'Will you have Isaac and Jacob also?'

Porto Farino is situated near the mouth of the Bagrada,[1] where Attilius Regulus, the Roman consul, lay encamped in the first Punic war, when the serpent attacked and destroyed several of his soldiers who came to the river to obtain water. . . . The ancient city of Utica, famous for the death of Cato in the civil war, was at no great distance from this port.

A short time before we sailed the Turkish governor paid a visit to the ship, with his retinue, among whom was the Turkish admiral—a fine looking fellow near seven feet high. We saluted the governor with eleven guns, and he minutely inspected every part of the ship and seemed highly delighted with the bread room, and also with the 68-pounders we had on the forecastle. One of his attendants spoke English, and said he was in England at the time the Foudroyant was captured by the Monmouth,[2] and that he lived at Wapping.

[1] Bagrada is the classical name; the river is now called Mejerda.

[2] In 1758.

We suspected he was an Englishman although he said his name was Mustapha.

Sailed from this port to cruise off the Island of Pantalaria. You that are fond of romance are aware that in this island the famous captain of banditti met his death; all Italy speaks of him, from the Apennines to the Straits of Messina, and the shepherds of the Sicilian vales sing the praises of the valoroso Capitano Rinaldini. But they did not (in this island) sing the praises of little Tommy Yates, our purser, who went on shore to purchase some articles, and put the whole island under quarantine when they found out we had just left the Turkish port; and if Tommy had gone on shore the second time he probably would have left his bones there.

We encountered off this island the heaviest gale I ever was in; particularly a squall that lasted from seven bells in the middle watch until two bells in the morning watch. The storm staysails were blown from the bolt rope, and the ship during this prodigious gust lay with her main-deck guns in the water. The sea was one white sheet, and during the whole course of my servitude I never witnessed anything equal to it; and many who had been in the hurricane of 1780 in the West Indies, declared that this squall was equally terrible. After the cruise we put into Trapani, the ancient Drepanum. It was here Aeneas landed, according to Virgil, when the fight with the gauntlet took place between Dares and Entellus, and it was also famous for that between Hercules and Eryx, in which the latter was killed. It was a noted place in the first Punic war for military events, as that of the defeat of the Roman fleet under the Consul Claudius Pulcher, wherein (according to Valerius Maximus) the Romans lost 90 galleys, 8,000 men killed or drowned, and

20,000 taken prisoners by the Carthaginians without the loss of a man or a single galley on their side.[1]

I must here relate an anecdote which will show how careful people ought to be when joking with those whom they think don't understand their language. The day after we arrived at Trapani, near thirty Sicilian clergymen came on board to see the ship, and while on the quarter-deck making their observations, Palmer, our fourth lieutenant, in a frolicsome mood, went up to one of them and, while bowing and scraping, said, 'Pray, sir, were you ever knocked down with a fathom of ——?' when, to Palmer's horror and amazement, the other answered in good English, 'Never in my life, sir,' and then addressed his companions, who cast their eyes upon Palmer and began to laugh at his expense. This he could not stand, and in going down the quarter-deck ladder declared he would sooner face the devil than a Trapani parson.

The islands Maretimo, Levanzo, and Faviguano are near this place; in the last-mentioned island the Turkish prisoners are sent as slaves. We saw several of them at work in the moat, one of them a man of prodigious stature. These islands were the ancient Ægades, where Lutatius Catulus, the Roman consul, defeated the Carthaginian fleet and put an end to the first Punic War.[1]

Before we left Trapani we went to see a church, or rather cemetery, where several rows of dead bodies were placed in niches one over the other. They were naked, some standing up and others lying at full length, and presenting an appearance truly horrible; we understood they belonged to a

[1] For the story of these very remarkable sea-fights, see Smith's *Dictionary of Greek and Roman Biography &c.*; *U.S. Mag.*, Oct. 1889, pp. 690–1.

particular order. While lying here, a mutiny took place among the ship's company, in consequence of some bullocks that were anything but fat being sent for the use of the people. Now John Bull, having more regard for fat and lean, swore he'd be damned if he'd have anything to do with skin and bone. A survey was then held and the report stated that as no other meat could be obtained, double allowance of this lean kine should be served out to make up the deficiency; but all to no purpose; and John Bull, forgetting his duty and only thinking of his maw, broke out into open rebellion. Some of the scoundrels were put in irons, but were immediately released by the others and the irons thrown overboard. They then assembled on the lower deck, got the hammocks down, and a breastwork made in the bay, with the two foremost guns pointed aft. The officers at last prevailed on them to return to their duty, and, Sir John Collins being an easy man, no examples were made. Sailed for Leghorn, where we arrived in Carnival time. We were not long at an anchor before the ship was surrounded by boats with musicians playing fine Italian airs and women singing most delightfully.

Several men of war were in the roads; among which was the Aquilon, 32, with Prince Augustus Frederick (now Duke of Sussex) on his travels. Got leave with some difficulty to go on shore with two messmates, Graves and Valobra; saw the brazen men so much spoken of, consisting of the father and three sons (Turks) in bronze chained to the four corners of a pedestal, with a marble statue of a Tuscan prince on the top. Visited the Jews' synagogue, which was well worth seeing, being a magnificent temple; also the churches, opera house and many other places, with fine paintings and statuary, and had glorious fun at the Carnival, where we met our little purser, Tommy Yates, with a mask and a black domino on, cutting such capers that Heraclitus would have wiped away his tears had he seen him, and joined in the laugh. He was a wet little soul and generous to a degree, and everyone respected him.

Early next morning, after a sumptuous breakfast, we set off for Pisa, about fourteen or fifteen miles from Leghorn, in one of the gilt coaches with horses that, had they seen the devil would not have taken fright. We were three hours going the distance and had full time to observe the beautiful prospect along the Vale of Arno. About ten we entered Pisa, where they were celebrating the Carnival in a magnificent style, and we were told that six hundred coaches were in the procession. The prince was among the number and appeared much gratified. Pelting with sugar plums is customary on this occasion; and one of our midshipmen pelted Lord Hervey in his coach; and when told it was the British ambassador, and that he looked very angry, he immediately hove another volley at Lady Hervey, observing that she looked better tempered than his Excellency.

We spent a very pleasant evening at the theatre, and next morning went to the cathedral—a gorgeous fabric, with gates of bronze highly decorated with passages from scripture in compartments in *basso relievo*. We also saw the baptistery with a whispering gallery, and the *campo santo*, with the paintings on the wall in *fresco* round the cloisters, the work of the oldest masters. One painting I well recollect, representing the Last Judgment—the work I believe of Buffalmaco, who in this painting drew all his friends going to heaven, and his enemies going to the devil; the faces of all being an exact resemblance of those of both parties. The tombs of some of the masters are at the foot of their works.[1] The *campo santo* is an oblong figure, and the earth in the centre was brought from the Holy Land some centuries ago, and people of religious celebrity are here interred.

We next visited the Observatory and Botanical Gardens, and then to the top of the Leaning Tower, 187 feet high, and whose summit overlooks the base fifteen feet. One of our party began ringing the bells, which brought up a posse of friars; and Graves, pointing to one of them, a very fat man, exclaimed, 'I'll be damned if that fellow is not fitted for foreign service with six months' provisions in his guts.' I suppose they did not understand him, as they behaved with great civility. Some in this country, who I could mention, would have behaved in a different manner. There's an old saying

That Pisa looks ill
If you sit still.

This was not the case with us, as we were constantly on the move and saw everything and enjoyed ourselves greatly, particularly among the masks while parading the Lung' Arno. The day before our departure we took a long and delightful walk upon the banks of the Arno and were within a few miles of the spot where Catiline and his whole army were destroyed 63 B.C., in the consulship of Marcus Tullius Cicero and Caius Antonius Nepos.

Pisa has a university and formerly contained 100,000 inhabitants, but has greatly fallen off and grass grows in the streets. It contains many churches and other superb buildings, particularly the Grand Duke's palace in the Lung' Arno, the

[1] The fresco is attributed to Nardo Daddi. See Kugler's *Handbook of Painting, Italian Schools* (5th Edit.), pp. 111, 112, where there is a drawing of 'The Last Judgment.'

Hospital, and Exchange. There are three bridges over the Arno, one of them of marble. Several Roman antiquities are to be seen. It was our intention to have gone to Lucca and from thence to Florence; but all sublunary things are vain, as we were ordered to sea sooner than was expected, and returned to Leghorn after five days' absence, where we dined at an excellent ordinary at one of the best houses in the city. We had a strong party of English officers at the dinner, some of whom got rather merry before the cloth was off the table, and catching hold of the waiter they rolled him in the cloth with plates and dishes, the fellow roaring out all the while to no purpose. One midshipman took a loaf and let if fall out of the window (we were on the second floor) upon the jaw of an Italian in the street, which floored him, while others pelted legs and wings of fowls at those looking out of the opposite windows; but to their kind forbearance everything was taken as a joke and only laughed at. Would this have been the case in England?—where every hole and corner has a board threatening prosecution, and if you pass two or three stopping in the street, their conversation will be about law, hanging, or trade.

Sallied out in the evening and went to a house in Scratch Alley—you that have been at Leghorn I daresay know the place well. In the middle of this lane lived an old woman of enormous size, who was named the Boatswain of Scratch Alley. Saw a figure there I never shall forget—a fellow dressed as a lady, with a fine cap trimmed with blue ribbon and a white frock on, a face like Vulcan with a long black beard. When he came in the room we were sitting in, he danced a fandango and cut such astonishing capers that my old messmate Vosper said drily, 'Gardner, if that fellow is not the devil he must be his near relation.' The next evening three of us took a cruise, and, it being very late before we returned, our lodging was shut up and with difficulty we got entrance to a house near the Mole. The accommodations vile in the extreme; only one bed, with sheets as if a sweep had slept in them. At this time it began to rain with drops as big as pistol balls, which obliged us to stay where we were. However, we sat on the chairs, but got very little sleep for the rats and people passing and re-passing to a sewer at the end of the room. The morning luckily turned out fine, and after clearing our uniforms of a few bugs that thought fit to billet themselves on us without being invited, we gladly started from this infernal hotel to breathe the fresh air. Went to Montenero, where the learned Smelfungus has a monument near his remains.[1]

Having received orders to sail immediately and join the squadron under Vice-Admiral Hotham off Toulon, we first put into St. Fiorenzo for a short time. Went to see the Mortella tower that beat off the Fortitude, 74, and Juno frigate; the former ship had upwards of sixty killed and wounded, and was on fire in several places from the red-hot shot. This tower had but two guns; one of them was dismounted during the attack and defended by twenty Frenchmen, only one of whom was killed. The tower was taken by mounting some guns on a spot that overlooked it.[2]

[1] Smollett, so called by Sterne in *A Sentimental Journey*. It is, however, a much disputed point whether he was not buried at Leghorn. See *Notes and Queries* (1898, i.), IX. i. pp. 201, 309, 510; but it will be noticed that the monument Gardner saw was earlier than that at Leghorn, and his mention of the 'remains' at Montenero is of earlier date than any evidence yet quoted in support of the Leghorn claim.

[2] *Cf.* James, i. 208. The effective defence of this tower—which took its name from the place (Mortella = Myrtle)—suggested

Sailed from St. Fiorenzo and joined the squadron. Our captain, Sir John Collins, being ill, we had Captain William Shield acting. Sir John soon after departed this life and was committed to the deep. Sixteen minute guns were fired at the funeral to denote the number of years he had been a post captain. Sir John was a well-meaning man, but fractious from long illness. He died with the gout in his head and stomach. The ship's company paid respect to his memory; they divided their black silk handkerchiefs,[1] and wore one part round their hats and the other round their arms, and requested they might see the corpse before the interment; which request was granted, and they walked through the cabin in ranks and bowed to the coffin while passing, and most of them in tears—a sight truly impressive. Billy Shield remained with us about a month after Sir John's death, and then George Campbell, as good a fellow as ever lived, took command.

I have already stated our reconnoitring the enemy's fleet in the roads. Out of many instances I shall mention one that had nearly been of serious consequences. Having stood in with a fine breeze, the enemy never fired a shot until we hove in stays. At this time it fell on a sudden a dead calm, and we were within gunshot. They then began to blaze away from all their forts, the red-hot shot flying in every direction. I was looking out of the gun-room port when a shot came right under our counter, which made the water hiss and had nearly struck the rudder. At this time things looked queer, all the boats were hoisted out and began to tow, but still we drifted in, the shot flying full half a mile

the erection, along our south coast, of those numerous, useless, and misnamed Martello towers, against which the poet Campbell vainly protested.

[1] See *ante*, p. 130, *n*.

beyond us, when luckily a breeze came off the land and saved the Berwick from being sunk or blown up, for she never would have been taken. Fortunately we had none killed or wounded, which was astonishing, as the shot flew like hail. Captain Campbell soon after left the ship, being appointed to the Terrible, 74, and Captain George Henry Towry succeeded him.

Our squadron under Admiral Hotham consisted of eight sail of the line, two of them three-deckers (the Britannia, 100, and St. George, 98) and two frigates; and, after several weeks' cruise, the French fleet put to sea from Toulon with seven sail of the line, one of them a three-decker, and six or seven frigates or smaller vessels. Now, mark me, several of those ships had been put down as burnt at the evacuation of Toulon, but now had the impudence to rise from their ashes like the Phœnix,[1] or like the snake that had slept the winter, but on the return of spring appears renewed in youth and with new fury burns:

> Qualis ubi in lucem coluber, mala gramina pastus,
> Frigida sub terra tumidum quem bruma tegebat,
> Nunc positis novus exuviis, nitidusque juventa,
> Lubrica convolvit sublato pectore terga,
> Arduus ad solem, et linguis micat ore trisulcis.—*Aeneid.*

June 1794.—We were at dinner when the drum beat to quarters, and on going upon deck saw the 'Resurgam Squadron' coming out, under topsails and foresail, on the starboard tack, in line of battle, the Sans Culotte,[2] 136 guns, their leading ship; the

[1] Nelson's comment on the reappearance of these ships was not so classical: 'Sir Sidney Smith did not burn them all—Lord Hood mistook the man: there is an old song, "Great talkers do the least, we see."'

[2] Formerly Le Dauphin Royal, and afterwards L'Orient, burnt and blown up at the Nile. She was really of 120 guns.

L

wind westerly; our squadron standing in on the larboard tack, and to the best of my recollection about three leagues from the enemy; and, had we stood on and tacked, we should have got in their wake. But our admiral made a signal—it being at this time evening—that a movement would take place after dusk. Now, what do you think this movement was? Why, to bear up and sail large! 'Tell it not in Gath, nor publish it in the streets of Askalon.' The Meleager, 32, was left behind to watch the enemy. All this appeared strange; but the admiral, we supposed, knew

> What was what and that as high
> As metaphysic wit could fly.

Now we had an opinion also, and that opinion was that the French might have been brought to action that evening; at any rate we should have prevented them from getting back to the roads, and could have attacked them in the morning if a night action was considered hazardous. It was said the admiral was fearful they should escape us and throw relief into Calvi, at that time besieged. Whatever was the reason, off we set as if hell kicked us and joined Lord Hood—I think the next day; and then, as brave as Hercules, crowded sail with fourteen or fifteen sail of the line and got sight of them the day after, in the morning, working in near Gourjean Bay,[1] where they anchored in the afternoon under the forts. Lord Hood made every preparation to attack them, and a general chase with some hopes of success took place. We were ordered to attack the fort on the starboard hand until the fleet had passed, and then to follow; and the Illustrious, 74, was ordered against the frigates in the other quarter

[1] Golfe Jouan.

in shore, near the other line-of-battle ships. But all this ended in disappointment, as towards night the wind blew strong off the land and the attack was given up in the morning, and we were detached with the sick to St. Fiorenzo, and then to Calvi to assist in the siege. It was here that Lord Nelson lost his eye and Captain Serocold his life. We remained but a short time at Calvi and then returned to St. Fiorenzo. The Yankee historian (James) gives a very incorrect account of this; in fact, he says little or nothing about our squadron under Admiral Hotham when the French put to sea; which appears strange, as this calumniator always felt happy in finding fault with naval officers, and here he missed a good opportunity.

While cruising in the Gulf of Genoa we picked up parts of the booms belonging to the Ardent, 64, who had been missing a long time; and from the appearance of the spars it was evident she was blown up with all hands,[1] as nothing has been heard of her since. It was a sad business that we did not bring the French to action the day they left Toulon; the disappointment was bitterly felt by those who expected prize money and promotion, and here a glorious opportunity was thrown away in the most unaccountable manner. For personal bravery Admiral Hotham stood pre-eminent; but it has been said he was not fit to command in chief, but very able as a second. In the American war he greatly distinguished himself, particularly when he was commodore on board the Preston, 50, he engaged and would have taken a French 84,[2] one of

[1] In April 1794. As no one was saved the details were never known. *Cf.* Brenton, *Naval History*, ii. 52.

[2] The Tonnant, of 80 guns, already dismasted in the storm. The capture was prevented, not by a gale coming on, but by the arrival of other ships to her assistance. *Cf. ante*, p. 74.

D'Estaing's squadron, which a gale of wind coming suddenly on alone prevented; and the public accounts respecting this action say, 'Now for the glory and honour of the British army.'

While speaking of the honour of the British navy, I must say a word or two more about the seamen and marines. When Lord Hood besieged Bastia he proposed to General Dundas, who commanded the troops, to make a joint attack; but the general thought it too hazardous. Now Lord Hood had a different opinion,

> and while General Dundas
> And his eighteen manœuvres sat still on the grass

he attacked the place with the seamen and marines who covered themselves with glory and carried all the works, and Bastia was obliged to surrender.

Having letters of recommendation to Lord Hood and to Admiral Goodall, I went on board the Victory and was told by the secretary (McArthur), that several were before me on the list for promotion; but if I would take my chance his lordship would remove me to the Victory immediately. This I thought would be of little service; and as the Gorgon, 44, was under orders for England I requested to be sent on board of her and try my interest at home. My request being granted, Captain Towry in the kindest manner recommended me to Captain Wallis of the Gorgon, which kindness I shall always remember, and am sorry that the service has lost by his death so good an officer. He served with his Majesty [1] in the Andromeda and Valiant.

Before leaving the Berwick I must mention a few droll hands that belonged to her; and first I shall bring forward old Bell, the mate of the hold.

[1] William IV., at that time Duke of Clarence.

We pressed him and several mates of merchantmen out of a cartel from Marseilles to Gibraltar, and put them on the quarter deck. He was a hard-drinking man and also a hard-working man. We had a set on board full of fun; and when old Bell was half seas over, they used to paint his face with red ochre, his eyebrows blacked, large moustache, with a flaxen wig made from the fag ends of the tiller rope; a cocked hat over all, tied under the chin; his shirt off and his body painted like an ancient Briton. In this costume I have seen him chasing the midshipmen through the tier with a drawn sword, a fit subject for a pencil like Hogarth's.

Next to him was old Collier, who drank like a fish, and when drunk used to sing the Thirty-fourth Psalm and prognosticate that the ship would founder with all hands. They used to make fast his shirt sleeves at the wrist and then haul the shirt over his head, so that he could not clear his hands. In this situation he would be powdered and painted, with a red night cap on his head, and placed alongside of old Bell, while the whole cockpit would be in a roar.

We had a little slovenly surgeon's mate whose name was Vag. The midshipmen annoyed him sadly by calling out Vag-Veg-Vig-Vog-Vug, while others in a cockney cadence would sing out Wig-Wag-Wog, which enraged him almost to madness. I happened to come into the berth where he was sitting at a time they were calling out as above, when he, without any provocation on my part, snatched up the snuffers and with the sharp end stabbed me in the chest and then run a-muck after the rest, who were glad enough to steer clear of him.

Some of our lads had a custom of taking an afternoon's nap, particularly Graves, who went with me to Pisa. The others, always on the watch for mischief, would clap a spritsail yard upon his nose. This was done by cutting a notch on the outside of a piece of hoop and bending it so as to form a forceps and then put it on the nose like a spring. The first time it was fixed he started up and swore lustily that a rat (for we had hundreds of them on board) had seized him by the nose. On another occasion some wicked fellow made a curious mark on his forehead with caustic that remained for several weeks.

Our chaplain was a learned gentleman and always going on shore to make researches after antiquities. When we sailed from Toulon he was left behind; and on making his escape (so we were told) when the enemy entered, he got upon a wall where a rope ladder was placed about ten feet high. When he got on the top the ladder gave way and he had no means of alighting on the other side, and was afraid to jump down. In this predicament a party of French came up and one of them let fly a stone, which fortunately for him first struck the wall and then hit him on the hip, and canted him the right way; and by that means he luckily made his escape to the boats with little hurt, but damnably frightened. In the gale of July 1793, when we carried away our main topmast and half the main top, an arm chest full of black pieces[1] fell out of the top with thundering sound upon the quarter deck, and several of the muskets stuck with their muzzles in the deck, which bent some of the barrels. Old Billy Chantrell, our first lieutenant, taking up one of them, said with a grin, 'I shall take this home; it will do when I go a-shooting to kill sparrows round

[1] So in MS. The name is now entirely unknown, but it may perhaps have some relationship to 'brown Bess.'

a hayrick.' When it fell it was within an inch of his head, and he was knocked down with a piece of the chest which broke through the netting. I passed a very happy life during the time I belonged to the Berwick and parted with many valuable friends with deep regret. Our first lieutenant (Chantrell), Mr. Chas. Duncan, the master, and Tomlinson, the clerk, left the ship at the same time and joined the Gorgon as supernumeraries for a passage to England; and also two of my old shipmates, Yetts and Allardice, formerly of the Edgar, invalided home, which made the Gorgon very agreeable to me. The following are the names of the officers:—

SIR JOHN COLLINS, Knt., Captain.

Dead. A good man but fractious from severe illness; he commanded the Ruby, 64, detached from the grand fleet at the relief of Gibraltar, 1782, being one of eight sail of the line sent to reinforce the fleet in the West Indies. On the passage she captured, after a smart action, the Solitaire, a French 64, for which Captain Collins was knighted.

WM. SHIELD, Esq., Captain.

A retired rear-admiral. [Died 1842.—Marshall, iii. 89.]

GEO. CAMPBELL, Esq., Captain.

Dead. A vice-admiral; a better fellow never existed. [As a rear-admiral, second in command under Nelson off Toulon 1803-4. Died, admiral and G.C.B., in 1821.]

GEO. HENRY TOWRY, Esq., Captain.

Dead [1808]. In him the service lost a most worthy officer

WILLIAM CHANTRELL, 1st Lieutenant.

Dead. See Barfleur.

WILLIAM BULLOCK, 2nd Lieutenant.

Dead. A commander; well-meaning and droll.

CHAS. STEWART [or STUART], 3rd Lieutenant.

Dead [1814]. A post captain [1796]; gouty and proud.

NISBET PALMER, 4th Lieutenant.

Dead [1811]. He commanded the Alacrity, an 18-gun brig, in the Mediterranean, and was captured by a French brig of the same force. In the action Captain Palmer was wounded and died soon after. James in his *Naval History* [v. 248 *seq.*] gives a sad account of this. He says, 'Capt. Palmer was only wounded in the finger, that he ordered the colours to be struck to an enemy of equal force, and that his death was occasioned by a locked jaw.' In justice to the memory of Captain Palmer it must be recollected that the Alacrity was weakly manned—a great number of her crew being absent in prizes. The Yankee historian must have known this, but he had not the generosity to state it. [James does state it; but nevertheless comments very severely on the conduct of Palmer; not unmindful, perhaps, of the fact that by the death of the captain, he was commanding officer of the Berwick when captured on March 7, 1795.]

THOMAS SHIRLEY, 5th Lieutenant.
Dead. Half mad, but good-natured.

CHAS. DUNCAN, Master.
A superannuated master attendant; a very good man.

[JOHN] DODGSON, Surgeon.
Dead. A worthy fellow.

THOS. L. YATES, Purser.
Dead. Generous and thoughtless.

[ALEXANDER JOHN] SCOTT, Chaplain.
A Doctor of Divinity; was with Lord Nelson on board the Victory at Trafalgar. [Died 1840.—*D.N.B.*]

[HECTOR] TAUSE, Gunner.
Dead. Crabbed.

PHILIP MYERS, Carpenter.
Dead. A droll fellow.

[JOSEPH] KEMBLE, Boatswain.
Uncertain. A snappish cur.

EDWARD HUTCHINSON, Mate.
A commander; a good officer; a good navigator; a good seaman and a most worthy messmate. [Captain, retired, 1840; died 1851. —O'Byrne.]

ROBT. TUCKER, Mate.
A commander; a good seaman, but given to drinking. [Died, retired captain, 1846.—O'Byrne.]

J. A. GARDNER, Mate.
A commander.

WM. VOSPER, Signal midshipman.
Lieutenant of the Royal Asylum, Greenwich Hospital. We were at three schools together at Gosport, and in two ships; a very able officer and seaman.

JAMES VALOBRA, Midshipman.
A commander; a very worthy fellow. [Died 1861.—O'Byrne.]

AUGUSTUS COLLINS, Midshipman; son of the captain.
Dead. I believe a commander.

JOHN GRAVES, Midshipman.
Dead. A lieutenant. Poor Jack was a worthy fellow.

JAMES GALLOWAY, Midshipman.
A commander [1806], out-pension. [Died 1846.—Marshall, x. 345; O'Byrne.]

JOHN LAWRENCE, Midshipman.
A post captain [1817]; C.B. [Died 1849.—Marshall, viii. 123; O'Byrne.]

[RICHARD] SCOVELL, Midshipman.
Killed in battle.

[NICHOLAS] LE BAIR, Midshipman.
Poor fellow! was taken in the Berwick, and died in French prison. [DD. in the pay-book, April 19, 1795. Toulon.]

ALEX. MACKENZIE, Midshipman.
Dead [1825]. A post captain. This man, when he was a midshipman, used to sneak after the lieutenants; when made a lieutenant, sneaking after the captains, and when made a captain, was at his old tricks, sneaking after the admirals. Had he lived to be made a flag officer, he would have sneaked after the devil.—[Marshall, vii. 75.]

JOHN ROSE, Midshipman.
A commander; a good fellow.

[WILLIAM] BARBER, Midshipman.
Dead. A lieutenant; a good fellow.

[THOMAS] PITT, Midshipman.
Uncertain. I believe a master.

[THOMAS] HEWLETT, Midshipman.
A master; I believe dead.

[JOHN] BELL, Mate of the hold.
Uncertain. A droll fellow; drank hard.

[WALTER] DEMPSTER, Midshipman.
Uncertain. A quiet, good fellow.

[JOHN] COLLIER, Midshipman.
Uncertain. Good natured; drank hard.

LORD PROBY, Midshipman.
Dead [1804]. A post captain. [William Allen Proby, eldest son of the first Earl of Carysfort.]

JOHN LAMBRICK, Midshipman.
A commander.—[O'Byrne.]

WM. MCCULLOCH, Midshipman.
Dead [1825]. A post captain [1814]; a smart officer.—[Marshall, vii. 398.]

JOHN BRIGGS, 1st Assistant Surgeon.
A surgeon R.N.; a most worthy gentleman.

[HENRY] VAGG, 3rd Assistant Surgeon.
Uncertain. A sloven; Vig-Vag-Vog-Vug.

GORGON, 44

UPON TWO DECKS

Adieu, ye vales, that smiling peace bestow
Where Eden's blossoms ever vernal blow,
Ye fairy scenes where fancy loves to dwell,
And young delight, for ever, oh, farewell!—*Falconer.*

In July 1794 I joined the Gorgon, Captain James Wallis, at St. Fiorenzo, and after considerable delay sailed for Gibraltar with the convoy bound for England under Vice-Admiral P. Cosby, who had his flag on board the Alcide, 74. The following men of war, to the best of my recollection, in company:—

Alcide	74	Vice-Admiral Cosby
Commerce de Marseilles[1]	136	
Gorgon	44	
Pearl[1]	36	
Topaze[1]	36	
St. Fiorenzo	36	
Modeste	32	

We had a very pleasant passage to Gibraltar, where we remained some time in the New Mole,

[1] French ships brought from Toulon. *Cf.* Schomberg, *Naval Chronology*, iv. 471. It will be seen that the lists of these squadrons differ from Schomberg's, which are probably the more correct. The Alert, for instance, had been captured on the coast of Ireland, in May.—James, i. 439.

and then started for Cadiz to take in money and to join the convoy assembling there for England. On the passage we got on shore a few leagues to the southward of Cadiz, and had very near taken up our quarters on the shoals, and, what was remarkable, a frigate had been sent before us for the same purpose, but got on shore in this place, and was obliged to return, and we (being clever) after laughing at the circumstance, were sent to repair her errors and went bump on shore on the very spot. The America, 64, having arrived at Cadiz to take charge of the convoy, we were put under her orders, and having got on board the money, sailed with the convoy for Lisbon.

> Farewell and adieu, ye fair Spanish Ladies,
> Farewell and adieu, ye Ladies of Spain;
> For we've received orders to sail for old England,
> In hopes in short time for to see you again.—*Old Song.*

After a passage of near three weeks we arrived in the Tagus, fortunately the day before a tremendous hurricane, which blew dead upon the shore, came on and lasted a considerable time. We remained several weeks at Lisbon collecting the convoy. At last when everything was ready we got under way, I think the latter end of September, the following men of war in company:—

America . . .	64	Hon. John Rodney, Commodore, having charge of the convoy
Gorgon . . .	44	Captain Wallis
Pearl	36	
Topaze . . .	36	
St. Fiorenzo .	36	Capt. Sir C. Hamilton (?)
Modeste . . .	32	Captain [Byam Martin]
Alert . .	18	

We had a most dreadful passage home, blowing a gale of wind the whole time with seldom more sail set than a close-reefed main topsail. The French squadron that captured the Alexander, 74, had been on the look-out for us. We had several French emigrants on board who were in the greatest tribulation for fear of being taken; and fortunately for them and for us the Jacobin squadron got on the wrong scent. I don't know how it happened, but some people kept an odd kind of reckoning, and we had some idea of making the banks of Newfoundland instead of the British Channel. However, at last we got to the northward and westward of Scilly, with the wind at SW; but it must be understood, to give the devil his due, that we had not an observation for a long time, and our dead reckoning was not to be trusted; but at last we found out by instinct or soundings that we were not in the right place. Now it so happened that we were lying to on the larboard tack, the wind, as I have stated, at SW, under a close-reefed main topsail and storm staysails, when in a thundering squall it shifted to NNW and took us slap aback. Over she went, with the upper dead-eyes on the lower rigging in the water, and we thought she never would right, but the old ship came to herself again. She was a noble sea-boat; it would have been worth any man's while to leave the feast, the dance, or even his wife, to have been on board this ship in a gale of wind to witness her glorious qualities. After standing to the southward for some time until we thought we had got into 49° 30′ by our dead reckoning, which is the latitude of mid-channel, we then altered our course to SEbE½E. I had a presentiment that something bad was hanging over us, and I went on the fore topsail yard (I think about 9 at night) to look out ahead, the ship scudding at the rate of eleven knots, which brought to my mind the following lines :

> The fatal sisters on the surge before
> Yoked their infernal horses to the prow.—*Falconer.*

But in this instance they were outwitted, for lo and behold, after running some time I saw a light right ahead, which I instantly knew to be Scilly light, and I called to Captain Wallis, who immediately hauled the ship off to the southward. If the weather had not cleared after the squall before mentioned we should certainly have made the port where Sir Clowdsiley Shovell took in his last moorings.

The gale separated the convoy, and in standing up Channel we had near run on the Bolt Head, but hauled off just in time. At last we arrived at Spithead, where a large fleet of men of war were assembled. Before we came to an anchor we had nearly run foul of several ships, and I remember the Invincible, 74, hailing us, saying, 'You have cut my cable, sir.' This was not all, for we shaved off the old Royal William's quarter gallery, which some shipwrights were repairing—who had barely time to save themselves. We were not allowed to anchor at Spithead, but to proceed to the Motherbank to perform quarantine on December 4, 1794, after the most extraordinary voyage that ever took place since the expedition of the Argonauts. Here I left the Gorgon and joined the Victory, who I found to my astonishment at Spithead.

But before I quit the Gorgon I must relate a few things that happened on and before the passage home. At the time we left Corsica we had forty-seven French prisoners on board. One of them could play the violin remarkably well. One morning on the forecastle, this man was reading to some of his comrades, and having his violin with him, Mr. Duncan (our late master in the Berwick) requested him to play *Ça Ira*, which he for some time refused, being fearful of giving offence. At last he struck up the Marseilles hymn accompanied by his voice, which was very good, and when he came to that part 'Aux armes, Citoyens, formez vos bataillons,' etc., he seemed inspired; he threw up his violin half way up the fore mast, caught it again, pressed it to his breast, and sung out 'Bon, Ça Ira,' in which he was joined by his comrades.

> Fired with the song the French grew vain,
> Fought all their battles o'er again,
> And thrice they routed all their foes; and thrice they slew the slain;

and seemed ready and willing for any mischief. But our soldiers were called up and the French were sent below, and not so many allowed to be on deck at a time.

On the passage we were frequently sent as a whipper-in among the convoy. On one occasion, a master of a merchantman was rather slack in obeying the signal and gave tongue when hailed; upon which Captain Wallis sent the first lieutenant and myself to take charge of his vessel. It was in the evening, blowing fresh, with a heavy sea, and we had great difficulty in getting on board; our boat cut as many capers as a swing at a fair, and in returning got stove alongside. We remained all night on board and had to prick for the softest plank. When Edgar, the first lieutenant, awoke in the morning, it was laughable to hear him exclaim, 'God bass 'e' (for he could not say 'blast ye,' and for this he was nicknamed little Bassey) 'What's got hold of me?' The fact was the night was hot, and the pitch in the seams waxed warm, and when he attempted to rise, he found his hair fastened to the deck and his nankin trowsers also. He put me in mind of Gulliver when fastened to the ground by the Liliputians. Captain Wallis having sent for us, we took this chap in tow. It blew very fresh, and the wind being fair, we towed him, under double reefed topsails and foresail, nine knots through the water, so that his topsails were wet with the spray. The master would sometimes run forward and hail, saying, 'I'll cut the hawser'; and Captain Wallis would reply, 'If you do, I'm damned if I don't sink you, you skulking son of a bitch; I mean to tow you until I work some buckets of tar out of the hawser.'

Our admiral (Cosby) was a glorious fellow for keeping the convoy in order, and if they did not immediately obey the signal, he would fire at them without further ceremony. While lying at Gibraltar a Portuguese frigate arrived, and one of our midshipmen (Jennings, a wag) was sent on board with a message from Captain Wallis. Having stayed a long time, the signal was made for the boat, and when she returned the captain asked Jennings what detained him. 'Why, sir, to tell you the truth, saving your presence' (for Jennings was a shrewd Irishman), 'the commanding officer of the frigate was so busy lousing himself on the hen-coop that I could not get an answer before.'

When we arrived at Cadiz to join the convoy and to bring home dollars, the merchants used to smuggle the money off to the ship to avoid paying the duty; and for every hundred taken on board, they would give as a premium two dollars and sometimes two and a half. It was a dangerous traffic, but very tempting; and some of our officers while lying there made sixty and others eighty pounds. On one occasion, my old shipmate, Lieutenant Chantrell, fell down in the street with six hundred dollars at his back—a moderate load—and sung out to some of the Spaniards who were looking on, 'Come here, you sons of ——, and help me up.' Had they known what he had at his back they would have helped him up to some purpose; imprisonment and slavery would have been the punishment. The manner they carried the dollars was this. A double piece of canvas made to contain them in rows, fixed to the back inside the waistcoat, and tied before. It was to an English hotel where they were sent to be shipped. This house was kept by Mr., or rather Mrs., Young, an infernal vixen, who would make nothing of knocking her husband down with a leg of mutton or any other joint she had in the larder, and he fool enough to put up with it. She used to charge us very high for our entertainment, which is the case in all English houses abroad; and if you have a mind to be treated fairly you must go to a house kept by a native, who will never impose on you. Having got a load of dollars to take off, we found our boat had left the landing place; so we hired a shore boat, and it appeared their custom house officers had suspicions, for they gave chase, and it was by uncommon exertion that we escaped, as they were nearly up with us when we got alongside. And yet those very men who would have seized us used to smuggle. I saw one of them come alongside and throw into the lower-deck port a bag of dollars containing, as I understood, a thousand, with a label on the bag, and then shove off his boat to row guard and prevent smuggling!

At Cadiz there is a beautiful walk with trees, called the Alameda, much frequented, particularly on a Sunday. It has three walks for the different grades of people. I happened to be on shore with some of our officers on the above day, and taking a stroll through the Alameda, we observed several well-dressed women in a balcony of one of the large houses that overlooked the walks. When they caught sight of us, they beckoned, and we went, as we thought, into the house. On going up two pairs of stairs without seeing any one, we imagined it was a trick, when casting my eye to a door that was partly open, I saw a fellow with a drawn stilletto ready to make a stab; upon which I called to the rest to make their retreat as fast as possible. One of them (a Mr. Crump) was deaf, and I was obliged to push him downstairs as I could not make him understand. This was a warning not lost upon us.

A droll circumstance happened while at Lisbon. A party of us had been to see the famous aqueduct over the valley of Alcantara, and on coming back, one of them (Tomlinson, of the Berwick) to show his dexterity jumped on the back of a donkey. He had on a round jacket and light nankin pantaloons; the latter he split from clue to earing, and was obliged to walk to the boat in that situation, and by way of helping a lame dog over a stile, we took the longest way, where we had to pass by several ladies, with his shirt sticking out and every one laughing at him. He declared to me it was the most miserable time he ever experienced in the whole course of his life.

We were one day accosted while walking in Black-Horse Square, by a genteel-looking young man who, in broken English, said he would be happy to show us about the city, which offer was accepted, though much against my will. As we were walking through the streets, I observed the people as they passed us to laugh and point to others and then at us. At last we met an officer belonging to our squadron, who asked if we knew the person we had in company, because, says he, 'If you don't I'll tell you. He is the noted pimp of Lisbon, and makes a trade of showing, not only the city, but all the ladies of easy virtue from the lowest brothel in Bull Bay to the highest in the upper town.' This was quite enough, and we told the fellow to be off, but he had the impudence to follow us to the boat for payment, and even got upon the gang board and was coming in, when Jennings, in his dry way, said to the bowman, 'Don't you see the gentleman is dusty? Have you no way of rubbing it off?' winking at the time. Upon this the bowman without any ceremony pitched him overboard up to his neck and then shoved off. We met the fellow several times after, but he took good care to steer clear.

I went with Lieutenant Chantrell to dinner at an ordinary at Lisbon. Among the company were several Americans. One of the dishes at the bottom of the table occasioned a dispute that had nearly terminated in a battle. A Yankee from the head of the table came and snatched up a beef-steak pie that an English master of a transport (one of our convoy) was serving out, and carried it off to his companions; upon which the Englishman stood up and harangued his countrymen as follows: 'I say, if you stand this you ought to be damned, and may as well take a purser's shirt out of the rigging.[1] Now, I move that all you that are Englishmen shall rise from the table and throw the Yankees out of the window.' This speech had the same effect as that of Nestor's to the Greeks, and the Yankees would for a certainty have been thrown into the street, had not Lieutenant Chantrell requested them to forbear, observing that abuse was innocent where men were worthless. This had the desired effect;

[1] A shirt in the rigging was the recognised signal from a merchantman for a man-of-war boat to be sent on board.

and the pie being restored to its place in rather a diminished state, and the Yankee who took it away saying he only meant it in Har-mo-ny, the war was put an end to, and the dinner ended in peace.

One of our men having deserted, I was sent with Ducker, the boatswain, and a couple of marines to hunt in Bull Bay, which is the Wapping of Lisbon, and after a long search we found him and were returning to the boat. In passing through one of their dirty streets, something which shall be nameless was hove out of a window and fell upon the shoulder of Ducker, about the size of a large epaulette. I wished him joy of his promotion and told him that he looked extremely well in his new uniform. A piece of the same material fell on his nose and stuck out like the horn of a rhinoceros. I never saw a fellow so vexed. He was going to break the windows, but I told him to consider, as Bull Bay was not to be attacked too hastily. I had hardly made the observation when his foot slipped, and he fell back in the gutter, where he lay cursing the whole race of Portuguese. Then

> Vigorous he rose; and from the effluvia strong
> Imbibed new strength, and scoured and stunk along.[1]

I thought I should have died a-laughing, while he was cursing every native he met with until he got to the boat.

As I have stated before, every ship has strange characters, and the Gorgon had her full share. I shall begin with the captain, who was a very good seaman and had many good qualities, but at times he appeared half mad. He once said to me, pointing to Ducker, the boatswain, on the forecastle, 'I'll hang that fellow; and you go down directly and

[1] *The Dunciad*, ii. 105. A reference to the original—of which only the tense is here altered—will show the strict appositeness of the quotation.

take an inventory of his stores.' I could hardly keep my countenance, but went forward, and as the captain turned his back I said to Ducker, 'You are going to be hanged, and I am sent for a piece of white line to tuck you up genteelly.' On my reporting progress, he seemed to have forgot that he gave such an order, and, taking a pinch of snuff, merely said, 'Let the fellow go to hell, and say no more about him.'

The first lieutenant, Edgar, was another strange and unaccountable being. He had sailed round the world with Cook, and was master of the ship Captain Clerke commanded. He was a good sailor and navigator, or rather had been, for he drank very hard, so as to entirely ruin his constitution. He and the captain often quarrelled, particularly at night. I have heard the captain say, 'Edgar, I shall get another first lieutenant.' The other would answer, 'Ye-ye-ye-yes, sir, another first lieutenant.' The captain again, 'Edgar, you are drunk.' 'No, sir, bass me if I am.' A day or two before we left Corsica, the captain ordered the sails to be bent and went on shore to St. Fiorenzo. On coming on board late at night he asked Edgar if the sails were bent. This question Edgar could not answer, his memory having failed him ; and on the captain asking him again, he said, 'Bass me if I know, but I'll look up,' forgetting it was dark. 'You need not do that,' says the other, 'for damn me if you can see a hole through a grating.' Then taking a pinch of snuff, part of which blew into Edgar's eye, he asked him down to supper. This the other readily agreed to, but said, Bass him, if he could see the way.

I must now speak of Jerry Hacker, the purser. He was a man, take him all in all, ye ne'er will see his like again. He messed by himself in the cockpit, and would sit in his cabin in the dark with a long stick in his hand, calling out to everyone that came down the cockpit ladder, 'What strange man is that?' He was in constant fear of being robbed or cheated, and lived in the most miserable manner. I have known him to corn meat in his hand-basin and in something else. He was suspicious to a degree and always saying he should be ruined, though there was little fear of that, as Jerry took good care to trust no one; and what he was only charged two shillings a gallon for, he kindly offered to let me have for five shillings, paying ready money; but I was not to be taken in so easy. He could not bear the sight of a midshipman in the cockpit, and did everything in his power to annoy them, and before I joined the ship, he used to sing a verse of an old song reflecting on the midshipmen. One morning while I was in the cockpit, he was quarrelling with some of them, and then struck up his favourite air, not thinking that any person knew the song but himself. However, in this he was mistaken, and when he had finished the following verse, I struck up another that settled him.

Tune, *The Black Joke.*

Ye salt beef squires and quarter deck beaus,
Who formerly lived upon blacking of shoes:
　　With your anchors a-weigh and your topsails a-trip.
If they call us by name and we don't answer, Sir!
They start us about till not able to stir;
　　A lusty one and lay it well on.
If you spare them an inch you ought to be damn'd;
With your anchors a-weigh and your topsails a-trip.

Our b—— of a purser, he is very handy,
He mixes the water along with the brandy;
　　Your anchors a-weigh and your topsails a-trip
The bloody old thief he is very cruel;
Instead of burgoo he gives us water gruel;
　　A lusty one and lay it well on.
If you spare him an inch you ought to be damn'd,
With your anchors a-weigh and your topsails a-trip.

After hearing the last verse Jerry's 'heavenly voice was heard no more to sing,' and he looked with an evil eye upon me ever after.

In the gale of wind near the Channel, when we were taken aback in the squall that I have mentioned, every article we had was broken with the exception of the cover of a very large mess teapot. This we handed round as a measure to one another with wine from a black jack. I remember being at supper soon after the squall, in the midship berth in the cockpit, the ship rolling gunwale under, when we heard a noise in the after-hold like the rush of many waters, and it struck everyone that a butt end had started and that we should founder in a few minutes. The alarm was given immediately. The sick and lame left their hammocks; the latter forgot his crutch, and leaped—not exulting—like the bounding roe. Down came the captain and a whole posse of officers and men. The gratings were instantly unshipped, and in rushed the carpenter and his crew, horror-struck, with hair standing on end, like quills on the fretful porcupine; when, behold, it was a large cask of peas that had the head knocked out, and the peas as the ship rolled rushed along with a noise exactly like that of water.[1]

After looking at one another for some time the following ludicrous scene took place, which I was an eye-witness to:—

The captain shook his head, took snuff, and went upon deck.

Old Edgar, first lieutenant, followed, and said 'God bass 'e all.'

Billy Chantrell gave a grin, and damn'd his eyes.

[1] At this time peas were issued whole. Split peas were not issued till about 1856—after the Russian war.

The parson exclaimed 'In the midst of life we are in death.

The carpenter said 'Damn and b—— the peas.'

Old Jerry Hacker, the purser, swore he was ruined, as no allowance would be made him; and cursed the field the peas grew in; and the French emigrant captain (Dubosc) said 'it was as vel for him to stay at de Toulon and be guillotined, as to come to dis place and be drowned in de vater.'

I never shall forget this scene as long as I live. I dined with Captain Wallis the next day, and he asked me, in a very knowing manner, if he should help me to some peas soup.

Our gunner was one of the drollest fellows I ever met with—it was his delight to come on the forecastle in the first watch and sing comic songs to amuse the midshipmen assembled there. 'Arthur O'Bradley' was one that he used to sing with a great deal of humour. I believe it contained forty verses. 'Bryan O'Lynn' was another which I shall relate, leaving out the lines that may not be liked by those endued with fine feelings.

Bryan O'Lynn and his wife, and wife's mother,
They all hid under a hedge together;
But the rain came so fast they got wet to the skin—
We shall catch a damned cold, says Bryan O'Lynn.

Bryan O'Lynn and his wife, and wife's mother,
They went in a boat to catch sprats together;
A butt end got stove and the water rushed in—
We're drowned, by the holy, says Bryan O'Lynn.

Bryan O'Lynn and his wife, and wife's mother,
They all went on a bridge together;
The bridge it broke and they all fell in—
Strike out and be damned, says Bryan O'Lynn.

Bryan O'Lynn and his wife, and wife's mother,
They all went out to chapel together;
The door it was shut and they could not get in—
It's a hell of a misfortune, says Bryan O'Lynn.

Bryan O'Lynn and his wife, and wife's mother,
They went with the priest to a wake together,
Where they all got drunk and thought it no sin—
It keeps out the cold, says Bryan O'Lynn.

Bryan O'Lynn and his wife, and wife's mother,
They went to the grave with the corpse together;
The earth being loose they all fell in—
Bear a hand and jump out, says Bryan O'Lynn.

Bryan O'Lynn and his wife, and wife's mother,
When the berring was over went home together;
In crossing a bog they got up to the chin—
I'm damned but we're smothered, says Bryan O'Lynn.

Bryan O'Lynn and his wife, and wife's mother,
By good luck got out of the bog together;
Then went to confess to Father O'Flinn—
We're damnation sinners, says Bryan O'Lynn.

Bryan O'Lynn and his wife, and wife's mother,
Resolved to lead a new life together;
And from that day to this have committed no sin—
In the calendar stands SAINT BRYAN O'LYNN.

I have left out four verses as being rather out of order. I have heard the old gunner sing this when the sea has been beating over the forecastle and the ship rolling gunwale under. We used to get a tarpaulin in the weather fore rigging as a screen, and many a pleasant hour have I passed under its lee, with a glass of grog and hearing long-winded stories. Alas! how dead are times now. Captain Wallis behaved very kindly to me. I used to dine with him two or three times a week. He had, as I have stated, strange whims and few men are without them, but his many good qualities threw them in the background, and I have, with grateful remembrance and respect for his memory, to be thankful for his kindness, and particularly for the certificate he gave me on leaving the ship.

Madame Trogoff, the French admiral's widow,[1] came to England and was a passenger in his cabin. She was a very agreeable woman. We had several French officers (emigrants) who had left Toulon at the evacuation. They were in the greatest tribulation all the passage for fear of being taken. We had also many invalids from the fleet, of very little service had we met with an enemy; and our effective complement I think mustered under a hundred, so that we should have stood but a poor chance had we met with the squadron that I have already mentioned. The forty-seven French prisoners that we had with us were left at Gibraltar, which was a great relief to the emigrants we had on board, as they were in constant fear of their taking the ship from us. The following are the names of the officers:—

JAMES WALLIS, Esq., Captain.
Dead [1808]. He had strange ways, but was an able officer and seaman. [Commander, 1794; captain, 1797. He was therefore only acting in the Gordon.]

THOMAS EDGAR, 1st Lieutenant.
Dead. A commander; was master of Captain Clerke's ship with Cook round the world.

THOMAS LYNE, 2nd Lieutenant.
A commander; a very good fellow.

WM. CHANTRELL, Supy. Lieutenant.
Dead. See Barfleur and Berwick.

WM. BRETT, Supy. Lieutenant.
Dead. A commander; a good fellow.

---

[1] Rear-Admiral Trogoff, with his flag in the Commerce de Marseille, left Toulon in company, with the English but he died within a few months.—Chevalier, *op. cit.* pp. 90, 91.

[JOHN] CHISSELL, Master.

Dead. A strange fellow; he could speak six or seven different languages fluently, and was well known in every part of the Mediterranean.

JERRY HACKER, Purser.

Dead. I believe Jerry was broke. The most strange and unaccountable fellow the world ever produced.

[WILLIAM] PHILPS, Gunner.

Dead. One of the drollest fellows I ever met with.

[JOHN] DUCKER, Boatswain.

Dead. Much respected.

[JAMES] JEZARD, Carpenter.

Uncertain. A good timber head of his own.

[WILLIAM] POOLE, Clerk.

Dead. Very good abilities, but killed by grog.

ULICK JENNINGS, Midshipman.

Dead. Was captain [commander] of the Woolwich, 44 [storeship], but broke by court martial [1, 2 Dec. 1803] at Jamaica, for thrashing some of the officers of the dockyard. Said to have been reinstated. A very droll fellow and great mimic. He was in the Dutch action under Duncan [*cf.* James, ii. 80, 88], and blown up; his face terribly scarred. Before that he was a very good-looking fellow. A native of Ireland, possessing great personal courage. [There was no thrashing, nor threat of thrashing, but much insulting and domineering conduct. He was found guilty of 'drunkenness and unofficer-like and irregular behaviour,' and dismissed the service. He was not reinstated.]

RICHARD CHISSELL, Midshipman; son of the master.

Dead. A lieutenant. [Borne as A.B.; native of Leghorn, aged 20.]

BRICKNELL, Supy. Midshipman.

Uncertain. The ugliest fellow the world ever produced. He used to dress with gold-laced hat, silk stockings, and full uniform upon every occasion, as if going to the queen's drawing room.

JAMES COURAGE, Assistant Surgeon.

Uncertain. A fractious little fellow.

J. A. GARDNER, doing duty as signal officer.

A commander. See Boreas, Conqueror, etc.

VICTORY, 110.

> Vides ut alta stet nive candidum
> Soracte, nec jam sustineant onus
> Sylvæ laborantes, geluque
> Flumina constiterint acuto.

In such a season, unexampled for severity, I joined the Victory in December 1794, in Portsmouth harbour, fitting for the Mediterranean and to receive again the flag of Lord Hood; John Knight, Esq., captain. Had I joined her in St. Fiorenzo Bay at the time I have before stated, I should have been promoted, as those who were before me and many that came after got their commissions as lieutenants; so by this I lost about five months' rank, and was obliged to go to London to pass my examination, as passing abroad is of no use unless you get promotion on the spot. On my representing to the first lieutenant (Hamilton) that I intended to apply to Captain Knight for permission to go and pass, and requesting him to forward my application, he in the most unhandsome manner said he would do no such thing, and would protest against my getting leave.

Now without flattering myself, I thought I knew the service (without being a conjuror) as well as Lieutenant Hamilton; and although he said it was his intention to send me on board the Commerce de Marseilles to assist in fitting her out at Spithead (notwithstanding that my right arm was hurt and obliged to wear it in a sling), I wrote to Captain Knight on the subject, who immediately granted my request. On my stating this to Lieutenant Hamilton, he said he should still oppose it, adding with a sneer that my promotion he supposed would not be so rapid as I expected. Without taking notice of his remarks I went on shore to take my place in the coach, and on my return the next morning to get my things I found that the ship had gone into dock, and that my chest, and that of another gentleman's who had lately joined, had not been removed to the hulk, but left in the ship, where it was broke open, and everything I possessed, with the exception of my quadrant, stolen. The other poor fellow suffered the same misfortune.

This was a heart-breaking circumstance to me, as I had just fitted myself out, and, with what I brought home, my loss was considerable. I had nothing left but what I stood in, and most of my pay that I received for the Berwick was expended. My messmates said they were very sorry for the loss I had sustained. Instead of being sorry, they ought to have been ashamed of their gross neglect. One of them had been in the Barfleur with me, and if possible, was more to blame than the rest who were strangers. I am not vindictive, but from that day to this I have hated the sight of a Portsmouth dockyard man. I had little time and less money to get fitted out again before the examination took place, which was early in January; so up to London I went 'with a heart rather sad.' I had on a mate's coat, a red waistcoat and grey trowsers, in which costume I passed my examination. I was so down in spirits before I went in that I made sure I should be turned back. My old and lamented friend and messmate, the late Captain Eaton, went with me and positively pushed me into the room where the commissioners were seated, saying, 'Damn your eyes,[1] Tony, what are you afraid of?'

One of the commissioners (Harmood) was an intimate friend of my father's; and Sir Samuel Marshall, the deputy comptroller of the navy, was a particular friend of Admiral Parry, my mother's uncle. To these I was recommended; but notwithstanding I could not get the better of my dread, until Commissioner Harmood, after a few questions had been put to me, said, 'I think we need not ask any more.' Captain Clayton, another of the commissioners, in reply said, 'I shall merely ask one question more. You have a close-reefed main topsail set, blowing a gale of wind; you cannot carry it. Pray, sir, how will you take it in, without splitting the sail?' Having answered this, but not exactly to his satisfaction, as I started the weather sheet first, and he the lee one, I was told they had done with me, and glad enough I was; particularly so, when they said the certificates I produced ought to get me a commission without interest.

On this hint I transmitted them the next day to Earl Spencer, the first lord of the admiralty. This was on the 9th January 1795, and I returned to Portsmouth on the 14th; but before I went on board I took a stroll in the dockyard, where I met two old messmates, the late Captains Lamb and Wolridge, and on my asking them for news, they said they had just left the commissioner's office and had heard nothing. However I thought I would

[1] A recognised form of encouragement. In the court martial on the officers of the Ambuscade, captured by the French on the 14th December, 1798 (James, ii. 273 *seq.*), the boatswain was asked, 'Did you hear Lieut. Briggs call to the people to encourage them to come aft and fight?' and the answer was, 'He called down to the waist to come up and assist. I believe it was "Damn your eyes, come up."'—*Minutes of the Court Martial. Cf.* Byron's *Don Juan*, xi. 12.

just call at the office and take a look, and on my entering the hall where the letters are placed on a table, the first I observed was directed to Lieutenant J. A. Gardner, H.M. ship Victory. I looked at it several times, rubbed my eyes and looked and looked again at what I thought an illusion; but I found what I considered shadow to be substance; for on opening the letter it ran thus: 'That Earl Spencer had received my memorial on the 11th, and that my appointment as lieutenant had passed the board on the 12th January.' This eased my mind of a load, and my prospects, that were dark and dismal from the loss I had sustained, brightened up, and with a light heart I waited on Captain Knight to thank him for granting me leave and to show him my letter. He wished me joy and expressed great indignation at the loss of my effects.

I must here state that, besides what I brought home from abroad, I lost twenty new shirts, two suits of uniform, trowsers, waistcoats, boots, etc., etc., in fact everything but my quadrant; and that no doubt would have gone also, but my name was engraved on the brass.

On my return to the Victory to report myself, Lieutenant Hamilton was all politeness. I was asked down to the wardroom, and Lieutenant Vincent, who had been a midshipman with me in the Salisbury, but who had hardly spoken to me before, forgot his pomposity and was as friendly as in times of old; but I disdained their kindness as well as the dinner they asked me to, and went on shore without taking leave of the men who suffered, by base neglect, an absent messmate to be plundered by rascally dockyard men. I was so short a time on board the Victory that I remember but few, and a great number were on leave who I never saw. Some of those in the mess I knew little of, and only remember the names of four.

With the Victory ends my servitude of mate and midshipman, but I never can forget the many happy days I passed in that capacity. It was some time before I knew what ship I was appointed to; but on the receipt of a letter from Mr. Harrison, Lord Spencer's private secretary, I was informed that it was to the Hind, 28, at Sheerness, and that I was to come to London to be sworn in without loss of time.

LORD HOOD, Admiral of the blue.
Dead [1816]. An admiral of the white and Governor of Greenwich Hospital; a most able tactician.—[*D.N.B.*]

JOHN KNIGHT, Esq., Captain.
Dead [1831]. An admiral of the red and K.C.B.: a very able officer; see his charts.—[Marshall, i. 154.]

EDWARD HAMILTON, 1st Lieutenant.
A vice-admiral; a baronet and K.C.B. He recaptured the Hermione. [Died, an admiral, 1851.—*D.N.B.*]

MARTIN HINTON, 2nd Lieutenant.
Dead. A commander; a good sailor.

RICHARD BUDD VINCENT, 3rd Lieutenant.
Dead. See Salisbury.

JOHN McARTHUR, Secretary.
A very clever fellow, and one of the first swordsmen in Europe [Died 1840.—*D.N.B.*]

LAWFORD MILES, Lieutenant of Marines.
Dead. A captain; good-natured and thoughtless.

WILLIAM RIVERS, Gunner.
Dead. See Barfleur.

JOHN MARR, Boatswain.
Dead. See Barfleur.

GEO. WOLFE, Midshipman or mate.
Dead [1825]. A post captain; a worthy fellow.—[Marshall, iii. 310.]

H[ENRY] VANSITTART, Midshipman.
A rear-admiral. [Died, a vice-admiral, 1843.—O'Byrne.]

G. E. HAMOND, Midshipman.
A vice-admiral, Bart., and K.C.B. [Died, an admiral and G.C.B. 1862.—*D.N.B.*]

RICHARD W. SIMMONDS, Midshipman.
Dead. See Barfleur.

WILLIAM PYE, Schoolmaster.
Dead. See Salisbury and Barfleur.

J. A. GARDNER, Midshipman.
A commander.

I remember no more.

HIND, 28

AFTER being sworn in at the admiralty,[1] I left London to join the Hind, 28, Captain Richard Lee, at Sheerness, in January 1795. The Medway and Thames being frozen over, there was no communication with the men of war.[2] I proceeded on my journey by coach as far as Sittingbourne, and then walked most of the way through deep snow to the King's ferry, which was also frozen over. At this time my health was very bad, and coming from a fine climate to one noted for gloomy skies, fog, rain, bitter cold and everything else that was damnable, I had nearly sunk under it, and I have to acknowledge how much I was obliged to Mr. Poulden, an officer in the navy, and brother to Captain Poulden,[3] R.N., for his kind attention. He was a fellow traveller going also to join his ship at Sheerness. The snow was several feet deep, and the cold dreadful, and it was with the greatest difficulty and

[1] It is only by the aid of such occasional and incidental notices that we can now realise what a very real thing the Test Act of 1673 was, and continued to be, till its repeal in 1828. It required 'all persons holding any office of profit or trust, civil or military, under the crown, to take the oaths of allegiance and supremacy, receive the sacrament of the Lord's Supper according to the rites of the Church of England, and subscribe the declaration against transubstantiation.'

[2] As was the case in January, 1855.

[3] Richard Poulden. Died, a rear-admiral, 1845.

fatigue that we reached the public-house near the ferry without being frost-bitten.

You who are not too young (for it's difficult now to find an old person), must remember the cruel winter the latter end of 1794 and beginning of 1795.[1] To my surprise I met at the public-house an old messmate of mine (a Mr. Simmonds) formerly of the Panther, and going also to join his ship. We were half-starved and waited a considerable time for our host to bring in the dinner, which he did at last. To our horror and amazement, it consisted of a leg of pork of enormous size, without a bit of lean, and coarse white cabbage boiled with it, and as greasy as the devil. I shall never forget the consternation we were in; nothing else could be had, and what made it more vexatious was the praises the great fat fool of a John Bull landlord was passing on it. We were obliged to swallow this greasy morsel from downright hunger, and from its rancid taste in danger of cholera morbus.

The passage being frozen, we had no other

[1] Mr. Marriott, Assistant Secretary of the Royal Meteorological Society, has kindly supplied the following note:—The frost began about the middle of December 1794, was excessively severe in January, and continued till the end of March. There were large falls of snow, and the consequent floods were so great that nearly all the bridges in England were injured. The greatest cold recorded was at Maidstone on January 25, when a thermometer laid on the snow showed −14° F., and another, five feet above the surface, −10° F. There was a thaw on January 26–7, but on the 28th the frost returned and continued. Mr. A. Rollin, secretary to the captain superintendent at Sheerness, has also been so good as to send the following note, at the instance of Rear-Admiral C. H. Adair: 'In January 1795 King's Ferry was frozen and also Sheerness Harbour. People walked from ships in the harbour and from the Little Nore to Sheerness on the ice for provisions.' Mr. Rollin mentions similar frosts in January 1776, and January 1789; but has no record of the frost of January 1855, when the harbour, and seaward as far as the eye could reach, was frozen over, forcibly recalling Arctic memories.

resource than to cross the ice on foot, which we did at great hazard, it cracking and bending all the way. I had a small portmanteau, for which I paid a soldier to carry, as he was going the same way; but when we had crossed, his heart failed him and he refused to follow (for we passed over one by one), and it was a long time before we could prevail on him to make the attempt; but by promising him a shilling or two more he took courage until he got half way over, when he imagined the ice was giving way, and there he stood panic-struck. We really felt for the poor fellow, but at last he made a desperate effort and got safe over though dreadfully frightened. After a dismal walk we got to Sheerness, emphatically styled by the late Captain Gunter, R.N., 'the —— hole of the world.'

I found Captain Lee in lodgings; he seemed much surprised at seeing me as he had no communication with the admiralty for a long time. He seemed astonished at my walking across the ferry, which he considered a very hazardous undertaking. After waiting a few days we forced a passage through the ice and got on board; and soon after, followed his worship, old Stamp, the Mayor of Queenborough, as pilot, and well known as a most respectable boroughmonger of large property and powerful interest, and would be a pilot merely because he liked it. We soon got under way, and in a few hours anchored in the Downs, where we found the Leopard, 50 (the flagship), and several men of war. We remained but a short time and then proceeded to Spithead with a convoy.

We were on this service up and down Channel, and to Ireland, for several months without anything material happening, until being off Waterford, after seeing the convoy safe, we saw a suspicious lugger, which we gave chase to and, after a run of forty leagues, had the good fortune to capture—the Speedwell, smuggling lugger, pierced for eighteen guns which she had thrown overboard, as we counted the carriages that were disposed of soon after the guns. Her cargo consisted of spirits, tobacco, tea, nankins, etc., with thirty-nine gigantic smugglers; one we supposed was killed, as her muster roll had forty. We pressed the crew and took the vessel to Belfast, where her cargo was sold. Captain Lee, who was a good calculator, offered the first lieutenant, Hickey, and myself £58 15*s.* apiece for our prize-money, which after some consideration we accepted; but when the prize-money was paid, the share of a lieutenant was only £50, so that he lost by the spec. £17 10*s.*, besides losing with the marine officer. We kept the crew as part of our ship's company, but they contrived to desert at different times with the exception of four.

I well remember while lying in Dublin Bay, and being at breakfast with Captain Lee, in course of conversation he observed that the four remaining smugglers were the best men in the ship and that he was very proud of them. He had hardly made the observation when the officer of the watch reported that the jolly boat was missing; the hands were immediately turned up to muster, when it was found that the four worthies had set off in the boat, when or where nobody could tell. The captain looked at us, and we at him, but no one could keep countenance. It could not be proved in whose watch the boat was taken. We found her at Dunleary, but never heard of the deserters.

While at Carrickfergus the assizes were held and we had an invitation to dine with the grand jury. We passed a very pleasant day; upwards of two hundred were present, and several excellent songs were sung by one of the counsellors, who was considered equal to Braham or Incledon.[1] Having proceeded to Plymouth with a convoy we remained some time in the Sound, when the Medusa, 50, Captain James Norman, arrived with the West India convoy, part of which had been captured by the enemy's cruisers, and we were put under his orders to proceed with the convoy to the Downs.

It is well remembered by those who are not too young that the latter end of 1795 was a very tempestuous season, and it was a long time before an opportunity offered to sail; we once made the attempt and had nearly got on shore near the Mewstone. In working out, our main topsail yard was carried away in a squall, and we were obliged to anchor; but the gale increasing, the cable was cut, and we again anchored in the Sound. On November 3, the wind being favourable, the commodore made the signal to get under way, and we were ordered to lead up Channel. On the night of the 5th (it being light winds the whole of the time from our leaving the Sound), between Beachy Head and Dungeness it came on to blow a complete hurricane, with heavy rain at south; and on the morning of the 6th, it blew, if possible, harder, and our situation on a lee shore dreadfully alarming, in Rye Bay, with only storm staysails, which at last blew out of

[1] Two very well-known singers. There are probably many still with us who have heard Braham—he did not retire finally till 1852—if only in 'The Bay of Biscay.' Incledon, who died in 1826, served, when a very young man, as an ordinary seaman on board the Formidable, Rodney's flagship in the West Indies. According to the tradition still living 50 or 60 years ago, his talent was found out, and he used to be sent for, first to the ward room and afterwards to the admiral's cabin, to sing after dinner; and when the ship paid off, he came on shore provided with letters of introduction which made the rest of his way easy. The details of his service in the navy, as given in the *D.N.B.*, are certainly erroneous. The Formidable did not go to the West Indies till 1782; and Cleland did not then command her.

the bolt rope; the main topsail also split to pieces from the fourth reef, leaving not a wreck behind, and we expected the ship would upset under bare poles.

As second lieutenant, I was stationed on the forecastle, and seeing a light right ahead I pointed it out to Tim Coghlan, our master, who swore it was Dungeness light and that we were all lost; at the same time asking me for the key of the case, as he was going to step down for a lunch, being infernally hungry and thirsty. I asked Captain Lee, who was on deck all night—for he was an officer that never flinched, and where there was danger he was always to be seen cool and intrepid—to take some refreshment. 'Why,' says he, 'I don't know what to say about the eating part of the business, but I think we shall get plenty to drink, and that presently.'

Had the gale continued at south, nothing could have saved us. With a tremendous sea, and breakers at no great distance, there was no chance of reaching the Downs as we could not get round Dungeness; when in a dreadful squall of thunder, lightning, hail and rain, the wind shifted to north or NNW, which is off the land, and blew with the utmost violence. But towards daylight it got more moderate and we stood for the Downs, where we anchored with part of the convoy in a shattered condition, the remainder coming in soon after. Two of them were lost on the French coast when the wind shifted to the northward.

Captain Lee soon after left the ship, with the good wishes of every officer and man on board. He was a brave, generous, and meritorious officer, an excellent sailor and skilful pilot for the British, as well as Irish Channels, and well deserving of the honours he now enjoys. He was succeeded by

Captain John Bazely, who was one of the best officers in the navy for skill, activity, and high sense of honour, well read, and possessing an excellent understanding, and his death will long be lamented as a loss to the service and to society.

November 19th, another tremendous gale came on at SSW, which lasted the whole of the day and most of the night. This was the gale that Admiral Christian's[1] fleet suffered so much in. We expected every minute to part, and about the last quarter flood we began to drive; but before we could let go our sheet anchor she brought up. The Glebb, 74, the flagship of the Russian admiral (Henikoff) lying abreast of us, parted and brought up with her last anchor within half a mile of the Break. The Montagu, 74, under jury masts, from the westward, anchored in our wake,[2] and run her cable out to the clinch before she brought up. Had she parted, God knows what would have become of us, as it was the height of the gale, with thick weather, and nothing could have prevented her being on board of us, as all her sails were blown from the yards. Had the gale lasted much longer it would been of serious consequenee to the ships in the Downs.

Sailed with a convoy to the westward, which service we were employed on, cruising occasionally in the Channel and Bay, for several months. In May 1796, coming into Plymouth Sound from a cruise, and blowing hard, we anchored astern of the Alfred, 74, who had driven without our being aware of it, so that we found ourselves in an awkward berth without room to moor. We then attempted to get under way, but the gale increasing from the SW, we were unable to weather Mount Batten and

[1] Rear-admiral Sir Hugh Cloberry Christian. See *D.N.B.*

[2] So in MS., evidently a slip for 'hawse.'

came to again. We soon after parted, and let go another anchor and brought up between two rocks in a perilous situation, with two anchors ahead; but fortunately it got more moderate, and, observing there was an undertow, so that when she pitched there appeared no strain upon the cables, we thought there was no occasion to cut away our masts; and our opinion was right, notwithstanding the wish of the knowing ones who came down by hundreds and chalked in large letters on the rocks—'Cut away your masts.' This was dictating with a vengeance by a set of vagabond landsmen, fellows that could rob a house easier than knot a rope yarn, and be damned to them. A lighter with an anchor and cable came out soon after; and the wind shifting, we got under way and anchored in a safe berth.

Sailed to the westward and cruised in the Bay, and on our return to the Sound received orders to proceed to Spithead and fit for foreign service, and about the latter end of August sailed with a small convoy for Quebec. Nothing particular happened until we got on the Banks of Newfoundland, when we fell in with a French squadron under Admiral Richery. It was in the forenoon watch, blowing very hard, the wind WNW with a heavy sea, under a close-reefed main topsail and foresail, when we observed a ship of the line to windward with her head to the SW, under the same sail. Made the private signal, which was not answered. Most of our convoy had parted company in the gale. Bore up and made sail. The enemy also bore up and made all sail in chase until sunset, when he gave over chase and hauled his wind to the northward. We hauled our wind also, and stood to the southward. Separated from the remainder of the convoy during the night, it blowing strong with thick weather. There was great exultation at our outsailing the enemy, and some on board were wishing to have another trial, and their wishes were not disappointed; for in three days after, about six in the morning, two line-of-battle ships were observed astern about two leagues off.

The private signal was made, but not answered. We were under close-reefed topsails and foresail, steering WSW, the wind NW. The enemy made sail and stood after us. We immediately let two reefs out of the topsails, set top-gallant sails and hauled the main tack on board, with jib a third in[1] and spanker. It was neck or nothing, and those who wished for another chase looked rather glum and had not quite so good an opinion of our sailing on a wind as they had when before it. For my part I expected we should upset, and it was with uncommon alacrity in making and shortening sail between the squalls that we escaped upsetting or being taken. The enemy knew well what he was about, for he kept rather on our lee quarter with his fore topmast studding sail boom run out, and the sail ready for setting in case we had kept away. At one time his weather main topsail sheet gave way and he was only ten minutes in setting the sail again; his jib also split, which he unbent and had another set in twenty minutes, which did him great credit. Luckily for us the sea was nearly abeam; had we been on the other tack we must have been taken, as we should then have bowed[2] the sea. I remember heaving the log and she was going ten knots. But notwithstanding our good sailing the

[1] The tack hauled out only two thirds of the length of the jib-boom. *Cf.* D'Arcy Lever's *Young Sea Officer's Sheet Anchor* (1808), p. 84 and fig. 450. Setting the jib in this way seems to have gone out of use in the navy with the introduction of flying jibs.

[2] *Sc.* had the swell on the bow.

enemy gained on us fast, and we should have been captured for a certainty if the Frenchman had possessed more patience.

> Festina lente, not too fast;
> For haste, the proverb says, makes waste.

And so it happened; for a little before six, when he was within gunshot, the greedy fellow let another reef out of his topsails, and just as he had them hoisted, away went his fore yard, jib-boom, fore topmast and main topgallant mast. The other line-of-battle ship was hull down astern. The chase lasted twelve hours, during which time we ran near forty leagues. Shortened sail and wore ship, and as we passed to windward, we counted fifteen ports of a side on his lower deck.

Nothing further happened, except losing a poor fellow overboard in the Gulf of St. Lawrence, until we got to Quebec. The convoy also escaped and came in soon after; one of them was chased, but by fixing a pole on a tub with a lantern on the top, and steering another course in the night, escaped. We remained at Quebec until the latter end of November, and then sailed with a couple of fur ships for England under convoy. We left Quebec in the evening. I had the first watch, and I never shall forget the cold as long as I live.

Nothing remarkable happened until we got to the southward of Cape Clear, which bore north according to our dead reckoning, and if I remember correctly on the 23rd of December 1796, about eight in the evening we saw a squadron of men of war, one of them with a top light, standing to the northward, the wind about west, and at no great distance. We immediately hauled off to the southward, put out all our lights and hailed the two vessels under our charge to do the same. After standing to the southward some time, we altered our course and saw no more of them. The wind soon after shifted to the eastward and blew a heavy gale. Lost sight of our convoy and after buffeting about for some days we were obliged, for want of fuel, to put into Cork, where we found several men of war preparing to sail in consequence of the French being off Bantry Bay. All the carriages and horses that could be found were put in requisition to take the troops to that quarter, and when we had completed our stores and water we sailed with a squadron of frigates under Captain Jon. Faulknor to the southward in quest of the enemy, but they had left Bantry, where Lord Bridport was off with the grand fleet, who we joined with our squadron. I believe this was the time that General Grouchy with eight thousand men (before the arrival of our fleet) anchored in the bay; but from fear, or some other cause, thought it safer to set off than to land; and at Bantry, as well as at Waterloo, shewed great want of judgment.[1]

We were attached to the grand fleet as a repeating frigate; and in January 1797, we chased by signal and captured the French privateer La Favorite, of eight guns and sixty men, out but a short time from Brest and had taken nothing. After removing the chief part of the prisoners, I was put on board as prize master with two midshipmen and twelve men, with orders to stay by the fleet; but on examining her defects I found her in a very bad condition, upon which I separated from the fleet in the evening and stood for the Channel (being then in the Bay). We had nearly been run

[1] This was evidently written with very imperfect knowledge of the facts in either case. From the naval point of view, the only good account of this expedition to Bantry Bay is that contributed by Admiral Colomb to the *Journal of the R.U.S. Institution*, xxxvi. 17 (Jan. 1892).

down by a three-decker—I believe the Prince George, commanded by the late Sir Joseph Yorke—in the rear of the fleet, and the night being as black as Erebus we had a narrow escape. Portsmouth being the place of rendezvous, we stood up Channel with the wind at SW the day after leaving the fleet, blowing a gale, under a close-reefed main topsail and foresail.

We had not an observation for several days before we parted from the grand fleet, and in running up Channel we got into Portland Race. I have been in many noted places, but this infernal race was worse than all, and I expected every moment we should founder. The privateer being deep-waisted, I ordered her ports to be knocked out so as to let the sea have a clear passage through; our hatches were battened down, but we were in danger of being washed overboard. The sea appeared like a pot boiling, and the spray beat over our topsail yards. Hauled off to the southward, and fortunately got safe out of one of the most damnable places I ever was in. The Frenchmen were in the utmost terror and cursed the hour they ever left Brest. By our account we were half-way between the Start and Portland, which was very fair considering everything. During the night it fell calm and towards morning the wind freshened at SE with thick weather; at daylight, stood in and sounded fifteen fathoms near St. Alban's Head, and, it clearing away, bore up and made sail for Plymouth. When near the Start we hoisted the union jack over the French at the gaff end; but the jack blowing away, and the halliards getting foul, we could not for some time haul down the French colours, which frightened a brig that was near, and a frigate coming from Torbay under jury masts fired (I believe) at us but at too great a distance to take effect. However, we got our colours to rights and I hailed the brig, who seemed very much alarmed until I informed him we came from the grand fleet, a prize to the Hind. In the evening we anchored in Cawsand Bay, and next morning I waited on Sir Richard King, the port admiral, who behaved in the kindest manner, and on my explaining my reasons for leaving the fleet he said I did what was very proper.

As no despatches had arrived, I was ordered by Sir Richard to write an account of what happened in the fleet from the day we joined Lord Bridport until I left with the prize, and also to give an account of our proceedings from the time we fell in with Richery's squadron until our arrival at Cork. I was put into a room and desired to take my seat at a table with a quire of foolscap placed before me; and like a fool I looked, for it was a long time before I knew what to write, or how to begin. At last I took courage, and filled three or four sheets; bad grammar, no doubt. Sir Richard read the whole and said it would do very well—many thanks to him. He laughed heartily when I told him I got into Portland Race and what a panic the prisoners were in.

I had sent a pilot off to take the brig into Hamoaze and walked down with Sir Richard to Mutton Cove, as he wished to see her as she passed. He told me he was once put prize master when a lieutenant, on board of such another and had left the fleet as I had done and for the same reason. This made me easy and quieted my fears. Captain Bazely's father was port admiral in the Downs, and I wrote to him stating our arrival and received an answer thanking me for the information respecting his son. We had not been long at Plymouth before the Hind left the fleet and put into

Portsmouth, and not finding me there supposed we were lost, until Captain Bazely received a letter from his father saying he had heard from me, and that we were all well and safe at Plymouth, and in a few days I received the following letter from Captain Bazely :

Hind, Portsmouth, February 1797.

'Gardner, my good fellow, I am truly happy to find you are in the land of the living, and that it was through necessity you put into Plymouth. We are ordered to Sheerness to dock, where I shall be devilish glad to see you ; so get on board some vessel bound to the Downs with your party, and be sure to call on my father, who will be very glad to see you and will send some craft to take you to the Nore. We are all well.—Believe me to remain, with best wishes,

'Yours most faithfully,

'John Bazely, Junr.'

After clearing the prize and delivering her up to Mr. Hemmings, the master attendant at Plymouth and agent for Lord Bridport (who I have every reason to thank for his great civility while I remained in Hamoaze, in the many invitations I had to dine at his house, where he made a point to introduce me to the captains who visited there) I was put on board the Medusa, 50, commanded by my old messmate Jack Eaton, who was to take us as far as Portsmouth. On our arrival at Spithead we were put on board the Weasel, commanded by Captain Lewis, and sailed for the Nore, where we soon arrived and joined our ship at Sheerness, and I was well received by the captain and my messmates. Went into dock and when refitted proceeded to Portsmouth, where we remained but a short time and sailed with a convoy for Oporto. We had a very pleasant passage and took out Captain A. Ball on his way to join his ship, who left us off Oporto. On our return we recaptured a brig in the Bay of Biscay, and I was put on board as prize master; but from ill-health I went back to my ship and the first lieutenant took charge of the prize in my room.

On our arrival at Spithead, the latter end of April 1797, we found the fleet in a high state of mutiny. We had orders to fit for foreign service, and I had directions to go with a party of seamen and marines to the dockyard for new cables and stores. The mutiny, which in some measure had been suppressed, broke out afresh on board the London, 98, Vice-Admiral Colpoys, and some of the mutineers were killed; but the officers were overpowered and the admiral's flag struck by the scoundrels, and the bloody flag of defiance hoisted in its room. I went with my party to the yard in the morning and began to get off the stores, when a marine said he would not assist in rousing the cable into the lighter and advised the others to knock off; upon which I told him if he did not immediately take hold of the cable with the rest I would cut him down (which was my intention). This had the effect and he went to work with the others. When I got on board our men were in a state of mutiny, and every ship at Spithead and St. Helen's the same. I had the first watch that night, and the master relieved me at twelve, and everything seemed quiet; but about three bells in the morning watch I was sent for by the captain, and on my coming on deck I found the ship's company assembled there and the captain, in the most impressive manner, requesting them to return to their duty, but all to no purpose. Had we been the only ship, we should soon have driven the scoundrels to the devil; but as we were situated, surrounded by line-of-battle ships acting in the same disgraceful manner, it would have been of little use to resist. About six a paper was handed up to the captain with the following order in writing :—

'It is the unanimous opinion of the ship's company that Captain Bazely, Lieutenants Hickey and Gardner, Mr. White, the purser, and Messrs. Kinneer and Allen, midshipmen, are to quit the ship by 6, or violent measures will be taken to enforce the order.'

Soon after 6 the barge was manned and armed; every vagabond had a cutlass, and our trunks were handed in, with orders from the delegates not to carry them anywhere for us. I had a brace of pistols with a double charge which I put in my great-coat pockets in case I should want their assistance. It was blowing a gale of wind at NE when we left the ship, and near ten o'clock before we landed on Point beach; our things were handed out, and I desired the bowman and one or two more, who I knew to be great scoundrels, to take them to Turner's (living on the beach, and only a step from the boat) shewing them at the same time my pistols and saying, 'You understand me.' They then most reluctantly took our things to the place I directed. This was all I wanted, as I heard some of the ringleaders say as we were quitting the ship 'that if any of the boat's crew assisted in taking our things to any place after landing they should be severely ducked on their return'; and they were as good as their word; for those fellows got a fine ducking the moment they got on board, the others having reported them.

We left the Hind in May 1797, but before I close my account I must relate a few anecdotes as they come to my recollection. I shall begin with the surgeon, who was a very worthy fellow and much respected, but was strange, so that we thought him half cracked, and he had the name of Benjamin Bullock the Madman (a character in some work that I forget). I was one morning walking the deck with him when the postman came on board and presented a letter directed to 'Robert Anderson, Esq., or Benjamin Bullock, Esq., Surgeon of H.M. ship Hind. With speed.' The letter ran thus: 'Take care when you are going on shore, and do not on any account pass the Devil's Point where Bullocks are put to death daily for the use of the fleet. So no more at present from yours to command, J. TALGOL, Slaughter House, Devil's Point.'

He accused me of writing the letter, but he was mistaken, and from that day to this I know nothing of the author. He was greatly enraged and vowed vengeance against me and my friend Harley the purser, who was the person that gave him the name of Ben Bullock. It happened some time after that Harley and myself were going on shore and Anderson said he would take a passage with us. When near the Devil's Point, which we had to pass, I gave orders to the boat's crew to pull with all their might, 'Give way, my lads, give way until we pass this place.' Anderson looked at me and said, 'What the hell are you afraid of now? You are always croaking about some damned thing or other.' 'My good fellow,' says I, 'it is on your account that I am so anxious. Don't you remember the friendly letter you had warning you to beware of the Devil's Point? It is on this account that I want to pass it in such a hurry, as you may be taken out and cut up for fresh beef.' And what made things worse, on our landing the first object that drew our attention was a large board over a warehouse, with 'Bullock and Anderson' on it in gilt letters of immense size, to his astonishment and vexation.

At another time, when we had a large party on board I was sitting at the bottom of the table and Anderson at the head as caterer. I happened to be in conversation with Harley, who in the heat of argument was energetically moving his hand up and down; which Anderson observed, and leaving the head of the table with a knife in each hand, he placed himself between me and Harley, and holding a knife against our breasts says he: 'That's for thee, and that's for thou; I know well what you meant by moving your hand up and down like a cleaver cutting up bullocks for the fleet, and be damned to you both. Now do it again if you dare.' After some difficulty we persuaded him to go to the head of the table again; but those who were strangers to his whims looked on him with an evil eye.

Our master (Coghlan) was a very droll fellow and fond of carrying sail in a boat. Being sent from the Sound to the dockyard on duty, it came on to blow a heavy gale of wind, and we struck yards and topmasts. In the first watch about six bells I was walking the deck with Captain Lee, who observed how glad he was our boat was safe, as he had no doubt Mr. Coghlan had gone on board the flagship in the harbour. He had not long made the observation, when I thought (it being moonlight) I saw something in the direction of Drake's Island and pointed it out to Captain Lee, who said it could not be a boat, as nobody would be mad enough to risk his life on such a night. By this time the object drew near, when to our astonishment we were hailed by Coghlan to throw a rope, and in a moment he flew alongside. We got the yard and stay tackles over instantly, got the men in, and ran the boat up in safety although a heavy sea was running. When

Coghlan came upon deck, the captain asked if he was not ashamed of himself in risking the lives of the people in the wanton manner he had done. Tim with the greatest simplicity said, 'Sir, if you had seen her (meaning the boat) fly from the top of one sea to another without stopping between, you would really have admired her. She darted through the breakers when crossing the Bridge (a dangerous reef of rocks between Drake's Island and Mount Edgcumbe) like a race horse. I never was in such a boat in my life.' Captain Lee, vexed as he was, could not help smiling, at the same time telling Tim if he did so again strange things would take place. Coghlan's name was John, but someone had written to Steel saying his name was Timothy and it was put so on the list. Coghlan on this wrote to say it was not his name and requested Steel to alter it; but the same wag who had written before did so again, and when the list was printed his name stood as John Timothy Coghlan, and remained so, and we always called him Tim.[1] He has gone to his long home and has left behind the character of an honest and worthy fellow. He left the Hind to be master of the Trent, 36, going to the West Indies. I dined with him a short time before he sailed, and he was pointing out the different members of the mess, saying that none of them could live in such a climate. Poor fellow, he little thought while making that remark that they all returned and he the only one that sunk the victim of all-conquering death.

At the time we had nearly got on shore and lost an anchor near the Mewstone, when working out with the convoy, I was sent the next morning to

[1] Possibly; but on joining the Hind, his name was entered John Timothy Coghlan in the pay-book.

acquaint Commissioner Fanshawe[1] of the circumstance, and to request he would order a lighter with a new cable and to weigh the anchor we had lost. I recollect he was dressed in an old blue coat with a red handkerchief about his neck, and in a very crabbed humour. After staring at me for some time he roared out, 'I shall do no such thing. What brought you there? Go and tell your captain if he gets into a hole he must get out of it again. I shall give him no assistance and you may be off and tell him so.' I told him that we were out of the hole and that I only delivered my orders as I was directed. At the same time I would thank him to write down the words he had just made use of, as verbal messages were uncertain. 'Be off, sir,' says he, 'and if your memory is good enough to recollect what your captain said you cannot forget what I have stated; so no more palaver'; and grinning at me with a horrid set of teeth, he concluded by saying, 'I have other things to think of than bothering my brains about people who get into a lubberly situation and don't know how to get out.' I looked at him without making any reply, when, turning on his heel, he said, 'Aye, you may look';

> Nor more he deigned to say,
> But stern as Ajax' spectre, strode away.

As I am not fond of making mischief, I thought it best to say nothing to Captain Lee but merely state he refused to send the lighter. This put the captain in a terrible rage, but the lighter being sent off the next morning, the matter ended. Commissioner Fanshawe was one of the first seamen in the

[1] Captain Fanshawe commanded the Monmouth in Byron's action at Grenada, July 6, 1779, and the Namur on April 12, 1782. He was for many years resident commissioner at Plymouth. *Cf. N.R.S.* vols. xii., xix. and xxiv.

navy, and also one of the bravest officers that ever did honour to the service, a rigid disciplinarian, and to sum up all, a tight hand of the watch, as the saying is.

Coming from the westward to the Downs and when round the Foreland, the captain ordered the colours to be hoisted, when up went a swaggering French ensign and jack, which at first was not taken notice of, but was soon observed by the captain, who ran forward calling out to me, 'Look at the French jack, sir; haul it down directly.' 'Sir,' said I, 'the French ensign is at the mizen peak.' This he had not seen, and I thought he would have gone jumping mad. However, they were hauled down; but as if the devil would have it, instead of our own, up went Dutch colours. Nobody could keep their countenance, and a general laugh went through the ship and also in the men of war lying in the Downs who had observed the transaction.

While at Carrickfergus we were on very friendly terms with the officers of the Irish militia and dined often at the different messes. I remember on a rejoicing day calling with some more on the officers of the Cavan militia. On going upstairs to their messroom, we found several seated round the fire with a half barrel of gunpowder busily employed making fireworks for the evening amusement. Our visit was not of long duration, and I can truly say for myself that I only made one step downstairs and was off like a shot—

> Nor cast one longing, lingering look behind.

When in Hamoaze our boatswain was tried by a court martial for repeated drunkenness and dismissed the service. At the trial the captain of the Tremendous, 74, was unable to attend from indisposition, and the surgeon being sent for to attend the court and give in his report, he happened to make some remarks that the court considered disrespectful; upon which he was given in charge o. Lieutenant Richards, first of the Cambridge, 84, on board of which ship the trial took place, until the court should determine. He was not long kept in suspense, for on the court opening he was sentenced to three months' imprisonment in the Marshalsea for contempt of court,[1] and sent off that day. People should be careful.

On the passage to Quebec, after parting from our convoy, about eight in the evening, with little wind and going two knots, and nothing in sight, a voice was heard astern hailing, 'On board the Hind, ahoy!' I must confess I was a little staggered, and some curious remarks were made by the seamen. One fellow said, 'I'll be damned if we were off the Cape but I should think it was the Flying Dutchman.' 'As to that,' says another, 'he has got a roving commission and may cruise where he likes.' 'Bad luck to me,' says a marine, 'if it's not a mermaid.' 'And to sum up,' says old Macarthy, the quartermaster, 'it may be the poor fellow that fell overboard the other day.' However, the voice hailed again, saying, 'Bear a hand and send the boat, for I'm damned if I can keep up much longer.' The jolly boat was immediately lowered down from the stern and sent in the direction of the voice; and will it be believed that the fellows were afraid to take into the boat one of the main topmen (who had fallen overboard out of the main chains, being half asleep) until he had told his name and answered several ridiculous questions?

[1] This power of committing for contempt belongs inherently to a court martial, as a court of record, though it is now seldom, if ever, called on to exercise it (Thring's *Criminal Law of the Navy*, 2nd edit, p. 103).

At the time we took the privateer, it was given out by our lying newspapers that the French were starving. On the contrary the French officers told me that everything was abundant in France, and—if I may judge from what was on board—their account was correct; for she had barrels of meat of every description—alamode beef, ham, fowls, and tongues, casks filled with eggs, coffee, tea, and sugar, all kinds of cordial, with plenty of brandy and different wines; so that instead of starvation, there appeared the luxury of Lucullus, when supping in the Apollo.[1] The French officers belonged to some of the line-of-battle ships at Brest, but had leave from the French Government to go on board privateers for a certain time and cruise after our merchantmen. When we arrived at Plymouth they requested me to state this to the proper authorities in the hope of getting their parole. This I accordingly did, but without success, as they were given to understand that being taken in a privateer they could not be considered as officers entitled to parole.[2]

I found them very intelligent gentlemen; one of them spoke English remarkably well and gave a very interesting account of the revolution and of the leading characters then in power without any partiality. The opinion, he said, in France was that the nobles and the clergy were the instigators of anarchy and confusion, and the people did not know how to put a stop to it. I must here mention that one of our men who I had placed as a sentry,

[1] This has no meaning, unless we can suppose 'Apollo' to have been written inadvertently for 'Favorite.'

[2] On the part of the French this was a very old contention; sometimes, as here, with a view to obtaining better treatment as prisoners; at other times, with a view to being exchanged on more favourable terms. *Cf.* Laughton's *Studies in Naval History*, pp. 258–9.

fell asleep at his post, which was observed by a French officer who, to his honour, informed me of the circumstance. I need not say how I thanked him. When they were sent to Mill Prison I went with them and did everything in my power in recommending them to the officers belonging to the prison, who promised to make them as comfortable as they possibly could. I had but little money, which I divided among them. We shook hands at parting and they gave me their address, saying how happy they should be to see me in France when the war was over. One of those gentlemen had been a prisoner before in England and had his quarters at Petersfield.

RICHARD LEE, Esq., Captain.

An admiral of the blue, K.C.B., Knight of the Tower and Sword. An excellent officer and seaman. He commanded the Courageux, 74, when Sir Richard Strahan captured Dumanoir's squadron. [Died 1837.—Marshall, ii. 568.]

JOHN BAZELY, Esq., Captain.

Dead [1827]. A vice-admiral of the blue. He was one of the best officers in the navy, and much lamented by numerous friends and particularly by his old shipmates.

FREDERICK HICKEY, 1st Lieutenant.

A post captain and magistrate at Swansea; an excellent officer. [Died 1839.—Marshall, vii. 227.]

JAS. A. GARDNER, 2nd Lieutenant.

A commander.

JOHN COGHLAN, Master.

Dead. A most worthy fellow.

[GEORGE] PATON, Master.

Dead. A quiet, good sailor.

CHRISTOPHER NOBLE, Lieutenant of marines.

Dead from his wounds. A major; as brave and generous a fellow as ever lived.

GEO. WHITE, Purser.

Dead. He had many good qualities, and many bad ones.

ROBERT ANDERSON, Surgeon.

Dead. A very strange and worthy fellow.

ROBERT DUNHAM, Acting Lieutenant.

Dead. A lieutenant. He was made lieutenant in 1781, but broke and was reinstated in 1795; a very clever fellow, but as obstinate as the devil.

[JAMES] MOORE, Gunner.

Dead. A very good sailor.

[ARCHIBALD] FREEBURN, Gunner.

Uncertain.

FLEMMING, Boatswain.

Uncertain. Broke by court martial; a very good seaman but drank hard.

[CHRISTOPHER] HUMPHRIES, Boatswain.

Dead. A very good seaman and much respected.

[ROBERT] BIGGERY [or BAGRIE], Carpenter

Superannuated; a very worthy fellow.

[GEORGE] PORTER, Mate.

A commander; a smart officer.

[JOHN] NAZER, Mate.

Dead. A lieutenant; a very good and very ugly fellow

[THOMAS] ALLEN, Midshipman.

Drowned. A fine spirited young man.

[BENJAMIN] BADCOCK, Midshipman.

Drowned. A fine spirited young man.

[JAMES JERVIS] KINNEER, Midshipman.

Drowned in the Lutine, 36; a lieutenant.

FRANCIS GEARY GARDNER LEE, Midshipman.

Sir F. G. G. Lee; a major in the royal marines and lieutenant-colonel in the Spanish army.

CHUBB, Clerk.

Drowned in the cutter with poor Allen.

[JONAS] TOBY, Clerk.

Dead. A purser. [Purser of the Euryalus at Trafalgar; author of the plan of the battle which was sent home to Lord Barham, and published as a separate sheet and in the *Naval Chronicle*, vol. xiv.]

BLONDE, 32

I WAS appointed first lieutenant of the Blonde, 32, Captain Daniel Dobree, and commissioned her at Chatham early in March 1798, and soon after got a draft of twenty-seven hands and a midshipman from the Standard, 64, which was all I had to fit her out with, and of that number, only five knew how to turn a dead-eye in. However, we contrived to get her hold stowed, sails bent, and topgallant yards across, before we had any addition of men or officers. At last our complement was completed by a draft from the Dordrecht,[1] 64, and went to Black Stakes, where we took in our powder and proceeded to the Downs. We had a crack ship's company with our last draft, and in getting topgallant yards up the morning after we arrived, we crossed ours, sent them down again, and then swayed away and had them ready for crossing before the flagship and the rest of the men of war at anchor. Vice-Admiral Peyton[2] was the port admiral, and had his flag on board the Overyssel,[3] 64, commanded by my late worthy friend Captain John Bazely. I expected we should have got a reprimand for being too hasty in our movements, especially when I saw a boat

[1] One of the Dutch ships taken at the Cape of Good Hope in August 1796.

[2] Joseph Peyton; admiral, June 1, 1795.

[3] Taken possession of in Cork Harbour, Aug. 22, 1795.

coming from the flagship; however, instead of a rub down, it proved to be a visit from Captain Bazely, who paid us many compliments on the good order the ship appeared to be in. He told me there was a vacancy on board the flagship for a lieutenant and that he would apply for me if I wished it, at the same time stating that he was on bad terms with the admiral, who was at all times a harsh and disagreeable officer, and in the event of his getting a frigate (which he was in expectation of) he had no doubt would prevent me (to annoy him) leaving the flagship, and advised me to remain in the Blonde until he had an opportunity of serving me.

Having received orders, we proceeded to Spithead and took command of a small squadron of gun-boats and cutters to guard the Needles passage, and anchored off Jack in the Basket, near Lymington, which service we performed very agreeably for several weeks. The rebellion in Ireland taking place, we were ordered with several men of war and transports to proceed to Weymouth and embark troops for that country. The king, being at Weymouth at the time, with the royal family, it was expected he would review the squadron; but the news from Ireland being very serious, the troops were embarked in a hurry, and we got under way in company with the men of war and transports for our destination.

I must here mention that the commodore of the squadron (Captain Hardy,[1] commanding a 64) came on board with several other captains, and after going round the ship and mustering us at quarters, he addressed me, saying, 'Sir, I feel great satisfaction in stating that the Blonde is in the best order of any ship in the squadron and the fittest to receive

[1] James Hardy, of the Dictator.

his Majesty, should he go afloat; and for the short time your ship has been in commission she does great honour to her captain and officers.' This he said before the rest of the captains, and among the number was my old captain (Towry) formerly of the Berwick. In fitting out the ship at Chatham, I did everything I could to keep on good terms with the officers of the yard by asking them down to our mess and paying them every little attention in my power; and by that means I had an opportunity of getting many things done to beautify the ship.[1] I had the head painted in colours, the quarters friezed, a famous stand made for the arms on the quarter deck, and trophies painted on our scuttle-butts, with half circles and circles for our pistols and cutlasses, which made the old Blonde cut a dashing appearance.

Just as we were getting under way, Captain Hardy sent me four or five buckets of paint, with his compliments, saying I should stand in need of it after getting rid of the soldiers, which was really the case, as on board they were the most helpless and dirty devils I ever beheld—except the Russians. It was impossible to get them up from between decks without burning green wood in the stoves, which the devil himself could not stand, the smoke was so intolerable.[2]

After a quick passage we landed the troops at Waterford, where we remained a short time and then returned to our station, to guard the Needles passage for a few weeks. The Europa, 50, being sent to relieve us, got aground near Gurnet Point, and after lying there some time was got off and

[1] A similar method of beautifying a ship fitting out was the rule rather than the exception till long after Gardner's time.

[2] In 1852 the crew of a whaler in Baffin's Bay mutinied and struck work, till a pan of burning sulphur 'cleared lower deck.'

returned to Portsmouth to refit. More troops being ordered to Ireland, we were put under the orders of Captain Geo. Burdon and sailed with a small squadron consisting of the following men of war :—

Alkmaar[1]	54	Capt. Geo. Burdon, commodore
Tromp[2].	54	Capt. Worsley
Blonde	32	Capt. Dobree
Weymouth store ship	—	

On the passage we had near got on the Seven Stones. I had the morning watch, and soon after I relieved the deck I observed breakers upon the lee bow and beam and at no great distance; the wind about NNW, and our heads to the westward, blowing fresh with a chop of a sea. The Alkmaar was ahead, on the weather bow, and the Tromp to windward, the Weymouth astern of all. We were under double reefed topsail and foresail and no time to be lost; immediately set topgallant sails, jib and spanker; hauled on board the main tack, kept her rap full, and when she had fresh way, put the helm down and she stayed like a top. We made the signal for standing into danger, and when the Alkmaar put her helm down she missed stays, and when they got her head round her stern was close to the breakers. The Tromp, by being to windward and carrying a press of sail weathered the shoals and parted company. In consequence of foul winds we put into Scilly for a few days, and then sailed for Dublin, where we landed the troops.

We were employed upon this service from Dublin to Cork and then to Guernsey, and up and down Channel with convoy, until August 1799, when we received orders to proceed to the Baltic to

[1] Taken at Camperdown. [2] Taken at the Cape.

convey the Russian troops to Holland. Sailed from Spithead, and having taken in pilots proceeded to Elsinore and then to Reval, with some transports. Found lying in the roads the Russian fleet consisting of 15 sail of the line besides frigates, etc., under Admiral Henikoff, and several British men of war and transports. Having embarked some thousands of the Russian guards we left Reval for the Texel, in company with British and Russian men of war and several transports. We had on board a Russian captain, two subs., a surgeon, and 296 privates, all hoffs, choffs, and koffs. The captain's name was Peter Glebhoff, who never pulled his boots off the whole time he was on board. The men were the most filthy I ever met with. They used to scrape the tallow out of the bottoms of the lanterns and make it up into balls, which they would swallow and wash down with a drink of train oil. They had bread made on purpose, of the coarsest flour mixed with vinegar, and their cookery it is impossible to describe; so that the Spartan black broth must have been a luxury (however unpalatable) to their abominable messes. I have positively seen them pick the vermin off one another's jackets, which they would eat without ceremony.

On our arrival at the Texel the whole were immediately landed, and were soon after in action, and the most of those we had on board put *hors de combat* by the next day. Poor Peter Glebhoff, who had been sharpening his spear at the grinding stone a few days before the landing, and vowing to sacrifice every Frenchman he met with, was one of the first that fell. He had been in most of the battles under Suvorof against the Turks and Poles, and had left a wife and family at Riga to lament his fate. He was much liked while on board of us and we all felt heartily sorry for him. I was several times on shore and saw the numerous waggons of wounded soldiers from the scene of action which by no means corresponded with the accounts given in our Gazettes. . . . I had two cousins, captains in the 17th regiment of foot—one of them (Knight) was killed just as I was going to see him.

A short time before we left the Texel the Blanche, 32, Captain Ayscough, got on shore on the Haaks—a dangerous shoal near the Texel, and some of the boats that were sent to her assistance unfortunately upset, and several officers and seamen perished, owing to the surf which ran very high on and near the shoal. The Blanche got off, and returned to the New Deep, and sunk just as she entered, but none of her crew were lost.[1] At this time things looked rather queer, and it was found out after hard fighting that it was not so easy to beat the French out of Holland as at first expected; and we were ordered to take a cargo of runaway Dutchmen on board, with their wives and families —about 400 altogether. A short time before we sailed we saw the Lutine, 36, Captain Launcelot Skynner, at the back of the Haaks, and, if I am correct, the evening she was lost[2] and only one saved, who died soon after.

We left the Texel in November 1799, and in standing over to our own coast had nearly struck by the blunder of our pilots on the Gabbard. After escaping from this first blunder we anchored near the Shipwash, another shoal by far more dangerous than the former. It was in the evening that we took up our quarters in this precious situation, intending to get under way with the morning tide. I must here mention that we had

[1] September 28. [2] October 9. *Cf. D.N.B.*

two pilots; one of them had been a branch pilot for more than twenty years. I had the morning watch, and on relieving the deck I observed to this branch pilot that the weather had a very suspicious appearance. The wind at this time was favourable for getting to sea, and we could lay five points to windward of the tail of the shoal. I strongly urged the pilot to get under way, pointing out the danger of our situation should the wind get dead on the shoal, but all to no purpose. He said there was no fear and he must remain where he was, as he was sure the weather would be fine, and that it was only a light haze over the moon; upon which I went to the captain and gave my opinion. He agreed with me, but did not like to take charge out of the pilots' hands, saying he was fearful, in getting under way, that the ship might get on shore should she cast the wrong way. Now there was no fear of that, as a spring on the cable would have cast her the right way, and the loss of an anchor was of little consequence compared with the risk of losing the ship and our lives.

Far be it from me to reflect upon Captain Dobree, who was a good officer and seaman; and taking charge from a pilot was a great reponsibility; but when a pilot is guilty of a gross error, I should never hesitate to take charge of the ship, if I knew I could do so with safety, which was the case now. But it was neglected, and as I foretold, the wind soon after backed round and blew dead upon the shoal, so that we could not weather either end. At this time we were at single anchor about two or three cable's-lengths from the breakers, blowing strong, and the sea getting up; at half cable; but let go another anchor and veered to a whole cable on the former, and half cable on the latter, bringing two anchors ahead. Sent topgallant masts upon deck, and struck yards and topmasts; the wind increasing to a gale, with a hollow sea and great strain upon the cables. There was no alternative but to cut away the masts, which was immediately done; but owing to an error of one of the officers, who ordered the lanyards of the main stay to be cut before the lanyards of one side of the main rigging, the main mast, in consequence fell aft, and carried away the mizen mast, which stove the boats on the quarters and did considerably damage to the upper works; and some of the rigging caught fire, from the stove in the cabin having the funnel knocked off; but this was soon got under, and with great exertion the wreck was cleared. 'And now, Master Pilot,' says I, 'after getting us in this damnable situation, what next is to be done?' The son of a bitch could make me no answer; but the junior pilot exclaimed '——— seize me if we sha'n't be on the sands.' I could not help saying they deserved to be hanged as drowning was too good for them.

I have already mentioned that we had Dutch troops on board with their families, and of as much use as Castlereagh would have been with the same number of his Lancers or Prancers.[1] The few marines we had were worth a thousand of such live lumber. It was ludicrous to see those Dutchmen coming upon deck with their hat boxes, boots, trunks, flutes and music books, ready to go on shore, when the sea was running mountains high, and a tremendous surf of prodigious height on the sands close under our stern, and no chance whatever, if

[1] Castlereagh was at this time lieutenant-colonel of the Londonderry militia and acting chief secretary for Ireland. The reference would seem to be to the discreditable conduct of the militia in 'the race of Castlebar,' in the previous year. Castlereagh, of course, had nothing directly to do with it.

the ship parted, of a soul being saved; which made Captain Dobree observe to me, 'Where ignorance is bliss 'tis folly to be wise.'

About half-past ten A.M. we parted the best bower, and let go the sheet anchor; and at the greatest risk—it was neck or nothing—veered on the small bower to a whole, and half cable on the sheet, which brought us very near the shoal but there was no help for it. About twelve o'clock we observed that the small bower was stranded; and at the moment when nothing but a miracle could save us, in a terrific squall of thunder, lightning, hail, and rain, the wind suddenly flew round and blew with violence off the shoal, which saved H. M. ship Blonde from destruction. It soon after got moderate; we had an excellent ship's company, and in less than three hours we had jury masts rigged and both anchors hove up—having saved the small bower; made sail and anchored in a safer berth to await the tide.

About eleven P.M. we were surprised by a boat coming alongside with four hands, who stated they belonged to a galliot that had struck upon the tail of the shoal and had beat over into smoother water, where she sunk. The crew had taken to the boat and were six hours beating about before they got alongside of us, and thought we were a floating light. As soon as the morning tide would allow we got under way and followed some merchantmen—for I am certain the pilots did not know the way without having a leader—and arrived at Sheerness in the evening;

> Ragged, and shabby, and all forlorn,
> By wind and weather tattered and torn,
> Occasioned by pilots who treated with scorn
> The good advice that was given that morn;
> For which a rope their necks should adorn,
> The damnedest lubbers that ever were born.

Captain Dobree soon after left the ship to proceed with Sir Home Popham and other captains to Russia, and I acted as captain for several weeks until another was appointed. Having business on shore, I wrote to the admiralty requesting to be superseded, which after a little delay was granted, and Lieutenant Edwin James was appointed in my room. I left the old Blonde and my worthy messmates early in 1800.

I shall now relate a few anecdotes as they come to my memory. When near the shoal I have just mentioned, our surgeon's mate and the ship's cook were almost frightened out of their senses. The former, who would fight any man, or face the devil as soon as let it alone, was not equal to this; and when the junior pilot said, '—— seize me if we shan't be on the sands,' he clapped his hands and ran down to the gun room, with his hair standing on end, crying out, 'Lost! Lost! Lost!'—and then flew on deck again; and when the wind shifted, he cut several capers and said 'I'm a man again.' As for the cook, he had saved a sum of money by keeping shop on board and selling things to the ship's company. At the time the best bower parted, he was on the forecastle in the greatest tribulation; says he, 'Betty' (meaning his wife, who was on board) 'will go to a better mansion, but I'm doubtful about myself.' He had hardly made the observation when the sea broke over the bows that threatened destruction and with a faltering voice he said, 'Liver me! Liver me!'—meaning 'Deliver me,' but could not get the word out. 'Damn your liver, you croaking son of a bitch,' says the captain of the forecastle. 'Go into your coppers and be damned to you, and there you'll be safe, and don't come barking here like a tanner's dog.' I was on the forecastle with Captain Dobree at the time. He looked at me and for my life I could not help laughing.

While at Sheerness we had two courts martial held on board of us[1]; one on Lieutenant Brice, on charges brought against him by Captain Charles Brisbane while on the South American station. The charges being proved, he was sentenced to be dismissed the service and rendered incapable of serving his Majesty, his heirs or successors. This was most unfortunate for Lieutenant Brice, as his commission to the rank of commander only waited the result of his trial. The next was on Captain George Tripp, for the loss of the Nassau, 64, on the Dutch Coast.[2] The court having heard all the evidence came to the following conclusion:—That H.M. ship Nassau was lost through the gross ignorance and inattention of Captain Tripp, and that he did not set a good example to those under his command; and for such conduct he was sentenced to be dismissed from the service as unfit and unworthy, and rendered incapable of serving his Majesty, his heirs or successors.

I promised (page 12) to speak of Pat Gibson when I came to the Blonde. He was at this time (1799) purser of the Pallas, 38 (formerly the Minerva), having given up the Princess Royal as too great an undertaking for his age, being, as he told me, eighty. The Pallas being alongside the same hulk, we were constant visitors. As every circumstance, however trifling, may be interesting, I shall relate a few anecdotes. Gibson was a tall raw-boned Irishman

[1] Gardner's memory is here in fault. The court martial on Brice (for 'having at different times uttered words of sedition and mutiny . . . and for behaving in a scandalous manner unbecoming the character of an officer and a gentleman') was held on board the Blonde on 12, 13 June 1798; that on Tripp, on 6–11 Dec. 1799, was held on board the Pallas. [2] October 14, 1799.

from the county of Tipperary; very powerful, with an Herculean grasp, and woe betide those who got into his clutches if roused to anger. He was a very jovial companion, droll in his manner, full of anecdote, and sung in the Irish language, of which he was a perfect master. He used to go on shore to bring off the drunken Irish who had stayed above their time, and I remember his saying to me, 'Arrah, don't you think, my dear fellow, that it's a hard thing that nobody can manage those spalpeens but an ould man like me, now eighty years of age? Och, By the Holy Father, how I knocked their heads together, and left the mark of my fist upon their ugly podreen faces, bad luck to them.'

He was at the taking of Quebec and was one of those that assisted in carrying General Wolfe off the field when mortally wounded. His account of the battle was very interesting, and in it he fought most manfully. It was amusing to see him sitting in his cabin with his legs stretched outside the door singing Irish songs. The steward once interrupted him, for which he got a thump on the back that sent him the length of the gunroom, Pat saying, 'To hell wid you! take dat till the cows come home.' There was a countryman of his by the name of Fegan, who, in the American war, was sent by Sir John Fielding (the celebrated magistrate of Bow Street) on board the Conquistador, 60, then lying as a guard ship at the Nore with Admiral Roddam's flag. This Fegan was a shrewd, keen fellow, and made a song on being sent on board of a man of war, and Gibson was very fond of singing it. I only remember a few verses:—

The beginning of the war they hobbled poor Fegan,
And sent him on board of the Conquistador;
That floating old gin shop, who struck upon her beef bones,
While laying as a guard ship near the buoy of the Nore.

When first they lugged him before Justice Fielding,[1]
Fegan thus to him did say:
You may be damned, you old blind b——,
I will be back again before Christmas day.

By my sowl, Mr. Fegan, you are a fine fellow,
It's you that have done the king much wrong;
Call Kit Jourdan, the master at arms, sir,
And put Mr. Fegan in double irons strong.

Step here, boatswain's mate, and give him a starting;
Says the first lieutenant it's always my way;
And you shall have many before the day of parting—
I think, Mr. Fegan, you mentioned Christmas day.

Etc., etc., etc.

When I called on him about three months before his death he told me he was then on his last legs; that he had enjoyed an uninterrupted state of health for upwards of ninety years; that he never had the headache, rheumatism, toothache or spasms, and that he had nothing to do with doctors' bottles with collars round their necks, and look, says he, if you can find any of that craft on my chimney-piece. Before I close I must give another song of his:—

There was a wedding at Baltimore,
Of three score people lacking of four;
And you're kindly welcome, welcome all,
And you're welcome, gramachree, welcome all.

The priest of the parish got up at the dawn,
To marry brisk Flemming to sweet Susan Bawn;
And you're kindly welcome, welcome all,
And you're welcome, gramachree, welcome all.

There was Tyghe, and Dermot, and Madam Shevaun,
And they all rode on a long-tailed gar-ron;[2]
And you're kindly welcome, welcome all,
And you're welcome, gramachree, welcome all.

---

[1] Sir John Fielding, brother of the better-known Henry Fielding the novelist, was blind from his birth. It was said that he knew 3,000 thieves by their voice.

[2] Nag.

There was sneezing galore, with full madders [1] of ale,
Which made maidens stagger and men for to reel;
And you're kindly welcome, welcome all,
And you're welcome, gramachree, welcome all.

Potatoes and herrings must please the men,
But madam the bride, she must have a fat hen;
And you're kindly welcome, welcome all,
And you're welcome, gramachree, welcome all.

There was long kail, and pottage, with good pishochbey,[2]
And the rarest colcannon [3] that e'er you did see;
And you're kindly welcome, welcome all,
And you're welcome, gramachree, welcome all.

When the feasting was o'er, from the room she was led,
Where they lay head and points as if they were dead;
And you're kindly welcome, welcome all,
And you're welcome, gramachree, welcome all.

. . . .

Our master, Henry Webb, was a very worthy fellow, but had strange fancies. When we were going from the Downs to Portsmouth, and about three leagues to the southward of Beachy Head, he had the first watch, and having after supper taken his drop, he dropped asleep while sitting on the gun-carriage and had a dream that the ship was on shore. Up he started and ran into the captain, who had gone to bed, and called out, 'Get up, sir, we are all lost.' The captain jumped out of bed and went upon deck in his shirt, and ordered the hands to be turned up, and sent for me. I flew up with only my trowsers on, found everything in confusion, and I really thought that madness had seized the

[1] Milk-pails.

[2] The word is 'piseachbuidhe,' porridge made of Indian meal. A hundred years ago, possibly peas pudding.

[3] Potatoes stewed in butter, with cabbage or onions.

whole. 'Put the ship about, sir, immediately,' says the captain. This I complied with, and when on the other tack I asked him if anything was the matter. 'Mr. Webb, sir,' says he, 'must be sent to the madhouse.' I confess I was not well pleased, as I had the middle watch and this happened at six bells, so I had an hour more than I expected to trudge the deck. I should have stated that the wind was westerly and we were beating down Channel with a moderate breeze. The captain was much inclined to bring Master Webb to a court martial, but we interceded for him and the business was looked over, but he never heard the last of this, and would frequently be greeted with the well-known words, 'Turn out, we are all lost'—a compliment he could well dispense with.

He gave us a droll account that when at Lisbon he missed the boat that was to take the officers off in the evening who were on shore upon leave, and was engaging a shore boat for that purpose; but suspecting from something the boatmen were saying that their intention was to murder him, he took to his heels and hid under some logs in the neighbourhood of Bull Bay and remained there all night in the greatest terror. When he sallied out in the morning he was covered with filth of a yellow hue and appeared at a distance as if he had been dipped in Pactolus! His fright was so great that he was not aware of the bed of roses he had reposed on for so many hours, until he started in the morning with blushing honours thick upon him.

On another occasion, coming up in a small fishing boat from Sheerness to Chatham, he heard two of the men whispering, which he imagined was about himself, and when making a tack and near the mud, out he jumped and began to crawl upon his hands and knees as fast as he could for dry land. The poor fishermen, not knowing what to make of such conduct, ran the boat on the mud and two of them went after him, but to no purpose, it being dark. They called repeatedly, but got no answer from Webb, who was making off in terror and dismay; and what alarmed him more was hearing the men say, 'D'ye see him now? Where the hell can he be got to? He must be hereabouts.' At last he got out of the mud and set off for Chatham in a nice pickle, and told his tale; but the boat had arrived before him and the men in great tribulation had given their version, being fearful of prosecution, expecting that Webb was smothered or drowned; and glad enough they were when he arrived at Chatham and also to join in the laugh against him. One of the fishermen happened to know him by sight and where he lived, and by that means it got publicity.

In cases like this, and where ghosts were introduced, Webb's courage would be put to the test; but in every other respect he was as brave as a lion. While at the Passage of Waterford, he had a dispute with our second lieutenant, and a challenge was the consequence, and they asked me leave to go on shore. As I had the greatest friendship for them both, I refused their request, and went below to the gunroom. Soon after one of the midshipmen came down and informed me they were going out of the ship. Up I went and found them in the jolly boat just shoved off. 'Come back,' says I, 'immediately, or I'll make the sentry fire.' On their return I told them if they did not make it up instantly, I would try them by a court martial for going out of the ship contrary to orders and taking the boat. This had the desired effect, and I had the pleasure of making up the dispute between two as good fellows as ever lived.

The second lieutenant (Jack Derby) was a noisy droll fellow, always keeping the mess in a roar of laughter. The first day he joined the ship we had roast beef for dinner, and when brought to table it was little better than half done by the neglect of our black cook. Now this cook's name was Jack Derby also, whom I sent for, and calling him up to the head of the table close by Lieutenant Jack Derby, says I, 'I am sorry, sir, you should have such a dinner, particularly the first day of your coming on board; but you have to thank that black son of a bitch, Jack Derby'—an emphasis on the word—'whose grog shall be stopped for such neglect.' 'Don't mention it, sir,' says he laughing; 'I shall make a very good dinner, and suppose my name will be inserted on the ship's books as Jack Derby the Second.'

While lying off Lymington our launch was sent to Portsmouth yard for stores, and Derby was sent in her. On her return, our purser (Huish) took a passage. On leaving the harbour the weather was moderate, but soon after came on to blow from the westward. Now the purser was very fearful in a boat, and Derby carried more sail than he ought, on purpose to alarm him. From the harbour to Lymington, the distance is twenty-six miles, and the wind being dead on end they had to beat all the way. Sometimes the boat would be gunwale under, and Huish, terrified almost to death, would every moment rise from his seat and fall again, exclaiming, 'Jesus, Jenny, Jesus, Jenny' (common words of his when things went wrong), and cursed the hour he was fool enough to trust himself with Derby, and if it pleased Providence to spare him now he would never put his foot in a boat with him even in a calm. But his troubles were not yet over, for in getting into the Fiddler's Race near Gurnet

Point, on the Isle of Wight side, with the tide under their lee, there was such a sea breaking that the launch was nearly swamped, and Derby seriously repented his joke; while Huish in despair repeatedly ejaculated, 'Orontes' bark, Orontes' bark will be our fate.' (See *Aeneid* [i. 117]).[1] However, they got safe on board and created much amusement in the account Huish gave of Derby's wickedness.

Being ordered to embark the 23rd regiment foot for Guernsey, and after going through the Needles in the evening, it came on thick weather in the first watch; and about eleven the wind, at SE, began to blow a hurricane, with snow so thick that we could not see half the length of the ship. We sent topgallant yards and topgallant masts upon deck, and hove the ship to under storm staysails. The topsails and courses were frozen as hard as board, and being short of complement it took nearly the whole of the middle watch before they could be furled. One of our main topmen was frozen and died soon after. The officers were also aloft, and all hands suffered most dreadfully. I was speaking to the man at the wheel when a sheet of ice fell out of the mizen top and knocked both of us down. It gave me a severe blow on the shoulder and the other a staggering thump on the back. I was so benumbed when I got below that I had hardly life in me. The officers of the 23rd made me swallow hot brandy and water, and I went to bed, where I had not been above half an hour before all hands were called again, and I was obliged to go on deck. The fact was the fore topsail had got loose and

[1] Are we to understand that Huish also was well up in his Virgil, if only in Dryden's version? Perhaps rather the writer thought this was what he ought to have said.

blew to rags, and the main topsail was nearly following its example, but stopped in time, and we had to bend another fore topsail in this cruel weather. Towards morning it cleared up and got moderate. During the whole course of my life I never suffered so much as I did on that dreadful night. However, we got safe into Guernsey and landed our soldiers. The officers were a glorious set of fellows, and sorry I am that I cannot find any of their names on the list.

The last time we were at the Passage of Waterford was passed very agreeably. I had a cousin (the son of the late Alderman Bates of Waterford) who had an estate in the neighbourhood. He used to send horses and a carriage for the officers of our mess, who were frequently at his house. He was field officer of the district and kept a great deal of company, and gave many parties in honour of the old Blonde. On one occasion he came on board to invite us to an evening party, when he and Jack Derby got into conversation, and at last got so drunk that it was evening before they got sober enough to leave the ship. It was then time to go, and off they started, Derby in full uniform. When the boat landed, he, with all the politeness imaginable, wanted to hand Bates out. This Bates declined. 'Then,' says Jack, 'we'll go together.' Now the gang-board was hardly broad enough for two, and the moment they stepped upon it over they went where the water was four feet deep and got a fine ducking. Derby would not return to the ship, but, mounting a horse belonging to Bates, set off in his wet clothes to meet the party, and there Bates dressed him in regimentals, and a precious figure he cut. We passed a very pleasant evening, there being near seventy present. One of the ladies sung the beautiful air of 'Eileen Aroon' in Irish—

a translation of which I met with a few years ago and give it as follows :—

I'll love thee evermore,
        Eileen aroon.
I'll bless thee o'er and o'er,
        Eileen aroon.
Oh, for thy sake I'll tread
Where the plains of Mayo spread,
By hope still fondly led,
        Eileen aroon.

Oh ! how may I gain thee,
        Eileen aroon ?
Shall feasting entertain thee,
        Eileen aroon ?
I would range the world wide,
With love alone to guide,
To win thee for my bride,
        Eileen aroon.

Then wilt thou come away,
        Eileen aroon ?
Oh ! wilt thou come or stay,
        Eileen aroon ?
Oh yes ! oh yes ! with thee
I will wander far and free,
And thy only love shall be,
        Eileen aroon.

A hundred thousand welcomes
        Eileen aroon.
A hundred thousand welcomes,
        Eileen aroon.
Oh ! welcome evermore,
With welcomes yet in store,
Till love and life are o'er,
        Eileen aroon.

We had a fidgety and crabbed commodore (Captain Stevenson of the Europa, 50) who neither enjoyed pleasure himself nor would let anyone else do so : who kept Blue Peter flying the fortnight we remained, which said No! to every invitation to the city.

In going from Portsmouth to the Downs we gave a passage to an assistant surgeon, red hot from the land of cakes, who had never been on board of a man of war, and had now an appointment to a gun vessel. Seeing that he was a complete greenhorn, we took him into our mess that the midshipmen should not make a butt of him, for which he was very thankful. On leaving the ship in the Downs, he took the surgeon aside, saying, 'You have all been very kind to me, particularly the purser, and I would wish to make him some acknowledgment. D'ye think if I gave him three pounds of cheese!!! it would satisfy him?' After he landed at Deal he put up at the Three Kings. Captain Dobree, happening to go into the coffee room, observed him in one of the boxes, and hearing him ask the waiter what there was for dinner, stayed to hear the result. The bill of fare being given him, he ordered an apple pie, which was brought him made in a good-sized dish. This he devoured in a short time, and ordered the fellow to bring him another, which he demolished also, and then rang the third time and asked him if he had any more of those pies. On the waiter saying they had, he said, 'You may as well bring me one more,' upon which Captain Dobree exclaimed 'Merciful father!' and left him in his glory. The captain told me this the moment he came on board, saying he never met the fellow of him in all his peregrinations.

About six months after this a small squadron of gun vessels were ordered from the Downs to cruise on the French coast. It happened that his appointment was dated before the other assistant surgeons in the above squadron, and will it be believed that he considered himself entitled to the same rank and emoluments as physician of the fleet, and made application for the same, and got for answer (as we were told) that the board disapproved of the whole of his practice.

DANIEL DOBREE, Esq., [Acting] Captain.
Dead [1802]. A good officer, seaman, and gentleman. [Post-captain, April 29, 1802.]

J. A. GARDNER, 1st Lieutenant.
A commander.

JOHN WORRALL, 2nd Lieutenant.
Dead [1831]. A commander; crabbed.

JOHN DERBY, 2nd Lieutenant.
Dead. Warden at Portsmouth yard.

HENRY J. LYFORD, 2nd Lieutenant.
Dead [1830]. A post captain.—[Marshall, vii. 170.]

WM. GIBSON, 2nd Lieutenant.
Broke by court martial and rendered incapable of serving, for going on shore without leave to fight a duel.

EDWIN JAMES, 2nd Lieutenant.
Dead [1829]. A commander.—[Marshall, xi. 156.]

HENRY WEBB, Master.
Dead. A worthy, honest fellow.

ROBERT HUISH, Purser.
Dead. A droll fellow and good mimic.

[JOHN] TUCKER, Purser.
Dead. Thoughtless and extravagant.

J[AMES] MILLIGAN Surgeon.
Dead. A worthy fellow.

[JOHN] HARRISON, Gunner.
Dead. A very good warrant officer.

JOHN BLACKFORD, Boatswain.
Dead. A willing man, but drank.

[THOMAS] NEWPORT, Carpenter.
Dead. Broke by court martial.

[JAMES] THOMAS, Mate.
Uncertain. A good-natured Irishman.

[Edward] Caulfield, Midshipman.
Dead. A lieutenant.

[Charles] Doncaster, Midshipman.
Dead from yellow fever at Jamaica. A fine, promising young man. [Borne as 'boy of the 1st class'; afterwards midshipman.]

Frederick Houghton, Midshipman.
Drowned. A lieutenant.

Chas. Houghton, Midshipman.
A lieutenant. They were sons of Major [Daniel] Houghton [*cf. D.N.B.*], the African traveller.

Daniel Dobree, Midshipman; son of the captain.
Dead.

[William] Blackford, son of the boatswain.
Dead. A lieutenant; a worthy character. [Borne as 'boy of the 3rd class'; afterwards midshipman.]

BRUNSWICK, 74

> This flat-floored tub that rolled like the devil,
> Was planned by Black Dick in an hour most evil.

In April 1801 I was appointed to the Brunswick in Portsmouth harbour and did duty as first lieutenant until the senior officer made his appearance, which was not until I had fitted the ship out. This officer was my old shipmate, Jack Key, formerly of the Barfleur, and one totally unfit for the situation. In consequence, Captain George Hopewell Stephens, who commanded the ship, was obliged to apply to the admiralty for an officer senior to Key, and Emanuel Hungerford was appointed first lieutenant, Captain Stephens expressing his regret at the circumstance, observing that it was a hard case but that he would do everything in his power to serve me. He was as good as his word, and I found him through life a sincere friend. Hoisted the flag (red at the mizen) of Rear Admiral John Holloway, as junior port admiral, and received orders to proceed without loss of time to Spithead; and having struck the flag, sailed to join the North Sea fleet under Admiral Dickson, who had his flag (blue at the main) on board the Blenheim, 74. After cruising several weeks and putting into Yarmouth Roads occasionally, we were next ordered to join the grand fleet under Admiral Cornwallis (Billy Blue) off Brest blockading the French fleet until the negotiations for peace; when, in consequence of the French sending a squadron to the West Indies, our admiral detached from the grand fleet five sail of the line in October 1801 for the same destination. The squadron consisted of the following men of war:—

Goliath	74	Captain Essington, as commodore
Captain	74	Captain C. Boyles
Elephant	74	Captain Thos. Foley
Brunswick . . .	74	Captain Geo. Hopewell Stephens
Ganges	74	Captain Fremantle

We had a pleasant passage down the trades and made Deseada some time in November, and had a beautiful view of the West India Islands; and in about a week after making Deseada we arrived at Port Royal, Jamaica, and found lying there the following men of war:—

Sans Pareil . . .	84	Rear-Admiral Montagu—Captain Jas. Katon
Carnatic	74	Captain H. W. Bayntun
Cumberland . . .	74	Captain Penrose
America	64	A hulk
Admiral de Vries .	56	A cooperage
Abergavenny . .	54	A guard-ship
Vengeance . . .	44	A French frigate: a prize
Melampus . . .	36	Captain Thos. Le M. Gosselin, etc.

We remained about ten weeks in sweet Port Royal harbour, until the arrival of Rear-Admiral

Sir John Thomas Duckworth, K.B., as commander-in-chief, who had his flag (red at the mizen) on board the Leviathan, 74, and then sailed with a small squadron to cruise off the Island of Navasa, Cape Tiburon, etc., for several weeks under Rear-Admiral Montagu. In 1802 (I don't remember the month) Rear-Admiral George Campbell arrived with the fleet from England, which cut a very fine appearance.[1] The like had not been since the days of Rodney, viz. :—

Leviathan . . .	74	Rear-Admiral Duckworth, K.B. Captain Richard D. Dunn
Sans Pareil . . .	84	Rear-Admiral Montagu Captain Jas. Katon
Temeraire . . .	98	Rear-Admiral Geo. Campbell Captain [C. Eyles][2]
Princess Royal . .	98	Captain
Formidable . . .	98	Captain [Rich. Grindall][2]
Carnatic	74	Captain
Cumberland . . .	74	Captain Penrose
Goliath	74	Captain Essington (then Brisbane)
Spencer	74	Captain [Henry D'E. Darby][2]

[1] Attention is called by Ralfe (*Naval Biography*, ii. 286) to the remarkable fact that a fleet of 28 ships of the line should be under the command of a rear-admiral.

[2] The captains' names, left blank in the MS., are filled in from Schomberg; but it should be noted that when rapid changes are being made, it is frequently difficult to say who commanded a ship at a particular time. Some of the names given by Gardner do not agree with Schomberg's lists.

Captain	74	Captain C. Boyles
Ganges	74	Captain Fremantle
Elephant	74	Captain T. Foley (then Dundas)
Brunswick . . .	74	Captain Geo. H. Stephens
Vengeance . . .	74	Captain Duff
Audacious . . .	74	Captain S. Peard
Orion	74	Captain Oliver
Edgar	74	Captain Otway
Bellerophon . . .	74	Captain Loring
Robust	74	Captain Hon. Alan H. Gardner
Resolution . . .	74	Captain
Majestic	74	Captain D. Gould
Theseus	74	Captain John Bligh
Zealous	74	Captain S. H. Linzee
Warrior	74	Captain Chas. Tyler
Powerful	74	Captain Sir Francis Laforey, Bart.
Bellona	74	Captain Thos. Bertie
Vanguard	74	Captain Chas. Inglis
Defence	74	Captain Lord H. Paulett
Abergavenny . .	54	A guard ship
America	64	A hulk
Admiral De Vries .	54	A cooperage
Hindostan . . .	54	A store ship
Vengeance . . .	44	A prize
Decade	36	Captain Rutherford
Melampus . . .	36	Captain Gosselin
Trent	36	Captain Perkins
Naiad or Néréide .	36	Captain Mends
Æolus	32	Captain Walker
Druid	32	Captain
Thisbe or Dido (?)	28	Captain

And other frigates I do not remember.

Pelican	18	Captain Geo. McKinlay
Calypso	18	Captain
Lark	18	Captain
Raven	18	Captain James Sanders

Came into Port Royal the Française, 36, French frigate, to purchase different articles for Madame Le Clerc, the wife of the commander-in-chief of the French army at St. Domingo, and sister of Napoleon (then first consul of France). A court martial was held on Captain Thomas New for the loss of his ship,[1] on which charge he was acquitted. During our cruise off St. Domingo we could observe the devastation occasioned by the war with the French and the blacks; several plantations and villages on fire. At this time sickness began to make its appearance in the fleet, and the Brunswick had 287 men on the sick list, and buried a great many. The Vengeance, 44, a prize, tailed on shore and many lost their lives in endeavouring to get her off, particularly the party of thirty-four from the Brunswick, the greater part of whom died; and this for an old French frigate not worth repair, being rotten and useless.

A short time before we arrived, the Topaze, 36, on a cruise, buried all hands except fifty-five; the captain (Church) and all the officers died, and the ship was brought in by the gunner. Eight sail of the line having been surveyed and ordered home, we were one of the lucky squadron. Each ship was directed to take on board four tons of iron hoops lying at a place called Greenwich; and our launch took several trips for this precious cargo; the

[1] Bonetta sloop, 25th October, 1801.—James, iii. 482.

thermometer generally 112,[1] and I have to remember many damnable roastings I got in grubbing for rusty hoops not worth their carriage. So much for the wisdom of Sir John. What could induce him to think of such a thing was only known to himself. Everyone at first thought it a hoax until they took the trip. I have heard many men say how dearly they liked the West Indies; the heat was so fine and conducive to health. Much good may it do them; and I, for one, shall never envy them taking up their quarters with Shadrach, Meshach and Abednego.

The day before we left Port Royal happened to be sweet May Day and I shall never forget it. The squadron ordered home had to send as many of their stores as they could spare to the dockyard. I had to tow our spare topmasts and several spars, and with great fatigue got them landed and put into store; the heat beyond description; so much so that near thirty of the blacks belonging to the yard were taken ill and sent to the hospital. Captain Stephens was one of those who liked the West Indies, and coming into the yard at this time, when not a breath of air was stirring, I pointed out to him some fowls that had taken their station as well as myself under an archway, with their wings drooping and their bills open gasping for breath. 'Sir,' says I, 'the fowls wax warm although indigenous, and don't appear so comfortable in this fine climate as might be expected.' 'Let us be off,' says he, 'for there's no standing this.'

As several of our men had to receive extra pay for work they had been doing, I had to stay a considerable time in consequence of some of the

[1] A temperature so stated has no meaning. 112° is far above the shade temperature of Jamaica, and below the temperature in the sun. But it seems that these parties were working during the heat of the day.

Jacks-in-office waiting to get change to settle with our men; and I had a hot dispute with one of them (a Mr. Bull), who felt much hurt at my saying 'What a cow you are to keep us in this infernal oven until our faces are the colour of your own (he was a man of colour)—bad luck to you.'

A short time before we knew of our being ordered home I went to dine on board the Elephant with Lyford, the first lieutenant (my old messmate in the Blonde). They expected to be sent home, and were so sure, that Captain Peers of the marines, and Jones, the purser, said how happy they should be to take any letters I had to send to England, and would be certain to call on my friends as soon as the ship arrived. Poor fellows, little did they think that instead of going home their bones would be left at the Palisades. I am grieved to say that out of the whole mess only two or three returned. I was taken ill the day I dined with them, and I can truly say that I feel the effects of the wretched climate while I am stating this.

On the 2nd of May we left Port Royal and for two or three days were becalmed in sight of the accursed harbour. At last we joined Rear-Admiral Campbell off Cape Tiburon. On our sick list being shown to the admiral he seemed astonished at the number, and when he found it was so swelled with yellow fever patients he ordered our boat off immediately and would not suffer any communication with our ship. We remained cruising with the squadron for a short time, and then left the fleet for England with the following men of war:—

Bellona	74	Captain Thos. Bertie, commodore
Powerful	74	Captain Sir Francis Laforey, Bart.

Defence	74	Captain Lord Harry Paulett
Zealous	74	Captain Samuel Hood Linzee
Brunswick. . . .	74	Captain Geo. Hopewell Stephens
Edgar	74	Captain Robert Waller Otway
Orion	74	Captain Oliver
Vengeance . . .	74	Captain Duff

Went through the Crooked Island passage and parted company with the commodore, who, with five sail of the line, stood to the eastward and left the Powerful, Brunswick, and Edgar or Orion (I forget which) to get home as they could, being bad sailers. But Sir Francis Laforey, in the Powerful, knew well what he was about and stood to the northward. We had dreadful weather near Bermuda for three days, but moderate after, and when on the Banks of Newfoundland altered our course for the Channel and got there a few hours before the flying squadron, who we joined, and soon after arrived at Spithead after a passage of nearly two months, and went into harbour, where the Brunswick was paid off in July 1802.

But before closing I must relate a few occurrences, beginning with the captain. This gentleman was first lieutenant of the Janus, 44 (upon two decks) commanded by Captain Glover in the American war, and was one of the small squadron under the late Admiral Cornwallis, who at this time was captain of the Lion, 64, in the action with the French under Lamotte-Picquet,[1] who had a much

[1] Off Monte Christo, 20–21 March 1780. See Beatson, v. 96; Chevalier, i. 193.

superior force. As the action commenced, Captain Glover (who had been ill some time) died, and Lieutenant Stephens fought the ship in a manner that will do eternal honour to his memory. He was opposed in the line to a French 74 and fairly beat her out of her station. When the battle was over he went on board the commodore and reported the death of Captain Glover, and that he had died below, as the surgeon had reported his being unable to be brought on deck. Now Captain Glover had been spoken of before as not having exerted himself so well as was expected; and Cornwallis (who was a friend of his) observed to Lieutenant Stephens that he ought to have let his captain die on the quarter deck, as he well knew what had been said of him on a former occasion; and notwithstanding the surgeon's report that he could not be removed from his cot, he never forgot it. This account I had from Captain Stephens; and when we joined the grand fleet off Brest under Admiral Cornwallis, we had not been there two hours before he made to us the signal of disapprobation for what in fact the ship ahead of us was to blame for. Says Captain Stephens to me, 'Gardner, did I not tell you that Billy Blue would hold me in his kind remembrance? See how he begins to compliment me before the whole fleet.'

Captain Stephens was a brave and meritorious officer, an excellent sailor, and a master in naval tactics. I found him, both on board and on shore, a sincere friend. He applied for me to go as his first lieutenant when he was appointed to command the Captain, 74, but from ill health I was unable to join. He died a rear-admiral of the white, lamented by numerous friends.

I shall never forget the morning before we took our departure from the grand fleet off the Black

Rocks. The signal was made to put ourselves under the orders of the Goliath, 74, with the ships I have already mentioned, and we imagined it was to go into port as the first division to be paid off. I had the middle watch and had turned in, when about five our master thundered at my door and calling out, 'Here's news for you, you ragged-headed rascal; turn out and hurrah for the back of the Point and Capstan Square! paid off by the hokey, in a few days.' He then began singing:—

> Jolly tars, have you heard of the news?
>   There's peace both by land and by sea;
> Great guns are no more to be used,
>   Disbanded we all are to be.
>
> Oh! says the admiral, The wars are all over;
>   Says the captain, My heart it will break;
> Oh! says the bloody first lieutenant,
>   What course of life shall I take?

He then began to cut such capers that I thought he was mad. For my own part, I was in high spirits and got up and roused out several more who had not heard of the good news, when unfortunately a cutter came under our stern and sent a boat on board. When the officer came on the quarter deck, our master, full of glee, went up to him and said, 'If you have any letters, give them to us and we'll take them in for you.' 'The devil you will?' says he. 'That would be a pretty circumbendibus, to send letters to Portsmouth *viâ* Jamaica. Why,' says he, 'you don't laugh.' And well he might say so, for no lame duck on change ever cut a more rueful appearance than the master, who damned his eyes, and went below to make his will, wishing bad luck to the fellow who brought the news.

We had to victual and get stores from the rest of the fleet, with a heavy swell and the ship rolling like a tub. She was the worst sea boat that ever was built, drawing less water by some feet than the other ships of her rate, but of great breadth and superior size. She had a trick of carrying away her main topmast close by the cap, by a particular jerk in pitching; and as we were informed by Mr. Yelland, the carpenter (who had been appointed to her for years before), could never be prevented; and here she played the same game, and laboured so dreadfully that it was with the utmost difficulty we could get the stores on board and another main topmast rigged, so as to be ready to join the squadron. She rolled so that the scuttle butts broke adrift, and a poor fellow got so much injured by one of them that he died soon after. She also held a bad wind, so that it was no easy task for an officer to keep her in her station; and to sum up the whole of her good qualities, on her last cruise she had nearly drowned all hands, and it was by uncommon exertion and good luck they succeeded in getting her into port, where they made her a powder ship, the only thing she was fit for.[1]

Before we left the fleet, one of our lieutenants was taken ill and sent home, and Lieutenant Hector Maclean came in his room—he was senior to me and appointed second. This was another hardship, but Captain Stephens told me not to mind it as he would do everything in his power to serve me. I told him that Lord Hugh Seymour, the admiral commanding on the Jamaica station, was an old friend and shipmate of my father's, and I would thank him to mention me to him when the ship arrived, which he said I might depend on. But, unfortunately for me, Lord Hugh died before we

[1] When writing this, Gardner seems to have forgotten that eight years before she had carried her 74 guns with some credit in the fleet under Lord Howe.

got out, regretted by everyone, and was succeeded in the command (until the arrival of Sir J. T. Duckworth) by a man[1] as proud as the mighty Prester John.

We had many strange beings in our wardroom —I shall begin with the master and surgeon. Our first lieutenant gave the former the name of Pot Guts, and the surgeon the cognomen of Bottle Belly. The master saved everything he could, having a family; and for this he was considered by some as very near. Now the surgeon was one that loved good living, and used to eat very hearty and seemed to devour everything with his eyes on the table. I remember his saying to the master in a satirical manner, 'Mr. Wills, don't you intend to purchase a black servant for your good lady?' 'Why,' says Wills, 'I had some idea of doing so, but to tell you the truth I am fearful you would eat him on the passage.' The surgeon had nothing further to say. While lying at Port Royal, Wills was caterer of the mess and went to Kingston to purchase dollar pigs; and going into a house he saw some people lugging a man downstairs, and on his asking what was the matter, they told him it was only a man who had died of the yellow fever. This gave him such a turn that to recover his spirits he was obliged to drink seven glasses of grog before (to use his own words) he could make his blood circulate, and for several days he was on the look-out for the black vomit.

One of the dollar pigs he brought with him was deformed, having a head as long as his body, and when put into the sty with the others he killed the whole of them; and some of the seamen got it into their heads that this pig was the devil. Now Wills

[1] Rear-Admiral Robert Montagu

was a bit of a methodist and did not like this, and one morning he had the devil knocked on the head and hove overboard, observing it was the last time he'd have anything to do with a shaver like that.

Our first lieutenant used to play many tricks with Wills. Once when the packet came in, we were looking at her out of the wardroom windows, when up started Hungerford, who swore that Mrs. Wills and her two daughters were in a boat under the stern and coming alongside, and that he saw them leave the packet which had just arrived from England. Out he ran from the wardroom to escort them, and poor Wills looked stupid with surprise. A few minutes after the door opened and in came Hungerford with three naked black fellows, who he introduced as Mrs. Wills and her two daughters in the newest fashion from England. Wills, angry as he was, could not help joining in the laugh. When the ship was in Portsmouth harbour, I went with Hungerford to dine with Wills, who lived at Portsea. He had on his door a large brass plate with 'Methuselah Wills' engraved thereon in capital letters. When we returned, Hungerford swore that old Wills had the following inscription on the above brass plate :—

> Methuselah Wills Esquire,
> Master in the Royal Navie,
> Passed for a first-rate ship of 110 guns,
> Him and his wife lives here.

Poor Wills was a very good fellow ; he died the senior master on the list at the age of eighty-three, and lies, with a great many more of my old shipmates, in Kingston churchyard, near Portsmouth. The last time I saw him was on the day the Princess Charlotte, 100, was launched. We were in the dockyard together and had just passed the bridge when it gave way with the gates belonging to the dock, by which accident near twenty people were drowned, and we escaped the same fate by about three minutes.[1]

I must now speak of a very different kind of being—poor unfortunate Jack Key, our third lieutenant. He had many vices, particularly hard drinking, but more his own enemy than any others. He was sent to Port Royal Hospital and invalided, and remained there after we sailed, in great distress, not being able for some time to get a passage home. One gentleman with feelings that do honour to him, took pity on the destitute. This gentleman was Mr. Carroll, assistant surgeon belonging to the Goliath, who, in the kindest manner, brought him on board his ship to provide for his wants, and did everything in his power to relieve him in his miserable situation; but the march of intellect among the superior officers rendered the good intentions of Mr. Carroll of little avail, as they ordered poor unhappy Jack out of the ship without loss of time.[2] Mr. Carroll is now a surgeon in the navy of long standing, and in extensive practice in Walworth. Key, from his dark complexion, had the nickname of Cocoa Jack, and was always, when the weather had the appearance of being bad, seen with a piece of wool between his finger and thumb ready to put in his ear, which made them say, 'We are going to have bad weather; Jack is wool gathering.'

[1] 15th September, 1825. See *Times* of 16th September and following days.

[2] It is easy to believe that the Goliath's officers did not consider this man of 'many vices' a desirable passenger, even in the gun room; but as he had not been found out by a court martial, it cannot but seem curious now, that he was not ordered a passage in the mess of his rank.

I once relieved Jack at 12 o'clock P.M. When I came on deck he was not to be found. It was blowing fresh, we were on a wind, the weather topsail braces gone, the yards fore and aft and the weather backstay falls overhauled. Why the topmasts did not go was no fault of Jack's. At last I found him asleep in the lee scuppers and more than half drunk. On another occasion, when with the grand fleet off Brest, the signal was made for the ships to send boats to unload the victuallers, and I was sent with the launch and an eight-oared cutter for that purpose. As there was a great swell we had a difficult task to clear them, and it was late in the evening before we could take our launch in tow, and then pulled for the ship (I think about 7 P.M.), which was about a league off. Now Cocoa Jack had the first watch, and the ship was lying-to for the boat until the captain went to supper; when Jack, thinking we were too far from the admiral, made sail for some time and left us to shift for ourselves. At this time the wind freshened and the sea began to break, and I had serious apprehensions for our safety, and we did not appear to near the ship, whose distinguishing lights were scarcely visible. At last after near five hours' labouring at the oar we got alongside. On going upon deck I found Jack had gone below without being relieved, and seated at the wardroom table with cold beef and a bumper of grog before him. 'Ah, Tony,' says he, 'you have got on board at last? I had almost given you up.' Although he was my senior officer I could not help saying, 'Damn your old cocoa soul, did you want to drown all hands of us? Why did you not heave to before?' 'Lord help you,' says he; 'we have been lying-to these three hours.' Now what Jack called lying-to was this: he let go the main-top-bowline, kept the sail shivering but not aback, and the helm a little a-weather, so that the ship forged ahead considerably. With all his faults he was a good-tempered fellow, and I said no more.

Our purser was a glorious fellow for keeping it up; and after taking his full share of Madeira would then turn to upon rum and water, and about two or three in the morning would give his last toast, 'A bloody war and a sickly season!' and then retire in a happy state. I once told him when he had the dry belly-ache after drinking port wine, that it was likely he'd go to the palisades (the burying ground), but that I would be happy to do anything for him in England that lay in my power. He gave me a look that expressed everything but thanks.

I must here relate a circumstance which took place on the evening of the day we made Deseada. We had a dog on board that in fact belonged to no one, but the ship's company were very kind to the poor animal, who used to get well fed from the different messes, and was quite at home fore and aft. The evening was fine, with light winds, and the ship going about three knots, when some wicked fellow (supposed to be the son of a clergyman) threw the poor dog overboard when several sharks were round the ship. It was naturally supposed they had made a meal of him, but that was not the case, as they had more mercy than the ruffian who was guilty of such cruelty. On the arrival of the squadron at Port Royal one of our officers went on board (I think) the Captain, 74, when to his astonishment, who should come jumping round him but the lost dog. On his relating the circumstance to the officers, they told him that about ten o'clock of the evening in question they were upwards of two miles astern of us when they heard a strange noise under their bows. At first they thought it was a man overboard until they heard the dog bark, when one of the men went down by a rope and caught hold of the poor creature by the neck and got him safe on board. A blanket belonging to a sailor was towing overboard which he got hold of with his paws and held on and by that means was rescued from a watery grave. His new shipmates wished to keep him and with them he remained. Of the young man who threw him overboard, if I were to pronounce an eulogy on his character I should without flattery say :—

> On Newgate steps Jack Chance was found,
> And bred up in St. Giles's pound;
> He learned to curse, to swear, to fight,
> Did everything but read and write;
> And bawdy songs all day would sing,
> And they all declared he was just the thing.

Our first lieutenant (Hungerford) was a very droll fellow but fractious from disappointment. He was in the Trusty, 50, when the late Admiral Walker commanded her at the time she put into Cadiz, where some of her officers were arrested and sent to prison by the Spanish Government for smuggling off money; for which Captain Walker was tried by a court martial and dismissed the service. He and Hungerford were upon very bad terms, and happening to meet in High Street, Portsmouth, Hungerford with a cane began to strike at him, when Captain Walker in his defence, caught hold of a hod belonging to a mason who was standing by, and made a blow at Hungerford, which, fortunately for him, missed the mark, and several officers coming up, a stop was put to any further proceedings. This business hurt Hungerford in the service and made him many enemies. Captain Walker was reinstated and died a rear-admiral.[1] He commanded the Monmouth, 64, in the Dutch action under Duncan and behaved with uncommon bravery. Hungerford was a very good officer and seaman and an indefatigable first lieutenant. In watching, quartering, stationing, and regulating the ship's company in every respect he showed great ability. He was a great mimic, and very droll in other respects. I remember at Port Royal, when he was ill, his pretending to be dumb and mad, and carrying on the joke for a whole day on purpose to annoy the surgeon. He put on a white great coat belonging to Captain Rea of the marines, with his sash and sword, and a large cocked hat and feather, strutting about the wardroom and making a dead set at Fuller whenever he came in. However, about seven in the evening he found his tongue and said to me, 'What a damned fool I made of Bottle Belly; how easily I humbugged him.'

The day we made the east end of Jamaica I had the forenoon watch, and was walking the deck with Captain Stephens, when Lieutenant Morgan of the marines called out from the gangway to the gunner's mate to get a gun ready and fire into the ship abreast of us. On my asking him what he meant by such extraordinary conduct, 'Sir,' says he, 'I am not accountable to you for my actions'; and going up to the captain he told him he was no longer captain of the Brunswick, but that he would take pity on him and suffer him to keep possession of his cabin for the present. The captain looked at me in amazement. 'Sir,' says I, 'Mr. Morgan is certainly deranged.' He was then sent below, and on going down the quarter-deck ladder, he roared out to the man at the wheel, 'Put the

[1] 1831. *Cf.* Marshall, ii. 848, 882.

helm a starboard, you damned rascal.' The captain dined with us that day, and, after the cloth was removed, Morgan came to the table, and on something being said to him he took up a glass of wine, part of which he hove in the captain's face, and the glass at Jack Key's head; and when we seized hold of him, he called me a damned conceited whelp, and that he always saw a little greatness about me that he never could put up with. This young man's brain was turned by diving into things he did not understand, and it may be said in truth of him:—

> A little learning is a dangerous thing,
> Drink deep or taste not the Pierian spring.

He was invalided and sent home, and got the retirement, but never recovered his reason.

Another of our marine officers (Augustus John Field) was a very strange being. He was on board the Quebec, 32, in the action with the Surveillante, French frigate, in the American war. Both ships were dismasted after very hard fighting, when the Quebec unfortunately caught fire. Her brave captain (Farmer) would not quit, and was blown up in his ship. Out of the number saved Lieutenant Field was one and got a considerable lift in his corps for his bravery. He was a very good fellow in many respects, but drew a long bow and kept it up too much. He had been through all the changing scenes of life, and told incredible stories—that he was descended from the Plantagenet family and could trace his genealogy to Henry the Second. By way of amusement I have seen him rest the calf of one leg on the knee of the other and then drive several pins up to the head in the calf of his leg, saying he would leave them to the mess as a leg-a-cy.

Our ship was full of rats, and one morning he

caught four which he had baked in a pie with some pork chops. When it came to table he began greedily to eat, saying, 'What a treat! I shall dine like an alderman.' One of our lieutenants (Geo. M. Bligh) got up from the table and threw his dinner up, which made Field say, 'I shall not offend such delicate stomachs and shall finish my repast in my cabin,' which he did and we wished the devil would choke him. When he had finished, he said one of the rats was not exactly to his taste as the flesh was black; but whether from a bruise or from disease, he could not say, but should be more particular in future in the post mortem examination. I never was more sick in my life, and am so to this day when I think of it. Our captain of marines (Rea) was a very worthy fellow. He had great antipathy to the West Indies, and was always cursing Venables and Penn for taking possession of Jamaica, and was sorry Oliver Cromwell did not make them a head shorter for their pains. I have often heard him repeat the following lines as a morning and evening hymn:—

> Venables and Penn,
> Two bloody-minded men,
> In an evil hour
> Those seas did explore,
> And blundering about
> This cursed hole found out;
> And for so doing,
> The devil has them stewing;
> And with him they may remain
> Till we come this way again,
> Which we think howsomdever
> (As our boatswain says) will be never;
> And let all the mess say Amen!

When cruising off Cape Tiburon I was sent in our cutter to board a Yankee about two leagues off and to purchase stock. Our surgeon by way of pastime took the trip with me. As the Yankee had plenty for sale, and it being a dead calm, I loaded our boat with live and dead stock until she was pretty deep in the water. On our return, the sharks began to muster and the live stock to ride rusty. The surgeon said it was a damned shame to trifle with people's lives in that manner by overloading the boat, and cursed the hour he ever came with me; and it by no means eased his fears when one of the boat's crew said, 'Please, your honour, if we don't cut the b——s' throats' (meaning the live stock) 'their hoofs will be through the boat's bottom, as they are kicking like blazes, and here's a bloody shark close alongside us.' However, we got safe alongside after a long tug. The surgeon with a woeful countenance told a lamentable tale, which made Captain Stephens and the rest laugh heartily. He took good care never to volunteer his services with me in a boat again. He has often put me in mind of the trip and I hope he will live long to do so.

We had a tedious passage home, and when off Bermuda it was a gale of wind and a calm alternately for three days and nights, with thunder and lightning. On one of the nights I had the middle watch and was obliged to clue down the topsails upon the cap eight or nine times, blowing a gale of wind one moment and a calm the next. The night was as dark as Erebus between the flashes, and then as light as broad day. Through one flash I saw our surgeon coming on deck rolled up in a white great coat, and I said to Captain Stephens (who was up most of the night and standing with me on the gangway):

> By the pricking of my thumbs
> Something wicked this way comes.

Captain Stephens would always repeat the above when he saw Fuller come on deck. I have often wondered that no accident happened to the ship from the lightning, which was beyond everything of the kind I ever saw. This was the only bad weather we had during the voyage, which was a lucky circumstance for the Brunswick; for had a gale of wind come on for any length of time we certainly should have foundered.

And now let me say in the language of the Romans when taking leave of their deceased friends :—

Vale, Vale, Vale, nos te ordine, quo natura permiserit, cuncti sequemur.

OFFICERS' NAMES

JOHN HOLLOWAY, Esq., Rear-admiral of the red.

Dead [1826]. An admiral of the red. An old messmate of my father's in the Princess Royal with old Vinegar (Hyde Parker), in 1779.—[Marshall, i. 101.]

GEO. HOPEWELL STEPHENS, Esq., Captain.

Dead [1819]. A rear-admiral of the white; a most excellent officer.

EMANUEL HUNGERFORD, 1st Lieutenant.

Dead. An excellent first lieutenant; strange and droll.

HECTOR MACLEAN, 2nd Lieutenant.

Dead.

JOHN KEY, 2nd and 3rd Lieutenant.

Dead. Cocoa Jack was no man's enemy but his own.

JAMES ANTHONY GARDNER, 1st, 2nd, 3rd, 4th, and 3rd Lieutenant.

A commander.

[THOMAS] LOWE, 5th Lieutenant.

Dead. A loss to the service.

GEO. MILLAR BLIGH, 7th and 6th Lieutenant.

Dead [1831]. A post captain.—[Marshall, v. 430.]

METHUSELAH WILLS, Master.

Dead. Poor old Wills was crabbed, but a good fellow.

ROBERT COOPER, Purser.
Dead. A very worthy fellow.

SMITHSON WALLER, Purser.
A very generous fellow, but kept it up too much; since dead.

WILLIAM FULLER, Surgeon.
A skilful surgeon, but crabbed as the devil at times; yet a very good fellow, always obliging, and the first to relieve those in distress.

[HENRY] REA, Captain of marines.
Dead. Much the gentleman.

AUGUSTUS JOHN FIELD, 1st Lieutenant of marines.
Dead. A very brave fellow, who drew a long bow, but would injure no one.

[JAMES] HOLMES, 2nd Lieutenant of marines.
Uncertain. A good-natured fellow.

[JOHN] ROBSON, 2nd Lieutenant of marines.
Uncertain. Very quarrelsome, and appeared to be half mad.

ROSS MORGAN, 2nd Lieutenant of marines.
Dead. Invalided for insanity, sent home, and got the retirement.

[WILLIAM] WISEMAN, Gunner.
Dead.

[JOHN] FOLLIE, Boatswain.
Uncertain. Drank hard; a sailor.

[WILLIAM] YELLAND, Carpenter.
Uncertain. Very much respected.

[WILLIAM] HARRISON, Mate.
Uncertain. A very active officer.

[HENRY] EDGEWORTH, Mate.
Uncertain. A very good sailor, but unfortunately drank hard.

METHUSELAH WILLS, Midshipman and then mate; son of the master.
A lieutenant.

PARDIEU [(?) SIMON PURDUE], Midshipman.
Dead. A commander; an officer, seaman, and gentleman. Highly respected, but unfortunately given to drinking.

[WILLIAM] ELLIOT, Midshipman.
Killed in battle. A lieutenant; a very worthy young man.

EDWARD MEDLEY, Midshipman.
A lieutenant.

[R. A.] TAYLOR, Midshipman.
Uncertain. Wicked and wild.

[G. J.] ARCHDALE, Midshipman.
Uncertain. Much respected.

[GEORGE] ROBERTS, Midshipman.
Uncertain. A steady youth.

[JOHN] LEMON [or LAMOND], Midshipman.
Uncertain. Very steady.

WILLIAM WADE, Midshipman.
Dead. A lieutenant.

[RICHARD] HORSLEY, Midshipman.
Dead.

[JOHN] HODGES, Midshipman.
Died of yellow fever at Jamaica.

[ROBERT] WILSON, Midshipman.
Died of yellow fever at Jamaica.

[JOHN] CONTENT, Midshipman.
Died of yellow fever at Jamaica. [Borne as coxswain. Aged 39. DD.]

[ROBERT B.] MATTHEWS, Midshipman.
Uncertain. I believe a lieutenant; he was one of those saved from H.M. ship Apollo that was wrecked on the coast of Portugal [1 April, 1804].

ROBERT ATKINS, Midshipman.
Dead. A lieutenant; steady fellow.

[MICHAEL] GOULD, Clerk.
Uncertain. Very clever. [Midshipman; afterwards captain's clerk.]

[J. H.] WADDLE, Wrote under the clerk.
Uncertain. This poor fellow was made a butt of and ran away from the ship. [Borne as L.M. Aged 30.]

[ANDREW] MARSHALL, 1st Assistant Surgeon.
Uncertain. This gentleman did honour to his profession.

DANIEL QUARRIER, 2nd Assistant Surgeon.
An M.D. A surgeon in the navy, and surgeon of the division of royal marines at Portsmouth; a magistrate for the county, and what not.

AGENT OF TRANSPORTS

I WAS employed on this service but a short time in Portsmouth Harbour and had several transports to superintend, and was in expectation of sailing to the Mediterranean; but as ill luck would have it, our destination was altered to that infernal bakehouse, Port Royal, Jamaica. I then thought it time to be off and I wrote to the board to be superseded, which gave great offence to Sir Rupert George[1] (the chairman). However, my request was granted and I left a service that I never would accept of, had I my time to go over again, upon any consideration. For the short time I was in it I saw enough to convince me that if an officer did his duty, he would be like the hare with many friends; and if he acted otherwise, he must lay himself open to any puny whipster who might wish to take advantage of his good nature. I was succeeded by Lieutenant Jump, who refused to take charge of the stores, saying he had enough hanging over his head already (being, as I understood him, in the transport service before). However, I settled everything to my satisfaction, returning into store all the articles I had drawn; struck my swaggering blue pennant[2] and resigned my command to the above officer, wishing him joy and not envying him his appointment.

[1] Captain, 1781; first commissioner of transport, 1796; knighted, 1804; baronet, 1809; died, 1823.

[2] See Appendix, p. 265.

SIGNAL STATION: FAIRLIGHT, NEAR HASTINGS, SUSSEX

From January 30*th*, 1806, *to December* 7*th*, 1814

As when high Jove his sharp artillery forms,
And opes his cloudy magazine of storms;
In winter's bleak uncomfortable reign,
A snowy inundation hides the plain;
He stills the winds and bids the skies to sleep;
Then pours the silent tempest thick and deep;
And first the mountain tops are covered o'er,
Then the green fields and then the sandy shore;
Bent with the weight, the nodding groves are seen,
And one bright waste hides all the works of men;
The circling seas, alone absorbing all,
Drink the dissolving fleeces as they fall.—*Iliad.*

In such a season as the above I arrived at Hastings on the 30th of January 1806. I was appointed to the station by Lord Garlies, one of the lords of the admiralty, who behaved to me in the kindest manner. After waiting on Captain Isaac Schomberg, who superintended the Sea Fencibles from Beachy Head to Dungeness, I proceeded to join my station about three miles to the eastward of Hastings. When I got to the summit of Fairlight Down, about 600 feet above the level of the sea, the first object that struck me was a hut, built of turf, in a ruinous state, and on the top a figure with a soldier's jacket on. 'Hallo!' says I; 'Is this the signal station?' 'Yes, zur,' says he. Why then, thinks I, I'm damned if I don't give up the appointment. 'Where's the midshipman?' says I. 'Midshipman, zur? why, there be only me and another soger, and I expects to be relieved to-day.' 'By whom?' says I. 'Vy,' says he, 'by two melishy men, and I thought you and that ere lad' (meaning my son, who was with me, and under six years of age) 'was them till you comed near.' I could not help smiling at this, and taking a turn round the premises I thought I would look at the interior. I did so, but backed out again in a hurry, from filth and wretchedness. [The detailed description of these is omitted.]

On coming out I happened to cast my eye to the SE, and there I saw another signal station; and on making enquiry, I was informed by a labourer that the station I had just observed was the right one, and that this was only for the fogeys to look out from; so away I trudged over several ploughed fields and at last arrived at my destination, in the room of Lieutenant Francis Gibbon, deceased, who had formerly been a messmate of mine in the Salisbury.

It would puzzle a Philadelphia lawyer to recollect everything that happened for the eight years and ten months that I remained in this place, and I shall merely relate a few occurrences as they come to my recollection. I had a midshipman, two signalmen, and two dragoons, under my superintendence; and when anything particular took place one of the dragoons was sent off with the despatch to the nearest commanding officer. We had the strictest orders to be on the look-out by night and by day, in consequence of the threatened invasion, and our being so near the French coast that on a clear day the camp at Boulogne could be seen without a glass,[1] so that the utmost vigilance on our part was required. Blue lights, fire beacons, etc., were in constant readiness, and the French flotilla at Boulogne, Calais, Ambleteuse, and Vimereux were hourly expected to make a start.

Independent of this, whenever the wind blew strong from the westward, so as to occasion the cruisers to take shelter under Dungeness, the French privateers were sure to come over and pick up the struggling merchantmen before the men of war could regain their station off Beachy Head. We had also to be constantly on the watch to give notice in case of smugglers being on the coast, and to prevent prisoners of war making their escape from the vicinity of our station, a signal for that purpose being made from one post to another; so that we had no relaxation from duty except in a thick fog, which sometimes would take place for nine or ten days together, during which time we had only to walk round the cliffs and along the seashore. I have heard many say that a signal station was an easy berth, and only fit for old and worn-out officers. This I flatly deny; and, without fear of contradiction, can safely say that I suffered more from anxiety at this station than ever I did on board of a man of war. In the latter, when one's watch was over, a little rest could be obtained; but at the station the night was worse than the day, as the flotilla were expected to take advantage of the darkness so as to be over in the morning, and the

[1] Gardner's memory must here have been playing him false. The distance from Fairlight to Boulogne and the adjacent coast is fully 35 miles: the camp had been broken up in the previous September, and the soldiers that had formed it were far away, at Vienna or its neighbourhood; as Gardiner, at the time, must have known.

night signal was more anxiously watched than that of the day. When Earl St. Vincent was first lord of the admiralty, Lieutenant John Henry St. John Page (an old schoolfellow of mine, who I had the following account from) applied to him for a signal station, stating that he was unfit for active service in consequence of a paralytic stroke which affected his arm and one of his eyes. His lordship wrote for answer, 'That an officer of a signal station ought to have two eyes, and damned good eyes they ought to be.' However, he complied with his wishes.

From our elevated situation I have often been in dread for the safety of the house, particularly in the SW gales, and have frequently expected that the board would be obliged

> To set a figure, to discover
> If we had fled to Rye or Dover;

and I'm astonished that the house did not blow away. I well remember one dreadful gale blowing down our chimney, which lay upon the roof without breaking through, forming an angle of 45°, and the midshipman, crawling out upon all fours (for we could not stand upright), declared he thought it was our 18-pound carronade that was blown there and had taken that position for a long shot. The fire blew out of the stoves, and the glass out of the window frames; the night as black as Erebus, with heavy rain which formed a river that swept everything before it; the chief part of our garden washed or blown away, leaving nothing but the bare rock behind, so that I wished myself in the old Bay of Biscay again.

To make up for this, the views about Hastings are remarkably fine, and in the summer well worth visiting; particularly the fish ponds, Dripping Well,

Lovers' Seat, Friar's Hill, Old Roar and many other romantic spots, one of which I must mention. About a mile to the NE of Hastings, from a place called the Tile Kiln House, the prospect is highly interesting; looking towards the town, is a valley with a thicket on the left, and at the bottom a stream that runs to the sea; in front, the west hill with the ancient castle said to be built by William the Conqueror soon after the battle of Hastings; and on the east hill, the remains of a Roman camp. One morning when the hounds were out, I was walking near the above thicket when an immense boar rushed furiously on the pack and the huntsmen had great difficulty in separating them. The boar belonged to the farmer near the spot, and some of the dogs had reason to remember him.

As I am better acquainted with handling a tar brush, strapping a block, or turning in a dead-eye, than describing green groves and gravel walks, I shall say nothing more respecting the face of the country, but begin upon other subjects. And here I must say that during the time I had the station, I was upon good terms with every individual from the mayor down to the fisherman. But I regret to state that death has made sad inroads among my worthy friends since my departure. In the summer, the cockneys would frequently come to take a look at the French coast and Bonaparte's tower on a clear day; and not content with asking ridiculous questions, would walk into the house without leave or licence, and seat themselves. On one occasion, when I had returned from Hastings, I found seated in my room a fellow with his coat off and reading one of my books. He took no notice of me for some time. At last he drawled out 'It's werry hot veather.' 'It is,' I replied; 'but pray what is your business?' This question seemed to startle him, and particularly so when I informed him I was a man of war's man, and never suffered myself to be taken by storm or boarded in the smoke. He took the hint and walked off.[1]

In stating this I only allude to a set who were unacquainted with common politeness. At the same time I have to acknowledge the civility and attention I received from many of the respectable families that visited Hastings.

The lower class at Hastings and in the vicinity believe in witchcraft, and several old women that lived in All Saints' Street were supposed to be witches. About a mile from my station lived a poor old woman named Hannah Weller, who was put down in the list; and many strange stories were told respecting her—such as pigs, and sheep, and sometimes oxen, refusing to pass her dwelling, until the drovers would go and beg of her to let them pass quietly. On my going one morning to market at Hastings, I bought with other articles some eggs, which I gave to Wm. Crump (one of the signalmen), who put them at the bottom of his basket well covered with straw so that they could not be seen. I then told him to make all haste he could to the station, and without his knowing it I returned before him. When I had got about a mile and a half from the town I met Hannah Weller, who, I knew, was coming in at this time with some clothes for the wash; and I told her, if she met Crump, to tell him to make haste out and to be careful of the eggs he had in the bottom of his basket, and not to say she had seen me.

[1] We are so accustomed to talk of 'Arry as a product of the late nineteenth century, railways and cheap return tickets, that it is neither uninteresting nor socially unimportant to note that he existed in 1806. Increase of population and excursion tickets have merely swelled his numbers.

Now Crump stood in great dread of Hannah, and was a firm believer in deeds of the black art. Soon after I had seen her she met Crump, and desired him to be very careful of the eggs and to make haste and not loiter by the way. Crump was terrified almost out of his wits to think she should know what cargo he had charge of; and, after wishing her good morning, strode off without looking behind until he got about a hundred yards from her. He then took out his knife and stuck it in the mark the ring of her patten (as he thought) had made, and a sure way—if she looked round—to prove witchcraft; and she, happening to look round at the same time and seeing him stopping, called out, 'Crump, what are you about?' and shakher hand, desired him to be gone, upon which he took to his heels in amazement and arrived at the station as pale as death, and told his woeful story to the midshipman with many illustrations, which the midshipman believed to be as true as holy writ.

We had a tame raven, the most sagacious creature I ever met with. He used to go every morning with the signalman to town, for the letters and to market, and would take his station at the butcher's shop long before we could get there; and when he saw us ready to return, would set off for home in a hurry. Sometimes we could see him fighting with the crows; and once he alighted on the head of a gentleman reading in a field; to his consternation, until we explained to him Ralph's tricks. Under the Lovers' Seat stands a house on the beach called The Govers, which was inhabited by a wicked fellow, a cobbler by trade. This man took it into his head to leave off his wicked ways, and went to church regularly every Sunday, and paid great attention to the service for about three or four months, and then relapsed to his former failings. On being asked the reason of his apostasy he replied that he went to church until he was tired; and seeing no use in it, he thought he might as well go back to sin and cobble again as he could get more by it than going to church. Early one morning this fellow was gathering sticks in the valley under the signal station, when our raven was on the prowl. The moment Ralph got sight of him he pitched on his neck and began to claw and tear him most unmercifully, which alarmed him so much that he had hardly power to defend himself. At last he got hold of the raven, and, with part of the thong he had to bind the sticks, he began to tie Ralph's legs, and when he thought he had him secure he gathered up his sticks and was stooping down to fasten them, when the raven broke loose, and seized on him a second time, and tore his breeches to rags after clawing him severely, and then flew away. The cobbler, dreadfully alarmed, went home without his sticks and told everyone that he met that the devil had attacked him and that he must alter his course of life, as he now believed something was in it. The joke was kept up, and I think he was never told it was our raven. Poor Ralph at last met with an untimely death. A farmer, shooting rooks, laid him low by mistake, which he was very sorry for when too late.

Notwithstanding the many cruisers that were on the station and the unceasing look-out on the coast by the officers of the customs, the smugglers contrived to make several runs. One morning in the month of November the midshipman called me up a little before daylight, and reported that fifteen horses were in the field near the station, with Flushing jackets strapped on their backs, and made fast to the hedge, without any one with them. As the day began to break, I went to the brow of the hill, and saw on the beach between two and three hundred people, and a boat a short way from the shore. The moment they got sight of me they set up a shout, and made use of horrible threats. However, I went down with the midshipman, and found some custom-house officers who had been up to their necks in water trying to get at the boat, but all to no purpose. The fellows on board seemed to be drunk, and held up some kegs which they stove; and making use of language the most vile, stood to the westward. I immediately dispatched the midshipman to give information to the custom-house and made the signal to the next station. A galley was soon after manned and armed, and after a long chase the smuggler was captured with several tubs of liquor. As I returned to my station the mob shewed their heads just above the brow of the hill, and complimented me with three groans and then dispersed; and glad I was to see them clear off. They appeared to be all strangers, the custom-house officers declaring they had never seen one of them before. Some of them swore they would be a shot in our locker the first opportunity, and we expected they would have attacked us in the night; but we heard no more of them.

I shall now mention a few friends; and first the Reverend Richard Wadeson, late Vicar of Fairlight, who died since I left the station, aged eighty-nine. He had formerly been second master at Harrow School, when Dr. Parr was usher, and was offered to be first master at the death or resignation of Dr. Sumner, but refused it.[1] He was one of the best

[1] There is some confusion here. Wadeson and Parr were both assistant masters when Sumner died suddenly in September, 1771. Wadeson was certainly not offered the succession, and his name does not seem to have been officially mentioned in connection with it. On the other hand, Parr's claims were strongly

men I ever met with, and one of the first classical scholars in the kingdom, and highly respected by his parishioners as the following account will shew. He had, as vicar, only the small tithes; and when requested by some of his friends to raise them he refused, saying, he had lived on good terms in the parish with every individual for a long time, and that he would do nothing to forfeit their esteem and would suffer anything rather than oppress them. When this came to the knowledge of those who paid tithes, they, as a mark of respect, immediately made a handsome addition to his income, with a high panegyric on his integrity. Nothing could put him out of temper except losing at backgammon. I well remember one evening his coming to the station and saying he was determined not to be vexed, let what would happen. We then began to play (not for money), and he lost twenty games running. At last he roared out, and on my asking him what was the matter, says he, 'He's here.' 'Who, sir?' says I. 'Why, the devil,' says he, 'is at my elbow, but he shall not make a parson swear.' I am sorry to say this worthy gentleman lost his sight some years before his death, and, in addition to this misfortune, had great domestic troubles which he bore to the last with unshaken fortitude.

I must not forget another worthy friend, the Reverend Webster Whistler, Rector of Hastings and New-Timber, who lately died at the advanced age of eighty-seven. He also was a first-rate scholar and a powerful preacher; a hater of bigotry

urged, and the refusal of the Governors to appoint him caused a violent 'meeting' among the boys. It is a very strange story, told at length in Johnstone, *Works of Samuel Parr*, i. 55 *seq.*; Thornton, *Harrow School and its Surroundings*, Chap. viii.; *Report on the MSS. of Lady Du Cane* (*Hist. MSS. Comm.*), 229 *seq.*

and clerical tyranny; possessing great personal courage, and one of the finest-looking men in the kingdom; with an athletic frame, upwards of six feet, and looked, when on horseback—as Napoleon said of Kleber—like one of Homer's heroes. His kindness and attention I never shall forget. I was always welcome to his house and he always sent me a large tithe, as he called it, of fruit and game, whenever he had an opportunity. I could mention many acts of this kind; but one mark of respect I cannot pass over. When my mother died, he selected a particular spot for her grave where he knew the ground was dry, refused all fees, and even assisted in placing the turf over her remains. He was not one of your dandy parsons either in dress or address; for he was not ashamed to wear a rusty black coat, or to knock down anyone that offended him. I remember a dragoon officer addressing him one morning with, 'Damn me, how are you, Whistler?' 'If you say that again, I will fell you to the earth,' was his reply. Going into a boat, and having on an old black coat and trowsers, he asked me who I thought he was like, repeating the following lines:—

> Sordid his garb, but in his looks were seen
> A youthful vigour, and autumnal green.

'Can you,' says he, 'with all the antiquity you smatter, find out who I allude to?' 'Charon, sir,' says I. 'Right,' says he, 'I'm the man; but I am not going on the Styx to-day. The Channel shall be my cruising ground this morning'; and off he started with some ladies in company. On his return he came up to the station, foaming with rage, requesting me to inform him the name of the cutter in the offing, that he might report her commander to the admiralty for daring to fire at him. Now the fact was this. The cutter had fired at some boats to bring them to, as the fishermen had frequently smuggled goods on board; and Mr. Whistler having boarded one of them to get fish, the commander of the cutter fired several muskets at his boat, thinking him a smuggler also, which made the parson pull to land as fast as possible. It was out of my power to give him the name, as I had not her number. 'Well, then,' says he, 'the first time I can lay hold of him I'll christen him in the Bourne stream, by giving him a good ducking.'

The beginning of December 1814 the admiralty directed me to pay off the station without loss of time, and the next day I received a letter from the navy board to the same purpose, and further directing me to clear the station of the stores under my charge, and to sell all unserviceable articles. Now all this was very well, and they concluded by saying,

We are your Affectionate Friends[1]—
(Signed by three commissioners);

but on the margin of their letter was a postscript as follows:—

'You are to discharge your midshipman and men on the receipt of this letter; and yourself, as soon as these instructions have been complied with.'

So by this I was to do everything myself, which was very kind, in the dead of winter, three miles

[1] At this time this was still the usual form of subscription from a superior, whether social—as a son of the king—or official, as the navy board (collectively)—to an inferior. Naval officers, at any rate, will scarcely need to be reminded of the story of the eccentric Sir John Phillimore (*cf. D.N.B.*) who signed a letter to the navy board in the same way; and on being censured for so doing, signed his reply 'No longer your affectionate friend.'

from Hastings, and a long way from the spring where we had our water, and nothing to be had in the neighbourhood; and upon a hill, said to be 650 feet above the level of the sea—so that if a snowstorm came on I might remain there alone and starve and be damned for what some people cared. However, I got a merchant at Hastings to send his wagons out and take the stores to his warehouse, until a vessel was sent to receive them; and after selling the coals and fire stack, I paid off the station on the 7th of December 1814.

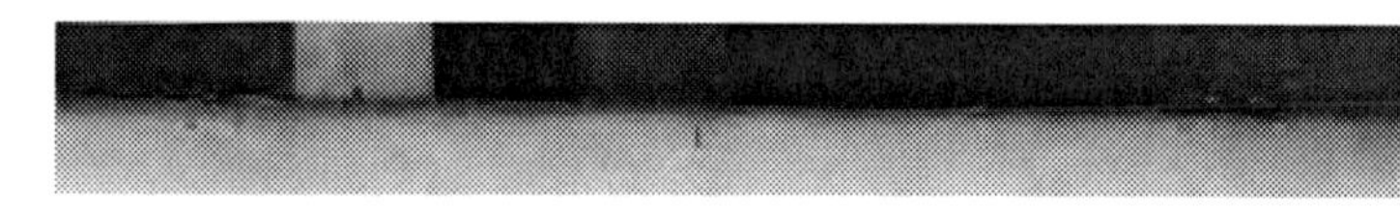

APPENDIX

(P. 250)

The 'swaggering blue pennant.'

[As the distinctive pennants for Transport Officers when afloat were done away with several years ago, and indeed Transport Officers afloat are now almost unknown, we are happy in being able, by the kindness of Vice-Admiral George T. H. Boyes, the present Director of Transports, to give the Regulations, as they stood in 1814, 'relative to the pennants of distinction' appointed to be used by transport agents when afloat.]

The principal agent, serving on any expedition, in order to be particularly known and distinguished, shall wear, on board the transport wherein he is embarked, a blue ensign, together with a plain blue broad pennant at the main topmast head, of the following dimensions, viz. eight feet at the staff, and twenty feet long; but, for foul weather, four feet at the staff, and ten feet long.

When there is but one agent to a division of transports, or when several agents are not serving under the immediate orders of other agents, a blue ensign with the common blue pennant at the main topmast head is to be worn as the only necessary mark of distinction. The broad pennant is never to be hoisted by any agent who has not another under under him.

All inferior agents shall hoist the blue ensign and a plain blue common pennant, two feet broad at the head, and thirty feet long. A smaller one, at discretion, may be worn at sea.

Should transports of different expeditions meet at the

same port, the principal agents only of each expedition are to hoist broad pennants at the main, fore, or mizen topmast heads, according to their respective rank in his Majesty's navy: and the inferior agents, belonging to each expedition, are to hoist common blue pennants at the same mast-head with their principal.

At sea, should a large fleet of transports, all on the same service, be classed in three grand divisions, the agent commanding each division may hoist the broad pennant at the main, fore, or mizen topmast heads, according to their rank, as aforesaid; and their inferior agents in like manner.

INDEX

CPSIA information can be obtained at www.ICGtesting.com
Printed in the USA
LVOW05*1943070514

384811LV00015B/801/P

9 780548 206461